THE FINANCIAL
ADVISOR
TO BUILDING
WEALTH

TM

PURSUING PROSPERITY
WITH FINANCIAL EDUCATION

Thomas Herold - Winter 2010 Edition

The Financial Advisor to Building Wealth

Pursuing Prosperity
with Financial Education

Winter 2010 Edition

Revision 1.0

Thomas Herold
Dream Manifesto, LLC.
© 2005-2011 All rights reserved.

www.wealthbuildingcourse.com

Table of Contents

INTRODUCTION

"Pursuing Prosperity with Financial Education"

Welcome to the Financial Advisor to Building Your Wealth

It's my pleasure to present the Winter 2010 edition of our quarterly publication 'Financial Advisor to Building Wealth'.

Just take a moment and think about what wealth means to you. If you're like most folk, you think it's all about money. It was for me too, until I decided to explore the topic more deeply and really consider what makes us wealthy, prosperous people. Wealth, for me, is not merely material possessions: it's your health, your lifestyle and relationships, even your mental abilities.

Curious yet? If you still think money has anything to do with wealth, you'll be in for a big surprise when you read this issue. My main aim, and the inspiration for my website and the whole of my work, is to help you learn about finance like I did – to help you transform your life, leave the past behind and take control of your wealth. Now, you might think financial terminology is about as interesting as a bag of rice falling off a shelf in China. But these days, one of the most essential and precious gifts you can give yourself is a financial education - especially given the worldwide economic crisis we are all experiencing.

Humanity is embarking on the biggest transfer of wealth in history. You may have sensed it already, and you're right: wealth is flowing at breathtaking speeds away from the financially uneducated towards people who know about finance and, crucially, how to use that knowledge to their advantage.

The current international financial crisis is a direct outcome of government and bank interventions. It's time for us to open our eyes to this and start to protect ourselves.

You might have heard the phrase, "If you always do what you've always done, you'll always get what you've always got." There's no question that, in order to secure your future and live a life that you're in control of, you must take on the task of understanding what is happening to your hard-earned money.

Once you grasp and unravel the hidden agenda of a few powerful people, you will be able to choose and reclaim your financial freedom. At the moment, this may all sound like a conspiracy theory to you; however, the research and facts contained in this book will provide you with enough evidence that there is a plan behind all this, which right now is serving other people, not you.

You'll realize that this plan is nothing new, and that the past shows similar attempts at monetary control and failure. Learning about these will make you better able to react to the present, and start creating wealth for yourself, rather than other people.

I've structured the articles into several categories. Feel free to skip between them and simply read what interests you most. Remember: this is not a course that you're doing for anyone else. This is a gift to yourself. Read the articles that apply to you, and in doing so you will broaden your knowledge and feel more qualified to keep learning and growing your wealth.

All the articles have been taken from the Wealth Building Course website and assembled here for you to make your financial learning simpler and more convenient. I've left out several articles which focused on issues that have now been overtaken by events. The situation is constantly changing, but the articles here have been carefully selected for their continuing relevance.

Enjoy your reading and always keep learning. Allow your mind to open up to new ideas. Believe that you can change your approach to wealth, and transform your life. As Steve Jobs once said: "Stay hungry, stay foolish."

Thomas Herold

Introduction

<u>INVESTING</u>

"Putting Energy to Work"

Introduction

The Two Investment Strategies: Capital Gain And Cash Flow

There are two principal classifications in any investment that you make. These are capital gains investments and cash flow investments.

While both are helpful to have and to be involved with, they differ drastically in their characteristics and approaches. In the following paragraphs, you will come to understand the differences between capital gains and cash flow investments.

Capital Gain Forms of Investing

When you make an investment with the strategy of achieving capital gains, you are pursuing appreciation in the underlying value of the investment. Simply put, you are looking to buy something cheaply and sell it more dearly. Probably a majority of the variety of investments fall into this category.

Most stocks, commodities, real estate, collectibles, and art would be considered capital gains forms of investing. A few of them are both capital gains and cash flow opportunities combined.

An easy way to understand capital gains investing involves looking at the example of real estate.

A real estate property that is bought with the goal of achieving capital gains is typically located near a major city, perhaps one to ten miles away.

The underlying value of such a property is more likely to increase in value because there proves to be a limited amount of these kinds of properties. Such properties in close proximity to the city are also in high demand. The type and size of the housing also plays into the potential future appreciation of the property in question.

You might buy such a house in this example for $250,000. After holding it for a few years, you are hoping that the scarcity and desirability of the property and its location will drive up the prices. If in a few years you are able to sell the property for $270,000, then a $20,000 capital gain has been realized.

It is important to note that this gain has only been realized when the property is actually sold. Buying a real estate property for capital gains is far different than buying one for cash flow, as you will see below.

The downsides to capital gains are several. These gains are paid out at only one time, and once they have been paid, the investment is no longer owned by you the investor. This means that pursuing this strategy will require constant searching for the next investment.

The upsides to capital gains are also noteworthy. The amount of money that is brought in with the single time disbursement can be significant. Capital gains investments can require less monitoring and upkeep than do many cash flow investments.

Cash Flow Forms of Investments

Cash flow investments take an entirely different approach than do capital gain investments. With a cash flow investment, the goal is not to seek out an appreciation in the underlying value of the investment at all.

Instead, you are looking to acquire an investment, asset, or property that pays you regular small amounts of money, creating a positive cash flow from the investment. The longer an asset pays out this cash flow, the better the cash flow investment it can be. There are cash flow types of investments that pay for an indefinite period of time. Real Estate Investment Trusts, Oil and Gas Trusts, bonds, and rental properties are all good examples of cash flow types of investments.

Look at the real estate example of investing again to better understand cash flow investing. A property that is a good cash flow type of investment will put money into your pocket every month after the rent is received and all expenses such as loan interest and maintenance expenses are covered.

For a rental property to be a positive cash flow investment, the property itself will need to feature a higher rent price than is typical for the property's purchase price. This is so that the rent will prove to be greater than all of the associated expenses attached to the property.

A positive cash flow property would be one that pays you $1,000 a month. The expenses on it, including loan interest and maintenance, could be $800 per month. This would leave you with a positive cash flow of $200 per month. So long as you own the property and continue to collect this rent on it, you will benefit from this regular monthly income.

It may not be as high as a capital gain investment one time sale would be, but it is steady income, and you get to continue owning the investment as you collect this income. Since money is being generated on the property to cover the mortgage payments, there are fewer limitations to how many cash flow investment properties that you can own at a time.

The upsides to this type of investment are several, and they are the opposite generally of the capital gains investments. On the one hand, you do not have to be constantly looking for a new cash flow investment property. So long as you own this one, the income will continue to be generated. At the same time, the money comes in on a routine basis. You can count on it regularly and periodically.

Even though it may not be a large amount at one time, over a long period of time, the money that comes in from a cash flow investment may be greater than the amount made on a capital gains investment.

The downside to a cash flow investment is limited. It may require a greater amount of upkeep, oversight, and maintenance than a capital gains investment would. With a rental property, the tenants will have to be found, screened, and kept for the property to continue producing income. The property will also have to be routinely maintained in order to keep it at a high income producing status.

Capital Gain Investment Versus Cash Flow Investment

As you have seen, there are advantages and disadvantages to each type of investing, be it capital gain or cash flow. Both types of investments are ultimately good, if they are well chosen. A greater amount of patience is likely required with capital gains investment, as for you to realize the appreciation in the asset can take several, or even many, years.

Cash Flow investments commonly produce quicker gains on a regular basis, but they are smaller in their nature and amounts. Cash flow investments do not require you to be constantly buying and selling, and having to do all of the significant amount of research that goes along with choosing a new investment every so often.

In the end of the debate, the truth is that both forms of investments are complementary. Since owning an investment for capital gains may take years to see the results, it is a sensible idea to be able to create regular income at the same time from a cash flow investment, property, or asset. Your personal investment style and goals in investing will determine to which of the two you give a greater priority as well.

Having both of them will shield you against the long amount of time that your capital is tied up with capital gains investments. Perhaps this is the greatest argument for having both cash flow and capital gains investments in your portfolio at the same time.

The History and Practice of Ponzi Schemes

Ponzi scheme is a term that you hear all too often in the media these days. Beginning back in the 1920's with Charles Ponzi, the number and dollar amounts involved with these Ponzi schemes have only increased dramatically, particularly in the last few years.

In fact, more than thirty-three Ponzi schemes have been discovered and dismantled in the first ten years of the twenty-first century. The most famous and highest dollar amount scheme, run by Bernie Madoff, is among them. In the subsequent paragraphs, you will see how the original Ponzi scheme came about, as well as the reasons that they are so effective, and some examples of other Ponzi schemes in the intervening years.

Charles Ponzi and His Scheme

Although the Ponzi Scheme is named for Charles Ponzi, he is not the man who invented the idea of deceiving people out of their money. Charles Dickins wrote about a Ponzi Scheme in his 1857 novel Little Dorrit. Charles Ponzi proved to be the man who built up the first such high dollar scheme in the United States.

Ponzi was an Italian man who immigrated to the U.S. in 1903. In less than twenty years, by 1920, Charles had figured out a means to make money by deceiving investors.

Within only six months time, he advanced from total obscurity to being a wealthy and prominent Boston millionaire.

Charles Ponzi's scheme involved international postal reply coupons. Investors were promised fifty percent returns on their investments in only a forty-five day time frame. They could double their money in ninety days time. The profits made were said to come as a result of exchanging such international postal reply coupons.

With his fantastic promises of returns, about forty thousand different people poured in approximately fifteen million dollars to his investment scheme. At one point, Ponzi was bringing in a quarter million dollars per day. Charles began turning his investors' monies to the use of paying off his earlier investors in order to keep the scheme going, and also of increasing his own wealth and personal needs.

When his scheme was uncovered and broken up, just five million of the fifteen million could be recovered and given back to the deceived investors.

Charles' crimes lay in promising returns that he did not plan on meeting. He willfully deceived and outright lied to investors. He used their money to support his own wealth and lavish lifestyle. He was first charged with eighty-six counts of mail fraud and sentenced to five years in federal jail.

After spending just three and a half years in jail, they let Ponzi go for good behavior. He was then charged with twenty-two charges of larceny by the state of Massachusetts. As it came out then that he was not actually an American citizen, he did not receive any more jail time, though they did attempt to deport him.

The Reasons that Ponzi Schemes Are So Successful

Ponzi schemes consistently work out well, at least for a while. The main factor underlying this is that the earliest investors really do receive the big returns that they are promised. As a result, they are generally easily persuaded to reinvest their capital back into the investment scheme, since it pays better returns than any other possible legitimate investment.

Because of this, a person running such a Ponzi Scheme will rarely end up having to pay back out much of the invested money on a net basis. Rather, all that they have to do is to give out statements showing the investors all of the money that they are making by leaving the money in the investment. This elaborate deception of an investment with tremendous returns can be maintained for years.

Examples of Ponzi Schemes

Another early Ponzi scheme was one run by a Swedish business-man Ivar Kreuger. He became known as the match king as he expanded his Ponzi scheme based on the unbelievably profitable nature of match monopolies. In the 1930's, his defrauding scheme fell apart and he killed himself.

A bigger Ponzi scheme emerged in the 1980's, when J. David and Company set up a supposed commodity and currency trading operation that involved many upper class people in San Diego, California. J. David Dominelli was working with the Del Mar, California Mayor as his partner.

Involved in J. David's scheme were a well known New York attorney firm Rogers and Wells that had advised him. J. David conspired to bring in two hundred million dollars, of which $120 million was returned to investors. With some of the missing $80 million, J. David ran to the Caribbean island of Monsterrat. He was extradited back to the states where he plead guilty to the federal charges levied against him. J. David went to jail under a twenty year sentence.

An unusual Ponzi scheme happened in the last years of the 1990's as a Scientologist minister named Reed Slatkin operated his setup. Although Slatkin did not prove to be a licensed investment adviser, he claimed that he was. Before his scheme was brought down in the year 2000, he had gathered in around $600 million from in excess of five hundred mostly wealthy Hollywood celebrities.

The Largest Ponzi Scheme of All Time

Perhaps the best known of recent Ponzi schemes is also the largest dollar amount fraud in U.S. history. You may remember the now infamous Bernard Madoff who, as a former chairman of the Nasdaq Stock Market Exchange, ran a Ponzi scheme of investing for around thirty years.

For literally decades, the man who began investing client's monies legitimately ran his investment business as a fraudulent operation that siphoned off hundreds of millions to billions of dollars for his own personal use and that of his family. The amount that was determined to be missed from literally thousands of investors' accounts proved to be an astonishing sixty-five billion dollars.

Much of this money turned out to be promised and artificially created gains, but in the end, trustees that the court appointed came to the conclusion that from eighteen billion to twenty-one billion dollars in actually invested money had vanished.

Madoff ran his investment operation as a private empire, with only a few trusted persons able to see the real books. He had a lavish building and employed staff who spent many work hours sending out statements to clients. The returns that he consistently generated were not so outlandish as with other Ponzi schemes, but still proved to be in the double digit returns per year over thirty or more years.

You may remember that his entire scheme collapsed not because he was caught, but because he admitted to his sons that his investment empire was all just a huge lie. They turned him in, he was arrested, and he was found guilty of operating this largest Ponzi scheme in history. For his eleven federal crimes, Madoff received the maximum allowable sentence under the law of one hundred and fifty years in Federal prison back in March of 2009.

This example of Bernie Madoff's Ponzi scheme proves that although such schemes typically collapse beneath their own weight, this can be avoided for many years. Madoff showed how a cleverly run Ponzi scheme can delude both savvy institutional and individual investors, along with overseeing securities exchange authorities.

His scheme may go down as not only being the largest financially, but also the longest running. In maintaining such an elaborate Ponzi scheme for around thirty or more years, Madoff showed how effective they can be at deceiving even the smartest of people.

Simplify Your Silver Investing With Exchange Traded Funds

If you have been following the news in the last few months and weeks, then you have likely seen that both gold and silver prices are making historic moves. While gold has already achieved price increases that put it well above its former all time highs, silver at $24.50 per ounce is still less than half way to its prior highs of more than $50 per ounce set back in the early 1980's.

This is a good argument for why silver now makes a better investment than gold. Still, you may not be clear on what is your most convenient way to invest in and trade the silver bull market moves. In the following paragraphs, two of the best Silver ETF's, or Exchange Traded Funds, are looked at and compared in detail to help you make the best decision.

Silver Exchange Traded Funds Explained

Exchange Traded Funds are a revolutionary idea that makes once inaccessible commodities like silver simple and convenient to invest in. As an investment vehicle, these silver exchange traded funds are traded principally on the major stock exchanges like AMEX and NYSE.

The real beauty of them is that they are comprised of shares that are bought and sold exactly like stocks. This means that any person with a common stock broker investment account is able to acquire them without difficulties. Unlike physical silver, which requires some effort to obtain, store, and then sell, the shares of silver exchange traded funds can even be bought and sold in a single day, if you so desire.

The SLV Exchange Traded Fund

The first such silver exchange traded fund that you saw created proved to be SLV. Barclays created and began trading this very first silver ETF on April 28th, 2006 in the United States. Since its inception, this iShares Silver Trust has been traded on the AMEX under the aptly identified symbol of SLV.

Even before this SLV ETF started trading, it had been eagerly awaited by silver investors ahead of its creation. The reason you saw for this lay in the fact that you would finally have an easy means for major money to move into the formerly hard to access silver markets. Institutional money that was capable of only investing in stocks and mutual funds, would now take on significant positions in silver using the new ETF.

Smaller investors who were wary of the COMEX futures and commodities exchange could now simply make a stock investment account purchase of silver. Even IRA funds are able to be placed in the SLV ETF without difficulty or expense. All of this signaled a new era in investing in the silver markets, that brought major money into the precious metal that had languished from lack of attention in the past.

The way that the SLV fund works is simple. With shares that investors purchase, the fund trustees simply buy physical ounces of silver and keep them in a vault. Literal silver underlies the actual SLV ETF to the basic ratio of more or less one ounce per existing one share. In such a way, SLV actually tracks the daily price movements of silver for its share holders.

In order to maintain this direct relationship, the trustees issue new shares and buy back redeemed shares whenever money flows into or out of the ETF fund. If many more shares are demanded, they simply create them and use the proceeds to purchase an equivalent amount of silver ounces. If many shares are redeemed, they simply sell an equivalent amount of silver ounces on the open markets in order to raise the proceeds to give back to the investors who are leaving the fund.

SLV can also be purchased on margin, giving a two to one leverage amount. This is because it is treated like a standard stock. In this way, investors are able to buy twice as much SLV as they would otherwise be able to, allowing them to attain greater profits as silver prices move higher.

The AGQ Exchange Traded Fund

Yet another silver exchange traded fund that is available to investors is the Pro Shares Ultra Silver ETF. The symbol of this ETF is AGQ. It began operating on December 1, 2008 and has traded on the NYSE ever since. This ETF is similar to SLV in that it follows the price of silver bullion as it is measured in U.S. Dollars, as fixed every day on the London Bullion Association exchange. This is where the similarities end, though.

AGQ does not seek to acquire physical silver ounces to underlie its shares at all. Instead, it buys silver futures and forward contracts from the COMEX with the proceeds of shares purchased. Similarly, when investors wish to redeem shares, the fund trustees sell a portion of their futures and forward contracts back on to the open market of the COMEX. So while the AGQ ETF is based on silver prices, it does not actual own any silver in vaults anywhere.

Another critical way that AGQ differs from the SLV ETF is in its leverage ratio. As you saw above, SLV is geared up at a one to one silver ounces to shares in the ETF fund ratio. AGQ shares are instead leveraged at a ratio of two to one against underlying silver prices and their daily movements.

This is accomplished using these futures and forwards contracts that allow the fund to control more silver than it actually has money to purchase. The goal of this leveraged ETF is simply to replicate two times the every day performance of the silver asset upon which it is based.

If you are extremely bullish on silver, then this AGQ ETF is a good vehicle for you to consider. It provides two times the leverage of the SLV ETF when purchased without margin. When margin is employed, it grants investors a four to one leverage against underlying silver prices. This is because twice as much of the AGQ exchange traded fund can be bought as you have money for when using margin accounts.

Learn The Two Main Strategies For Tackling Trading Stocks

When you are ready to start investing in the stock market, then you will need a way of intelligently approaching the many stocks available for you to buy and sell.

You will find that there are two main strategies for tackling trading stocks.

These are fundamental and technical analysis investing. In the subsequent paragraphs, the two drastically different strategies are explained and contrasted so that you may find the style that works best for you personally.

Fundamental Analysis Investing

With fundamental investing, you are interested in the fundamentals of a particular company and its underlying stock issue. This fundamental form of analysis looks very critically at the company's history and line of business, as well as its share of the market, style of management, and the amount of profits that the firm has realized over the past minimally three years time frame.

Other references considered are future projections for the company and the plans that it has for carrying out all outlined projects. The goal in pursuing this information lies in determining the company's future based on its current results, predicting its future profitability and associated stock price growth, and deciding how much risk there is for the company going forward.

Among these various measurements of how a given company is doing and will do is its future earnings potential. Fundamental investors are interested in reading the company's relevant financial statements before seriously considering putting money into it. The goal in this is to seek to lower risk in following both growth and value opportunities of the company in question.

Other fundamental investing factors besides the specific company's financial figures and prospects are considered as well. The overall economic outlook is considered. The future for the particular industry of which the company is a part is also scrutinized. Finally, fundamental analysis investing thinks about whether interest rates will go up or down, which can also impact the bigger economic picture as well as the particular company being studied. A role model in fundamental investing is Warren Buffet, who has been considered among the best of fundamental investors for decades.

Technical Analysis Investing

Technical investing is completely different in its approach and methodology. Technical investing may be said to require more training, as it is far more like a science of investing than an art. Supply and demand for a company's stock form the basis for this form of analysis and investing. Patterns of the corporation's stock as shown in its price are of critical interest to you as a technical investor.

Technical investors are looking to purchase stocks based on the sentiment of the market and their given price. You as a good technical investor would study the patterns inherent in the price of the stock to learn when the best time to purchase it would be. Real technical investors do not care about a company's internal business or affairs, like the fundamental investors do. They instead focus on the stock price and the market mood.

Technical investors understand that the prices of a given stock have little or nothing to do with random patterns of trends and price. They know that with the right charts and study, such trends and patterns can both be ascertained and taken advantage of to make profitable short term trades. With technical analysis, a wide range of charts and graphs tools are utilized.

You see many different methodologies used in practice. Whichever method is being employed in technical analysis though, you can be sure that examining charts for prior trading and pricing results will be in the forefront. Technical analysts and traders believe that the stock price currently takes into account all of the relevant information already. Because of this, they claim that fundamental analysis is simply wasting your time.

The old adage "the trend is your friend" is paramount to technical analysts. Technical investors believe that you can anticipate changes in the trend by watching for changes in sentiment. This is accomplished by reading the charts, since the emotional responses of investors to such changes in the stock price will cause patterns in the charts that can be recognized and utilized for intelligent and profitable trading purposes. Once again, technical investors shun a particular stock's actual worth or value. They are merely interested in conjuring up forecasts for future prices utilizing the historical patterns of the stock's price.

Why Many People Consider Technical Investing Risky

Many investors consider investing in stocks by any means to be risky. In most people's stock trading efforts, they act like technical investors, even though they are not remotely aware of the difference between technical and fundamental analysis and investing. To them, technical investing seems riskier, even though they are attempting to utilize it without clearly realizing it. This is because the prices of stocks do go up and down along with emotions in the market.

Examples of Factors Affecting Stock Market Prices

Many things can cause a stock price to rise and fall, and these factors do seem to be heavily dependent on perception and emotions. Take for example the fact that stocks might be substantially covered in the news one week and totally absent from it the next.

Large institutional investors, such as pension funds, mutual funds, or hedge funds also come in and sell or buy huge quantities of a stock, and this can significantly impact the price of the market. The companies themselves similarly affect demand and supply for their own shares by being involved with stock splits to create more shares, offering additional shares, and purchasing back their own shares.

Fundamental Versus Technical Analysis Investing

It should not come as a surprise to you at this point that the two camps of fundamental and technical analysts and investors at the least mistrust each other, and at the worst despise one another. Yet which method proves to be the more sensible one for investing in stocks?

Both of them will practice insuring themselves from catastrophic losses with stop loss orders and other risk management strategies. Only their approaches are completely different.

In the end, the answer to this question of who has the better idea for investing depends on your particular approach. Technical investors are purchasing their stocks like a person who goes looking for sales and bargains, using historical price and trend tools. This method has been proven to work well for investors who are only investing for shorter time frames such as days, weeks, or possibly even months.

Fundamental investors are like a quality driven shopper, whose biggest concern is the nature of the product, or company and associated stock, that they are getting for their money. You should not become a fundamental investor unless you are investing with at least a medium term time frame. Many months are required for this approach to yield results, and sometimes even years. Longer term investors should almost always be fundamental analysts, like our example of Warren Buffet.

A way to improve your chances of success is to try to combine the two approaches when you can. You might be a fundamental investor who finds a handful of stocks that are good long term values, then attempts to match these up with technical investing to determine if the timing to buy is right or not. Since both styles of investing have merits and significant followings, this would not be a bad idea for you at all, even though it requires time, study, and patience to master the two techniques.

The Four Streams of Income When You Buy Rental Property

You have possibly considered purchasing a second property in order to create passive rental income at some time in the past.

Buying property that you can rent out is an investment decision that actually provides you with four different benefits. Among these are cash flow income, amortization, depreciation, and appreciation, all of which are explored in the subsequent paragraphs.

Cash Flow Income Stream from Property

This cash flow benefit is the obvious one that you will have thought of already when you considered buying an investment property in the first place. A rental income steam is a terrific way to create cash flow. This income stream can actually be positive cash flow for you, if you are able to realize a rent that is higher than your monthly mortgage payments, taxes, insurance, and up-keep.

Even if the resulting cash flow only proves to be a break even, there are other benefits that you realize from cash flow. Perhaps the chief of these is that it looks good to banks and other lending institutions in case you decide to purchase another investment income property on top of your first one in the future. However you look at it, having additional cash flow is always a benefit for your finances.

When you are looking for such a cash flow income investment property, there are some things that are helpful to keep in mind. Ideally, you would like to know what similar properties in the immediate area are garnering in monthly rent from their tenants. This way, you can attempt to purchase the highest renting property for the most reasonable price.

It is sensible to keep in mind what the approximate monthly mortgage payments will amount to as well while you are figuring estimated expected monthly rent. By doing these two things, you can increase the chances of your monthly rental income exceeding your monthly outlay on the investment property.

Amortization of the Property

Another type of income stream that you benefit from when purchasing investment properties that you plan on renting out is the amortization of the property in question. Amortization is a complicated word that means the eventual paying off of a debt, like a mortgage, using monthly payments for a pre-set amount of time. These payments include both the principal borrowed on the investment property as well as all accompanying interest. An easier way of understanding this amortization concept is that the tenant is paying off your loan.

You may be scratching your head wondering how the tenant is actually paying off your loan for you. He or she is accomplishing this on your behalf with each and every monthly rent payment. Assuming the rental amount is enough to cover the mortgage payments, then you are not having to come out of pocket every month to cover them yourself.

As an example, if you found a tenant who loved your property and stayed in it for the twenty to thirty year length of the mortgage's life, then when you had made that last mortgage payment, the tenant would have paid for the entire property. The same principal is true if you have multiple tenants over the life of the mortgage.

If you sell the property before the mortgage is paid off, you have still realized this tenant provided amortization income stream. The money that you recuperate from the house, beyond your original down payment and any increase in property value will be the money that the tenant or tenants paid every month that you ultimately used to pay for the monthly mortgage payment.

Depreciation as an Income Stream

Another helpful income stream that comes front rental investment properties is depreciation. This depreciation refers to your ability to take off a portion of the cost of the property on your individual tax return every year. You are actually able to regain the expense of buying the rental income producing property through depreciating it.

This is possible because the Internal Revenue Service considers that residential real estate is declining in value every year, or depreciating. Since the general facts are that real estate actually gains in value with time, this amounts to what is called an accounting loss. The loss is not a real one and only appears on paper as if by magic, but it is certainly a helpful factor to have working for you when it is time to prepare your taxes.

Residential types of properties are allowed to be depreciated on your taxes as cost of purchase recovered over a twenty-seven and a half year amount of time.

So long as at least eighty percent of the building's income results from rent on dwelling units, then it is permissible according to the IRS.

The other advantage to this is that you are allowed to live in part of the property or building yourself and still count the fair value of rent for the part of the property that occupy as well. This means that while you can deduct only the portion of the property that is actually being rented out, you will be able to count the rental value of the portion of it that you occupy in the total along with it.

This depreciation amount can reduce your taxable income significantly for as many years as you own and rent out the rental property all the way until the recovery period is reached. Money that you save in taxes is ultimately another useful income stream in your pocket.

Appreciation as an Income Stream of the Property

Even though the IRS acts as though the value of your investment property that you rent out is declining in value, the truth is that real estate generally appreciates, or increases in value, over time. The beauty of this fact is that with consistent property appreciation, rental rates generally increase as well.

Since your monthly mortgage payments are fixed, higher monthly rent means that you have realized yet another income stream. In time, you may actually be making a significant amount of extra money per month as a result of this rising rental rate and yet fixed monthly mortgage payments.

There is yet another advantage to appreciation in your investment property that you may realize. This results from the property's rising actual value over time. As the property value gains, so too does your equity, or stake, in the property along with it. When your equity rises enough, you will be able to refinance your mortgage loan, which would allow you to take cash out of this extra value in the property, as well as to possibly lower your interest rate.

You might use this extra money taken out for potential investments, such as to purchase another rental income producing property. Whatever you choose to do with the extra equity value that you take out of your property, it makes another nice income stream that you realize from the property.

If you succeed in negotiating a lower interest rate on your refinanced mortgage, then your monthly payments will go down too, perhaps substantially. This will depend on how much lower the monthly interest rate is, and at what point in the mortgage that you chose to refinance your investment property in question.

The Three Personality Types of Investors

Investors of all kinds exist in the world. Still, practically every one of them can be classified into one of three particular types.

You are either someone who simply does not invest at all, a person who invests with the overriding goal of not losing money, or a person who invests to succeed.

All three of these investing personality types have different characteristics and modes of operating.

People Who Do Not Invest At All

There are two main types of people who fall under the category of those who do not invest at all. The first of these are those who are terrified of investing. Because they have no financial or investing education, they see investing as the unknown. It is easy to fear the unknown. Besides this, investing represents a dizzying series of terms and concepts to people who have never obtained any kind of background in it.

This is not a good reason to keep from investing for the long term, though it might be a good reason not to invest your money tomorrow. What this fear should do is to motivate you to acquire a financial education.

There are so many basic level guides written to help out novice investors available. A quick trip to your local library will yield several of these.

Other advice and education is available over the Internet and in seminars. Some of this may require membership fees or event fees, but these are a small price to pay to learn all about the means of bettering your financial future through investing.

The next type of person who does not invest at all is one who is infested with the entitlement disease. If you are this kind of person, then you are like countless Americans who feel that everything should be handed to you. The person who feels entitled believes that it should be the responsibility of someone else to take care of his or her retirement.

This individual simply does not feel like they should have to bother with investing at all. They will likely look to one of two different groups to provide for them in retirement. Either they will expect that the government should do it, and then they will simply wait around on social security to bail out their retirement. The problem with this lies in the fact that social security benefits are not enough money to cover much of a retirement, even a poverty level retirement, if you retire in the United States.

Not only this, but the GAO, or Government Accounting Office, has repeatedly said that Social Security will start to have problems paying out its full pledged benefits within thirty years. Depending on it and the government to take care of your retirement is a pitiful excuse for not investing. Other people expect that the company that they work for will take care of their retirement.

Maybe they anticipate having a pension at retirement age to cover their living expenses. Pensions are in similar trouble financially, in many cases. On top of this, many companies are doing away with them altogether to save on costs. In truth, you should not count on anyone else else to take care of you and your retirement besides yourself.

People Who Invest Not to Lose

The next category of investors that you might fall into is those who only invest with the goal of not losing their money. A person who is in this category will not take many, if any at all, chances with his or her investments. Rather than buy into an investment class that offers a potentially much greater return but entails some risk, they will opt for the safe, ultra low rates.

If you fall into this category, then you will shun stocks, mutual funds, commodities, and any other asset class that could realistically lose all or some of your money. Instead, you will go with guaranteed or practically guaranteed investments like Treasury Bills and Bonds, Money Market Funds, and Certificates of Deposit.

These are not inherently wrong investment concepts. They just do not pay returns that will keep you ahead of the ravages of annual inflation. Making sub inflation or at inflation returns on your investments is better than no gains at all, but not much better.

Your problem if you fall into this category of only being willing to go with safe investments is that you do not have enough confidence in your investing skills.

Maybe you are like many American who watched the Financial Crisis destroy major companies and venerable corporations and this only reinforced your idea that investing in anything that is not guaranteed is not a smart way to go.

It is important for you to remember that no one has ever became wealthy or financially secure by sinking their savings into Treasury Bills or money market funds. By increasing your financial education to learn about diversification and other sensible asset allocation strategies, you can learn the effective ways of minimizing your risk and of spreading your money around into a variety of investment categories that will balance each other out.

Once you have understood the ways that commodities like silver and gold can offset declines in stock portfolios, then you will start to have the courage to try some more aggressive investments. Another thing that will help you to overcome this timid mentality is to open a practice trading account and invest with pretend money for a while, even for months, until your confidence in your investing abilities and skills begin to grow with time.

People Who Invest to Win

The last category that you hopefully find yourself in is the one comprised of investors who set out to succeed with their investments. These types of people have overcome their natural inclination to depend on others, as well as any fear with which they might have started out investing. They have taken the time to study and broaden their financial and investing education.

They have kept themselves abreast of developing trends and ideas in the markets and investing world. It might be that they read newspapers like the Wall Street Journal or Investors' Business Daily. Whatever the source of current information, if you are in this ideal investing category, then you have learned that only through your financial knowledge and ability to invest will you be capable of getting ahead in your investments.

Investors who are at investing to succeed and outperform also seek more control over their investments. They realize that the fees charged by money managers and full service brokerages can be astronomical, serving to skim a large part of your investment returns off of the top of the account.

Between fees that are levied officially and spreads that are charged, the average investment broker company will take more than $300,000 in fees and spreads over the course of a thirty year investment management time frame. The amount is even higher than this if they are actively managing an account on your behalf. Savvy investors who are at it to succeed open self directed retirement and investment accounts to manage themselves.

Finally, these people invest for higher returns. They are willing to accept some degree of risk in exchange for better returns. They have effectively learned risk management techniques, and are poised to grow their investment accounts towards their financial independence over the medium to long term. This is where you want to find yourself as an investor.

Quantum Investing - The Future of the Stock Market

If you are a person who is always on the look out for future trends that make brilliant investing ideas, then you should consider the book Quantum Investing: Quantum Physics, Nanotechnology, and the Future of the Stock Market by Stephen R. Waite.

This is a work that deals with several subjects that many people are very unfamiliar with, quantum physics and nanotechnology.

The book offers a deep insight into these two still emerging fields that may change the corporate landscape for investing over the next twenty-five years. By exploring this book in the subsequent paragraphs, you may be able to gain an investment edge over the masses that have not yet caught on to this idea.

About the Author Stephen Waite

The author Stephen Waite is no stranger to financial and investment circles. He brings a seventeen year background of working on Wall Street to the researching and writing of this book. Stephen proved to be the managing director and co-founder of Trilogy Advisers, a firm that worked in investment advisory services and managed billions of dollars.

His prior book Boomernomics has been featured in Business Week, The Economist, and The Wall Street Journal. An adjunct Finance Professor at Quinnipiac University, Stephen Waite is also the Chief Knowledge Officer of a New York City headquartered technology research firm TheInfoPro.

Brief Background of Quantum Physics and Nanotechnology
Since this book deals with two subjects that are very unfamiliar, it is useful to review what the main focuses of the companies and fields in this book are about. Quantum physics turns out to be the science that works with tiny indivisible energy units that are referred to as Quanta and described in the Quantum Theory.

This theory contains five principal ideas. It states that energy is not actually continuous, but is found in tiny, discrete units. These basic energy particles act like waves and particles at the same time. These particles move in inherently random patterns. You can not know the momentum and position of such particles at once.

The atomic level universe is not at all similar to the world in which we live. This bizarre sounding theory actually helps to explain much about the true nature of the universe, and it has been called more significant to the understanding of science than even Einstein's Theory of Relativity. Companies that deal with Quantum Physics are working with these tiny energy units and particles to come up with new ways of doing things and revolutionary new products.

Nanotechnology remains study of how to manipulate matter on both atomic and molecular levels. In practice, it is used in the design and building of working systems and devices that are so small that they can not begun to be seen without the aid of powerful microscopes.

With nanotechnology, you may see enormous breakthroughs that lead to revolutionary new devices and materials that have a simply huge number of useful applications. These include the fields of electronics, medicine, energy production, and biomaterials. Nano-technology offers the potential to dramatically change the world in which you live forever.

Premise of Quantum Investing

The author Stephen Waite sets out to explain to you the ways in which quantum science and nanotechnology based ideas are set to make a tremendous and profound impact on the world around you, on corporations, and on investments.

With one volume that is easy to read and understand, he takes you through various critical points of major change in society, the underlying economics, and the production of wealth. This is a useful start to the book as it lays a helpful context for the scientific wave that is set to influence everyone.

Author Stephen Waite goes through the basis and relevance of Quantum Physics to make his case that these quantum and nano based technologies are set to create major long term investing and wealth possibilities for a great portion of the twenty-first century. He spells out the ways that you may begin to position yourself to benefit from this today.

Substance of Quantum Investing

Quantum Investing: Quantum Physics, Nanotechnology, and the Future of the Stock Market is a book about investing and so much more. Stephen Waite intently concentrates on the fields that present opportunities that you have never before seen in history.

Along with this, he shows you the massive benefits to society to which these advance in Quantum Physics based development will lead. In the work, author Stephen Waite references economists, physicists, historians, politicians, and even futurists. In such a way, he provides a many dimensioned view of the profound impact that these nanotechnologies and Quantum Physics breakthroughs are already starting to make even today.

Quantum Investing is not simply a book about the future, it is a book about today. It deals with the rising and already established industries that are based on Quantum Physics. Included in these are biotechnology, communications, and nanotechnology fields.

Throughout the book Stephen Waite explains and reinforces his point that all of these areas are in fact the most significant and potentially profitable places to invest in today, as they will have dramatic influence on the future of the American economy. It shows you clearly the big concepts that are going to lead to tomorrow's revolutions as well.

Layout of Quantum Investing

Quantum Physics proves to be very well organized in its layout. Each chapter includes takeaways sections at its conclusion. A chronology of Quantum Science's key events is presented, along with an extremely useful glossary of terms utilized in the work.

This makes digesting the fairly involved scientific concepts much easier.

Implications of Quantum Investing

The author Stephen Waite draws a series of conclusions in the book that are interesting and potentially earth shaking. As part of his depiction of the ways in which the next twenty-five years of advances in technology will change your life, the entire economy, and the composition of the stock market, he lays out some of the major business and investment evolutions set to occur.

Corporations that are not versatile enough to adapt to the relevant changes will likely disappear. He goes on to suggest that the changes that you have seen in the past years in indexes like the Dow Jones Industrial Average will only continue. In fact, he does not believe that most of the stocks that are presently listed on the S&P 500 will even be around in twenty-five years.

These are shocking claims to make. Stephen Waite says that a creation and destruction process will occur that permits corporations who are able to realize the benefits of technologies that have not even been invented yet to expand at phenomenal paces. They will take the places of the companies that can not keep up with the change.

Waite leaves you with some sobering thoughts about scientific advances and wealth creation. He makes the point that a greater amount of wealth creation occurred in the last hundred years than had happened in all of recorded history to that point put together.

He believes that this creation of wealth will only intensify and speed up, so that in the next twenty-five years, a greater amount of wealth will be created than all of that produced in the whole twentieth century. The author makes many convincing points that should lead you to read this book so that you are not left out of the greatest investing opportunity of not only our time, but possibly of all time.

The Guide Book For Investing In The Twenty-First Century

If you have become concerned about, or at least aware of, the tentative discussions that America's greatest days could lie behind her, then you should pick up the newest book that talks about this possibility. This is "The Great Super Cycle" by David Skarica.

In this intriguing work, the author goes through the declines and falls of the world's greatest empires and compares their decline to present day America's scenario. More than this, the book shows you the things that you must do to protect and grow your wealth in the difficult days that may lie ahead.

About the Author David Skarica

The author of "The Great Super Cycle" David Skarica has been called the most successful apprentice of Sir John Templeton, the legendary late investor. Skarica joined the elite ranks of the youngest people to ever pass the Canadian Securities course at only eighteen years of age. By nineteen, he was already a financial adviser.

The event that brought David into the spotlight proved to be a report that he wrote and issued in 1999 forecasting eight significant events in America that were soon to happen.

He predicted the following:

- Housing and real estate bubble would explode
- American stocks would go into a multiple year long bear market
- Real estate in exotic foreign countries would do better than that of the U.S.
- Bull run in commodities lay in the near future
- Gold would take off
- War would break out between the U.S. and countries in the Middle East
- The U.S. dollar would crash in value
- Major inflation would attack the country

With six of his eight unlikely events having already occurred, he quickly gained the attention of the investing world.

David Skarica possesses an uncanny capability of anticipating significant trends in advance of them happening. He has put this ability to work in picking out the best investments available at any given time. Skarica's work is showcased in such important places as Barron's and CNBC. Besides this, he is a routine contributor to the Financial Brain Trust of Newsmax Magazine.

Historical Background Highlighted in the "Great Super Cycle"
David Skarica spends a significant part of the book going through the greatest empires in history and what led to their inevitable declines and falls. First he takes you through their rise to power via military domination, economic leadership, and political and diplomatic accomplishments. Ancient Rome, The Ottoman Empire, Spain, France, and Great Britain are all examined along with the causes that led to their common demises.

The striking parallels of their mistakes stands out. Rome built up a great middle class that became threatened and disappeared, leading to their collapse. Both the Ottoman Empire and France fell apart as their interest rates exploded. Spain and Great Britain were bankrupted by expensive wars.

The Parallels Between the Great Empires and the United States "The Great Super Cycle" looks into the disarming parallels between these great empires of history and the present day United States. It compares the United States with Ancient Rome in the decline of the middle class in today's American society.

It looks at the costly war on terror and wars in both Iraq and Afghanistan that the U.S. has been forced to engage in and weighs them against the conflicts that pummeled Spain and Great Britain's formidable empires and economies. And chillingly, it looks at events in both The Ottoman Empire and the French Empire that led to sky high interest rates that broke the governments financially and shows how the United States is on the same path to this critical problem.

After this is done, David Skarica begins drawing conclusions from these other imperial lessons to show that the path that the United States is on literally mirrors the decline and fall of a great number of the most powerful and impressive empires that history witnessed.

The "Great Super Cycle" then ties all of this together to examine how the political, economic, and social choices that the U.S. government and Americans decided on decades ago that cut across both party lines have caused America to sit on the edge of a bankruptcy that could occur as soon as 2015.

Skarica shows that the Great Recession and Financial Crisis of 2007-2010 that the U.S. has struggled with is more than simply another recession, but that is is a probably total collapse into bankruptcy and irreversible decline. He outlines how this will lead to economic, social, and political crisis in the next few years.

Investment Advice from "The Great Super Cycle"

Skarica raises a good question as he transitions the book to investment advice and ideas for saving and growing your wealth in these likely circumstances. With the last two of his predictions yet to occur, namely those of severe inflation and the destruction of the U.S. dollar, how much of American's wealth will survive the collapse? Most Americans simply are not prepared for these tragedies. Those who read the rest of "The Great Super Cycle" can be.

David takes you through a series of important topics in the remainder of the book. Among them are the ways that you can make your investment portfolio truly protected from inflation. He goes through the best three means of using gold in order to save your investments and money from the coming attack of inflation. It may surprise you to learn that Skarica says that you should avoid American gold coins at all costs. He also give you a formula for forecasting the next huge price swing up in the timeless yellow metal.

More than this, "The Great Super Cycle" goes through what to do to survive the coming explosion of the bond bubble. The author argues that this will be ruinous for many people, individuals, and institutions that hold bonds as interest rates soar and bond prices plummet. In particular, he highlights two different securities that are created in order to withstand a bond collapse and to provide you with significant returns at the same time.

"The Great Super Cycle" even features a special section on foreign investing. Since it argues that the greatest days of the country are behind you, the book makes the case for investing in the world's best foreign markets and investments that will dramatically increase the returns of your portfolio. This Average American's Guide to Global Investing is an invaluable resource that all Americans should read now, while there is still sufficient time to diversify away from the U.S. dollar and dollar denominated investments.

Verdict of 'The Great Super Cycle"

"The Great Super Cycle" presents numerous lessons from history and shows how they relate to the current day problems and decline seen in the United States. It offers the lesson of learning from history's mistakes so that you do not suffer as they are repeated in modern day America.

The real value of this book is not in the gloomy predictions for the next few years and future of the U.S. though. It instead lies in the first of its kind detailed guide book for investing around the world in the twenty-first century.

"The Great Super Cycle" teaches you potent indicators, formulas, and trends that you are able to personally utilize in order to find and take advantage of cycles going on in all investment markets, whatever happens to the U.S. in the next decades.

Strategies of Successful Fund Managers and Future Traders

If you have ever dreamed of becoming a successful commodities' trader, then you will need a guide on how to do it. Such a guide is available from author Michael Covel in "The Complete TurtleTrader: The Legend, the Lessons, the Results."

The point and substance of the book is explored in the following paragraphs, so that you can see for yourself how this book can turn you into the accomplished commodities' trader that you have longed to be.

About Author Michael Covel

Michael Covel is both an author and even a movie director. Before his present work "The Complete Turtle Trader," he wrote "Trend Following." His documentary film is entitled "Broke: The New American Dream" and features more than one hundred on camera interviews filmed over three different continents. Michael Covel has also created successful web sites TrendFollowing.com and TurtleTrader.com(R).

The Legend Part of the Complete Turtle Trader

Should you have been involved with trading either stocks or commodities over the past twenty years, then you would have probably heard about Richard Dennis and his Turtles. The mystery of his nurture as opposed to nature experiment relating to trading is unveiled in Michael Covel's latest book "The Complete Turtle Trader." The legend goes back to a successful early eighties movie called Trading Places.

Trading Places addressed the story of a bet that two crusty old wealthy commodities brokerage owners made in their Chicago office. They made this bet that any people could be taken off of the streets and made into a successful trader of commodities.

The unbelievably successful commodities trader Richard Dennis actually entered into this bet with his business partner William Eckhardt. The substance of the bet surrounded the possibilities of instructing a random and diverse segment of people in their trading methods. To accomplish the experiment, ads for employment were set up and the experimental Turtles were brought on with the firm to trade.

This true story demonstrated that such trading could actually be taught. It had nothing to do with being born with the ability. Dennis' Turtles made enormous sums of money for him. One of them went on the be a greater success than Dennis even turned out to be.

The System of the Complete Turtle Trader

This trading system that Dennis and his Turtles used does not turn out to be so complex. It is centered on a formula that follows trends.

Money management proved to be the critical part of their success. The idea remains that you simply avoid trading when the markets sit within a constant range. You only engage in trading if they instead make new trends. This is the place where you have to pile into the trades without fear and reservations.

For any of you who have previously worked with futures and commodities, you understand that the majority of breaking out trends last for relatively short amounts of time. The Turtle trading system anticipates this and accounts for it. The vast majority of their actual trades represent small losing trades. The majority of their money made comes from only several powerful trend trades every year. The little losses are in fact not important, so long as they are kept small.

The Specifics of the Complete Turtle Trader

The Complete Turtle Trader and the Turtle Trading System features breakout rules that work on both four week and eleven week time frames. If the prior trade proved to be a winning trade, then they ignore the four week trade. In this case, they would wait for the eleven week trade trigger to make certain that a trend was caught and traded.

The particular rules of the system did not allow them to put any more than two percent of their capital at risk in any given trade. As such winning trades went their way, they would increase the size of positions to realize greater profits from the winning trend.

Warnings on the System Featured in the Complete Turtle Trader There is no doubt that the Turtle Trading System shows itself to be a winning system. It demonstrates this not on the majority of trades, but over time.

You can not be timid or fearful to follow it. You also can not be insufficiently capitalized to make it work either. Draw downs in losses taken on the system are significant. You need to have a big trading account so that you are able to be both frequently trading numerous markets and well diversified at once.

What Happened Following The Experiment

In 1988, Richard Dennis tired of the experiment and chose to end it. This proved to be only the next phase of the experiment though. Now the Turtles had to go it on their own. The question became one of what would these traders who had demonstrated success actually do with these impressive newly acquired skills in trading?

The balance of the book deals with this question. It generally concentrates on the story of Jerry Parker. He is the Turtle who turned his initial trading success into the major outfit Chesapeake Capital. Michael Covel estimated in the book that his net worth rose to somewhere between $770 million and $1.75 billion. Jerry Parker showed himself to be the first of the Turtles to cash in on the group's newly acquired fame. He demonstrated the intelligence to to do this in the most sensible and practical way possible.

As the book shares with you, Jerry Parker is not the only one of the Turtles who succeeded with the skills that Richard Dennis taught them. A number of the other Turtles eventually became managers of substantial sums of money as well. Curiously, the rest of them just decided to go back to living their regular lives.

Still, the experiment showed that it was a great success in that regular people could be instructed in this system of trading to realize greater than typical returns in trading commodities, stocks, and futures.

That some of the participants decided that this new life and occupation was not for them in the end is a commentary on human nature and not the viability of the experiment.

Verdict on the Complete Turtle Trader Book

The Complete Turtle Trader book is more than simply an interesting read. It is also a book that is both well researched and instructional for the reader who wishes to succeed at trading not only commodities and futures, but also stocks.

In writing this book, the author Michael Covel did not rely simply on second hand accounts. He interviewed a good number of the Turtles, and he relates his findings in these interviews, helping to give the book life and character. Besides this, author Michael Covel also has followed the story of these Turtles and the practice of following trends since 1996 on his website found at TurtleTrader.com.

The book represents a fascinating story that can encourage you through seeing how ordinary people went on to do extraordinary things financially. Such success stories can only build you up and help you to realize your own dreams.

More than this, it teaches you the strategies that a great number of the world's most successful hedge fund managers and futures traders actually go about using in trading the markets to realize consistent significant gains over time.

The 3 Best Silver Investment Strategies For Top Profits

There is a great number of different ways to get involved in the exciting silver bonanza that is just getting started.

At this point, you may wonder which of the many vehicles and means is the most appropriate one for your situation and investing background.

With so many alternatives, it is easy to be a little bewildered. In this summary, you will see the strategies that is best for beginning investors, intermediate investors, and advanced investors.

Investing in Silver for Beginners

If you are a beginning investor, then you do not want to expose yourself to scary amounts of risk or the volatility, price swings, and value changes that using leverage will bring. This may be an effective way to maximize your profits. Still, if it puts you on an emotional roller coaster ride that causes you to doubt your choices as the prices of silver temporarily correct, possibly even leading you to sell overextended silver positions at a loss, then it is counter productive.

You as a beginning investor need to focus on purchasing physical silver and holding it. Since you will own the silver, it will be easier to ride out any short term price movements without panicking.

In this book, we discussed many different methods of acquiring physical silver.

There are semi collectible silver coins, collectible rare silver coins, and bullion silver coins. Each of them have their advantages and appeal as we saw, but at this stage, you are looking for the most cost effective way to purchase as much physical silver as you can for the money that you have to spend. Because of this, your best way of purchasing physical silver is through buying silver bullion coins or bars.

In buying one or ten ounce silver coins, you have something that is not only a store of silver, but also beautiful to look at and enjoy. The premiums for these coins can be a little high, but they offer the advantage of small denominations of even a single ounce.

This is helpful if you later decide that you want to take some of your profits while keeping the rest of the investment for later additional price appreciation.

It will cost you from $2 to $4 per ounce if you buy the once ounce coins, depending on whether you buy the Canadian Maple Leafs or Austrian Philharmonics, the American Silver Eagles or Silver Buffaloes, or the Australian Rabbits.

By buying the ten ounce versions of these coins, you will save as much as half on these silver bullion premiums. This is your best way to go with the coins, since ten ounce silver denominations are still small and easy to part with for partial profit taking.

If you are willing to go with the silver bars, then you will get lower silver product premiums over the spot market price. On hundred ounce bars carry commissions of only $50 per bar. This amounts to a reasonable fifty cent premium per ounce. For the biggest bang for your silver dollar, these larger bars are the way to go.

There are storage facilities that will act as custodian for you. The most cost effective way of storing silver though is likely in your local bank's vault in a safe deposit box. This is also easy to access. You can get one of these sufficient for your storage needs for a reasonable $100 to $150 maintenance cost per year.

The last advice for you the beginner is only to buy the silver for which you have the actual money. Avoid margin accounts for now. These are more appropriate for intermediate and expert level investors.

Investing in Silver for Intermediates

As an intermediate investor, you are prepared to do some trading in and out of silver. For you, the best formula for silver fortune success lies in buying the SLV silver exchange traded fund. It tracks silver extremely closely every single trading day. It is highly liquid and easy to get in and out of five days per week.

Buy these SLV shares like you would stocks, with low commission rates through self directed investment accounts online, such as with TD Ameritrade, eTrade, or Scott Trade. The commissions on these trades will cost you around only $20 for each round turn in and out of silver, or about $10 for each purchase or sale.

As you use your charts for price movement, you will see that there are major dips and peaks in the price. You can increase your profits with silver by purchasing the SLV Exchange Traded Fund shares as silver pulls back. When the price of silver rallies towards peaks and highs, then you can sell part or all of your shares to lock in profits.

You can increase your silver holdings and potential profits through wisely using a margin account. This will allow you to buy up to twice as much silver as the cash value of your trading account. In this way, you will possibly double your profits from the time that you buy your SLV ETF shares to the point that you sell them. With this two to one margin amount, you should not run into any danger of margin calls or forced position sales if silver prices pull back temporarily.

Investing in Silver for Advanced

For those of you who are more advanced investors, there is another track for you that will potentially allow you to make even greater levels of profits since you are familiar and experienced with handling larger amounts of risk. You can purchase the silver ETF that offers greater leverage for starters.

The AGQ Pro Shares Ultra Silver Exchange Traded Fund will allow you to acquire double exposure to silver price movements. By using a margin account with this, you will be able to achieve four times the leverage and exposure to silver price increases. Four to one margin is still a low and relatively safe amount of silver that should not lead to margin calls.

A more aggressive means for you to build up silver positions is through silver options on the SLV ETF. As silver pulls back after price increases, you may feel confident that it will soon resume its upward price march. This is the time for you to buy option contracts on SLV, giving you a one hundred share position equivalent for every contract that you purchase.

Just be careful with these options, since they are only valid for a certain amount of time until the expiration date arrives. If the silver prices have not risen within your time frame, then you will either have to accept the loss of all the money that you spend on the options, or exercise them and take on the underlying SLV shares at a price that has you underwater on the ETF shares, at least for the time being.

The other method to acquire heavy leverage to silver is with futures accounts or FOREX accounts. They give you the ability to hold the positions as long as you wish. They also provide you with fifteen to one margin with futures contracts and twenty-five to one margin with FOREX spot silver.

Just remember to buy silver on pull backs and to only acquire positions that you can take some price declines on, since this higher margin will mean significant gains and losses as silver prices swing back and forth.

Do You Know The Three Stages of an Investment Bubble?

In the last ten years, you have watched as the economy entered into several different bubbles. From the dot com bubble, to the real estate bubble, to the stock market bubble, to the credit bubble, you have likely participated in them along with everyone else.

This does not make you naive when you are deceived; it is almost impossible to recognize a bubble when you are in the middle of one along with everyone else. Usually only outsiders are able to recognize these bubbles in progress.

The subsequent paragraphs go through the three stages of an investment bubble, using the current bull market it in gold as an example, so that you may recognize these bubbles in the future.

Stage One of an Investment Bubble

You first see a skeptical stage with bubbles. This is the point where most individuals are not yet involved. Maybe the sector that is starting to bubble up had been beaten down in the past. Something changes in the form of a displacement to make the bubble begin, even while most people are saying that the sector will not rise.

Maybe a company invents a new technology such as the Internet, or the government shifts economic policy by lowering interest rates.

Lower interest rates prove to be a common fuel for bubbles, since the government makes money available cheaply this way so that participants in the bubble can more easily bid up the prices.

In this first stage of the bubble, the prices are already going up. You could also call this the ground floor opportunity of the bubble, since the majority of people are not yet aware that the bubble even exists. As you see prices continue to go up, other individuals begin to pay attention little by little.

Gold sat at this stage in the year 2000. Prices had bottomed out at a multiple year low. Many people remembered that it had traded in the last bull market of the seventies and early eighties to as high as $850 per ounce and since then had gradually and steadily declined all the way down to $250 for each ounce.

Very few people believed in its gains at this point, even as gold rose over the next few years up towards $600-$700 per ounce. The financial pundits pointed to the previous all time high of gold and said that the opportunities had already passed.

Stage Two of an Investment Bubble

The next stage of the bubble proves to be the longest one. In this second stage, you see the sentiment towards the sector or market begin to change. Prices continue to go up, but many members of the public still feel fear and confusion.

Cheap credit is available then to make investments in the bubble sector possible, since no bubble can really take off without it. The insiders of the bubble are already invested and are riding up with the prices. As the prices continue rising even year after year, you begin to see the fear of the investing public gradually diminish.

While the smart money has been taking advantage of the bubble for years now, you and members of the public are generally still struggling with whether to get in or not. A few brave ones manage to take the plunge and realize some still tremendous gains along the way.

Gold moved back and forth in a range between $600 and $850 per ounce for more than a year before really beginning its dramatic ascent towards the $1,300 to $1,400 range that it runs in now. Many analysts believe that gold is only in stage two, as it still has many skeptics and doubters among the public.

The average person has not yet made his or her full commitment to gold investments. Gold has also not neared its inflation adjusted high of more than $2,500 per ounce in today's dollars yet.

Stage Three of an Investment Bubble

You finally see the third stage of euphoria when all of the skeptics in the bubble market at last grow silent. The market has gone up for probably years now. You have seen friends and neighbors realize enormous gains and finally acknowledge that something is going on. Outsiders to the market start to pile in along with you.

At this point, prices are sensationally high, yet the majority of analysts keep telling you that these moves higher will only continue. This euphoria phase of the bubble has a few lone critics saying that the price rises have been too dramatic and can not go on forever. The media interview these few wise people with less frequency as prices move higher still.

The problem to the final tragic stage of the bubble is that you and everyone else are now already in to the investment. No one else is sitting on the sidelines waiting to get in anymore. The gains in the sector can not continue like this when the public has already piled in, since these gains require more investors to bid up the price. But you find that there is no one left to buy and to support the incredibly high prices anymore.

The truth is that the insiders are quietly taking their profits at this point, as the public completes its great buy in. In the end, the idea that the financial talking heads encourage about this investment bubble area being unstoppable and impervious to collapse proves to be just another attempt to keep the bubble going.

At this point, the prices may hold up for a while before the air quickly deflates from the bubble. Sooner or later, the prices have only one direction to go, down. As you see prices begin to decline, many financial talking heads will be preaching that this is only a temporary price pull back. This only makes the bubble worse as it deflates.

You and everyone else on the outside of the bubble are either holding on for dear life, or buying more of it as it falls. The pundits are likely encouraging this, and they may even be arguing for a soft landing before the prices take off again.

Gold has not yet reached this point. It may be around the inflation adjusted high of $2,500 per ounce that it runs into the inevitable wall. When you see that even the common man on the street owns investment gold and follows its daily progress, then this will be the sign that the gold bull run bubble's end approaches.

The saying is that the public rides down the slippery slope of hope after the third stage of the investment bubble finishes. Oblivious to the insider profit taking, you and the public continue to hope that the bubble will pump back up before long.

The insiders take their money and run as unobtrusively as they possibly can, laughing quietly at the public's folly of false hope. Sometimes the outsiders see them leave, but most of them still refuse to accept the truth that the investment bubble party has ended. You can always say that the bubble is over when the insiders take their profits and leave the bubble sector.

The only question left to answer then is how far down will you and the rest of the public ride the bubble while it deflates.

Why Are Derivatives Such Powerful Financial Instruments?

When you turn on the financial news, you often hear them mention a term called derivatives. The financial pundits talk about them more all of the time because of the impact that they are having on the world economy now.

You should understand derivatives because they are also financial weapons of mass destruction that were responsible for the meltdown in the financial crisis of 2007 to 2010.

A Simple Definition of Derivatives

The simplest way to define for you the generally complicated subject of derivatives is with a single sentence. Derivatives prove to be any thing that bases its value on an underlying asset or condition.

Their value simply comes from the value of something else. You could also call them a gentlemen's bet as to the future of securities prices or risk. This means that you can use derivatives for both hedging positions and for speculating on the future values of different assets.

The Example of Wheat Futures Derivatives

The most easily understood example of derivatives also has to do with the less harmful form of them. Farmers working in the middle of the country utilize many of the derivatives in the nation. Farmers are generally interested in protecting their investments in the crops that they plant.

They want to figure out how much money they will make on their harvest. To do this, they engage in business with companies or brokers to make derivatives contracts on future markets on the commodities exchanges. These contracts will let them sell crops, such as wheat, in advance of growing them.

In other words, the farmers lock in the price for their wheat crops that are not yet ready to harvest, or even planted, for a pre arranged price. The farmers can then safely plant and harvest their wheat crops knowing that they will receive a certain price for them.

Even though the farmer is not concerned with the value of these wheat crop contracts once he agrees to them, the contracts do trade with values that go up and down. These values fluctuate with what happens to the underlying commodity during the life of this futures contract.

The contract might make money, break even, or lose money for you if you are trading it in that time period. This will all depend on the changing price of the wheat commodity to which it is attached.

Various Other Kinds of Derivatives

Just as a farmer utilizes wheat futures contract derivatives to protect himself from changes in the price of the wheat that might
move against him before the harvest, you can also use derivatives
to protect yourself from changes in interest rates. Banks are interested in this. They want to lock in future interest rate prices, and
they can use these derivatives based on interest rates to do it.

Oil companies also use futures contract derivatives to lock in oil
prices. If the prices are high now, you could see them choose to
enter a contract to guarantee those prices in the future when they
produce their oil barrels. Airlines might similarly use them to lock
in lower oil prices. Southwest Airlines actually did this when oil
sat at $10 per barrel, and this allowed them to continue paying this
price for their oil even a long time after the oil had jumped to more
than $100 for each barrel.

Still other forms of derivatives will permit businesses to protect
themselves from the possibility of bad weather. They can make
derivatives contracts against snow storms or even hurricanes. Once
again, the value of the derivative is based on the underlying condition of the storms.

The Danger of Derivatives

The derivatives that are useful to many parties who actually need
to eliminate their risk are very powerful, as you can see. For farmers, banks, oil companies, and businesses, they can allow them to
engage in transactions with certainty. The problem with such derivatives is that they can also create risk and uncertainty on a massive scale.

There are several problems that you see with derivatives. The one is that they are not transparent, since the parties make the majority of them as private contracts. These derivatives are not regulated or traded on exchanges. This is the reason that you saw them referred to as gentlemen's bets in an earlier paragraph.

Because these derivatives spread risk of prices or events around to parties that the markets do not fully know about, they create a great amount of uncertainty.

Besides this, firms have created an enormous number of derivatives based on the credit worthiness of other companies and even countries. This means that if these companies or countries fail financially, then the parties that sold such derivatives have to make massive payouts to the ones that bought them.

When you saw Lehman Brothers fail, this set off a chain reaction of fear and speculation as to how many derivatives existed on their credit worthiness. On just this one financial firm, companies placed hundreds of billions of dollars of these "bets" on the future of the company. You saw many months of uncertainty and panic as people waited to see what other companies these derivatives would financially devastate.

To make matters worse, only a couple of large financial companies sell or own a huge percentage of all of the derivatives on earth. This creates enormous risk in the banking and financial system, as only one of them going down can potentially take the others with them. When Lehman Brothers collapsed in the midst of the financial crisis, the whole financial system stood on the brink of total failure because of these derivatives.

If the Treasury, Federal Reserve, and FDIC had not stepped in to help out, then likely you would have witnessed all of these financial companies collapse under the weight of the derivatives that they sold on Lehman Brothers.

Financial Weapons of Mass Destruction

Critics have repeatedly said that these derivatives are so dangerous exactly because they do represent speculative bets. In fact, from one point of view, derivatives are not assets at all. You should know that in a sense they are constructed securities that do not have any intrinsic or tangible value. There are now dozens of different kinds of these trading on every asset that you can imagine. It may shock you to learn that some derivatives get their value from still other derivatives' values.

Depending on how you total the derivatives up, there are more than one quadrillion of them in existence too. The actual number is $1.4 quadrillion approximately. To illustrate why these derivative instruments are financial weapons of mass destruction, consider how much larger they are than other financial markets.

The total value of derivatives is equal to forty times the size of all of the stock markets on earth. It is more than ten times the value of all bonds and stocks traded around the globe. Astonishingly, these derivatives are more than twenty-three times the gross domestic product of the world.

Despite the danger that they pose, derivatives have evolved into the center of the world financial markets. This is regardless of what you have seen that they are only instruments based on the value of underlying instruments, assets, or conditions. Derivatives do not create any value or wealth in and of themselves. But they do have the power to destroy the world's financial system and even to bank-rupt whole countries.

The Three Risk Assessment Strategies Before Investing

It is important for you to know that all investments carry some amount of risk. These levels may vary with different investments, but they are always present in one form or another. You need to understand your tolerance for risk in investments before you start to invest.

You can assess this investment risk based on three strategies to help you to deal with it. These strategies include determining your financial risk tolerance, your emotional risk tolerance, and the business risk involved in the investment itself.

How You Assess Financial Risk Tolerance

Your ability to assess and to deal with financial risk is fairly objective. This assessment is a straightforward approach where you sit down and look at the numbers that surround your finances and investment money.

You should start out with this strategy by first writing out your monthly, near term, and medium term money requirements. Then you should list out your savings and resources for investing. It is also a good idea to make notes on your overall financial situation. In this way, you are able to decide if you can accept the amount of risk that an investment may entail.

Another way for you to understand the financial risk assessment strategy is to ask yourself two important questions. The first of these questions is how much money can you afford to tie up? The second one of them is how much money can you afford to lose?

Look at some examples for financial risk tolerance. If you are looking at putting three hundred dollars every month into the investment that you choose, and you know that it will not be available for months or possibly even years afterward, then you need to understand clearly if you can afford to be without this three hundred dollars every month.

Along the same lines, if you choose to place three hundred dollars each month into your retirement account, then this is another way that you lock up funds. You need to have the same ability to do without that money. Besides this, if you put a thousand dollars into an investment, then you need to know that you can afford to lose all or part of it before you make the investment in the first place.

Financial risk tolerance is not identical for every person. You might be someone with enough resources who can lose several thousand dollars and not be significantly impacted. If your portfolio and risk mindset is geared to the longer term, then this is more likely to be the case. You could also be a person who decides that you can not do without more than a few hundred dollars at a time.

Whether you are the former or the latter person, you need to contemplate these things before you make an investment. After you get a realistic and understandable view of your total financial picture, you will be better able to make investment decisions that are appropriate for your ability to absorb financial risks.

How You Assess Emotional Risk Tolerance

The next assessment that you need to do before you start investing is emotional risk tolerance. Everyone will tell you that you must remove all emotions from your investing. The reality is that it is almost impossible. You are impacted by the risk that you perceive. It is natural to contemplate what the future has in store for you and your investments. Money tends to magnify these normal fears. This is why assessing your emotional tolerance for risk proves to be nearly as critical as assessing your tolerance for financial risk.

Before you can start with an investment, you need to understand that investments can create stress. When you are stressed by the ups and downs of a risky investment, this will spill over into the other parts of your daily life. Stress that comes from investments will impact relationships and even your personal health. This is why you might have the tolerance for the financial risk of a given investment and still not be prepared for the emotions that you feel with some volatile markets and investments.

If an investment is going to consume you and make you upset, then it is probably not worth making this investment. When you find yourself in this place, then the best thing to do is to begin with safer investments and only gradually work your way in to investments with higher risk. If you determine that you are a person with a very low tolerance for emotional risk, you are probably better suited to sticking with safer and calmer investments.

How You Assess Business Risk

Business risk is actually the most well known of the various kinds of risks that deals with investing. Business risk is not difficult to understand.

Business risk simply has to do with the possibility that your investment might decline in value from financial problems at the firm, increased and fierce competition, and the company badly managing their resources. You usually see this type of risk most typically with stocks or bonds of companies that are publicly traded.

For you to assess the business risk of an investment, you will need to read and learn as much about the company and investment as you can. You can do this by staying up to date on company reports and news stories about the company. It is true that some sectors of the economy, and the companies that operate within them, come with greater amounts of business risk. This is something that you ought to contemplate when you begin investing.

The best way to assess business risk is to determine what a company's ability is to raise their prices when times become more difficult for them. Companies that have this price power are those that make and sell products that everyone knows for their reliability and quality. They would probably also have a large market share in their industry.

By measuring every company up by the power that it has to raise its prices, you will be best protected from business risk, overall economic risk that the economy will go through a down turn, and the risk that the government will decide to change economic policies, as when the government chooses to raise or lower interest rates and taxes.

How Can You Analyze an Investment for Risk?

The simplest way to determine how much risk an investment actually carries is to find out for yourself honestly what percentage of the investment that you can lose in a worst case scenario.

With U.S. government bonds, this is zero under the current circumstances. With corporate bonds, it might be seventy-five percent or more if the company fails. With stocks and options, the most that you can lose is one hundred percent.

This revelation about stocks could come as quite a shock to you. Think about General Motors three or four years ago. The stock proved to be strong and highly valued. During the financial crisis, it fell to a few dollars a share. Other well known and highly respected companies disappeared altogether.

Their collapse wiped out the holders of these stocks. Lehman Brothers, Bear Stearns, and Washington Mutual are all stunning examples of this reminder that the level of risk with stocks is high.

Will Manipulations of The Silver Market Drive Up Prices?

If you follow the silver market, then you may possibly have heard a suggestion or even a complaint over the years from silver insiders that the silver market is manipulated in order to keep the prices down.

For a long time, skeptics and detractors simply scoffed at this idea as the product of conspiracy theorists and crackpots.

In the last few months, you have witnessed the truth of the very real manipulation begin to be revealed. This manipulation has worked to hold down prices in the past, but with the advent of serious lawsuits being filed by the regulatory body of the silver futures market, it is set to change in a big way that could significantly impact any silver investments that you presently hold or choose to buy.

Silver Market Manipulation Allegations

The first serious allegations that you heard regarding someone manipulating the silver market came from a public hearing that the CFTC, or Commodities and Futures Trading Commission, held on Disruptive Trading Practices and Anti-Manipulation. At that meeting, the CFTC representative Bart Chilton announced that at least one party has manipulated the silver market.

If you heard his preliminary announcement, then you had to wait several more weeks to get the full prepared statement.

In Bart Chilton's full statement, he let out the Commodities and Future Trading Commission's research backed up opinion that various parties have engaged in repeated and successful attempts to influence the silver market prices. He said that these efforts were not only unethical, but that they are fraudulent. Chilton alleged that you have seen the Commodity Exchange Act willfully violated.

He further stated that these parties will be not only investigated for it, but also will be criminally prosecuted for the acts. At the time that this full statement came out, few analysts believed that the CFTC and Mr. Chilton would stick out their necks so far without significant documented evidence to prove such claims.

Later on you may have seen that the main party being accused of this is JP Morgan Chase. JP Morgan Chase has officially manipulated the silver markets for years, according to the suit being filed. The net result of their intervention is that silver prices have been kept artificially lower than they should have been for decades now.

If you were following the silver markets when these announcements came out, you saw that silver prices managed to move up fully five percent in a single session when gold had no real gains for the day. Since then, silver has smashed through its multiple year high, charging from the $21 previous decades long high up into the $28 plus dollar per ounce range.

Many analysts have concurred that with silver manipulators on the defensive, these parties will be looking to quietly unwind their positions and make a hasty retreat for the silver market exits.

This will likely lead to still higher prices in the future, especially as silver is able to rise to prices that are fair for the extremely limited inventories.

Naked Short Sales

Your first real proof that silver prices have been deliberately and artificially held down came from past evidences that something strange was happening in the silver markets. While you are probably aware of the fact that you can buy silver, you may not know that you can also take on negative positions of silver ounces or contracts.

This is called shorting, or short selling, silver. This is how the manipulation happens. Short selling silver when you do not have the silver to back up the positions is called naked short selling. Such naked short selling is illegal, even though the guilty parties have probably been doing it without punishment for decades.

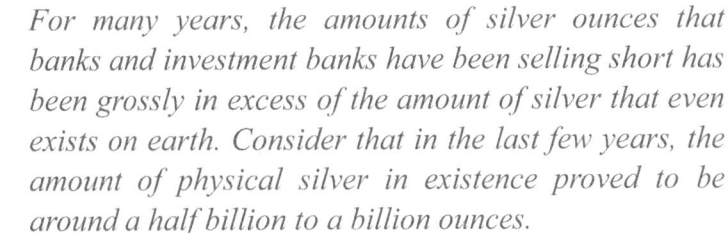

For many years, the amounts of silver ounces that banks and investment banks have been selling short has been grossly in excess of the amount of silver that even exists on earth. Consider that in the last few years, the amount of physical silver in existence proved to be around a half billion to a billion ounces.

Yet at this same time, the contract trading of silver in the futures markets amounted to thirty billion ounces of silver on the London Bullion Management Association. The Futures and Options exchanges also traded nearly sixty billion ounces of silver as well. Estimates for silver contracts trading over the counter amount to ten billion ounces besides this.

The basis for the charges of silver market manipulation becomes clear once you learn that speculators and so called hedgers are trading over one hundred times the amount of silver in a given year as actually exists. This is the essence of how silver prices are manipulated. In the end, the price of silver is set as though the actual inventory of silver is one hundred billion ounces. In reality, less than half a billion ounces exist today.

Other Silver Manipulators

Not only JP Morgan Chase is in trouble, as eight or less traders in the silver markets own the short silver positions that amount to roughly two hundred and ninety million ounces. This means that there are possibly seven other parties who may be charged with silver market price manipulation in the near future.

For now, the regulators at the Commodities and Futures Trading Commission have set their sites on Chase, since it is the largest player whose hand has been in the cookie jar too many times.

There may be still other penalties for JP Morgan Chase and the other silver market manipulators. The Commodities Exchange Warehouse holds almost the entire available silver inventories on the market, around one hundred million to one hundred and twenty million ounces. This means that just the largest eight short sellers of silver have positions that are one hundred and seventy million ounces more in the negative than actually exist in market inventories.

These firms who are short silver will not be able to find enough silver to cover their negative positions if they are forced. This means that they would have to cover their positions by settling the contracts at cash prices. Should a run of the limited inventories that exist happen, then the prices that they have pay to cover their positions at could be several times higher than they are presently.

What Max Kaiser Is Doing to Fight Silver Manipulation

Some large silver investors out there have set out to punish JP Morgan Chase for their likely manipulating the silver markets for all of these years. The financial analyst Max Kaiser started this movement that is growing and taking on a life of its own. He began with a goal to bankrupt JP Morgan Chase through encouraging you and others to buy silver to force them to have to cover their short positions at substantially higher prices.

No one can say with any certainty if his plan will work. One thing that JP Morgan can count on is the fact that the government backs them up for their help in the financial crisis and in helping to keep silver prices down, which makes the dollar stronger in contrast.

Many analysts believe that the government will find a way to help JP Morgan Chase out of its bind, if they get into real trouble. You will see what happens as this interesting drama of the silver market manipulation is played out.

The Trading Wisdom of Protective Puts And Covered Calls

You will have heard that stocks yield higher returns over the long term than do many safer investments like bonds, money market accounts, certificates of deposit, and Treasuries that the government issues.

This is only true for those investors who do not know how to hedge and protect their stocks properly using options. Because the stock market yields an average return of more than eight percent a year over longer stretches of time as compared to only a couple of percent for these other investments, you need to have exposure to good stocks in order to make returns that help you to achieve your financial goals.

The following paragraphs go through the ways of using options with stocks to protect your principal as well as to increase your returns on the investments.

What Are Call Options on Stocks?

You will see that there are two types of options that you can use to protect your stock positions and increase the returns on the stocks that you hold. The first of these is known as a call option. When you buy a call option, you obtain the right to buy one hundred shares of a specific company stock for a set price.

If you sell a call option, then you agree to sell the one hundred shares of the same stock to the buyer of the option at a set price. This price that you can buy the stock for, or sell the stock at, is called the strike price. The option runs for a certain amount of time to an expiration date. Expiration dates prove to be the third Friday of the expiration month. So a call option with a strike price of 50 and an expiration date of March gives a buyer of the option the right to purchase the shares of the stock at $50 per share until the third Friday of March.

When you trade call options, you might use them for speculation or for making profits from a position. You purchase calls to speculate if you believe that you will see the price of the stock rise so that you can sell the option for more than you bought it. You might also use this option to obtain the shares of the stock for a cheaper price than it is trading at before or when the expiration date arrives.

How to Use A Call Option to Make More Money on A Stock

Speculating with call options involves the risk of losing all of the money that you spend on the contract. This is not the way that you will want to use call options if you are looking to reduce risk. You have possibly never heard of the means that you can utilize a call option to profit from a stock that you already hold.

This is a very safe way to employ call options to make money. You do this by purchasing one hundred shares of the stock in which you want to invest. Then, instead of buying the call option and paying for the right to obtain the hundred shares of the stock at a certain strike price, you sell the one contract of the call option, and you receive a premium for agreeing to sell your one hundred shares of the stock at a certain price.

As long as you pick a selling strike price that is at the price or higher than the price for which you bought the stock, you will always make money with the option.

Take a look at an example of how this works to better understand it. If you decide that you like the ABC stock enough to buy one hundred shares of it and potentially hold the stock longer term, then you can sell a single one hundred share option contract on it. If you pay $50 per share for the stock, then you might safely sell the option for a $50 or a $55 strike price.

Imagine that the premium that you will receive upfront for selling a two month $50 call option is $5 per share, and a one month $55 call option is $1.50 per share. Just for agreeing to sell your stock at the $50 that you paid for it, you will receive the $5 per share premium. This represents a ten percent profit on the transaction if the stock price stays the same or rises and you are forced to sell the shares.

If the stock price goes down, you still keep your shares that you meant to hold long term, but you also get to keep the $5 per share premium of $500. You might pick the higher $55 call option strike if you want to keep the shares. In this case, you would still receive the $1.50 per share premium up front if the stock price does not rise to $55 per share or higher.

If it does go up that amount in the two months time frame, then you sell the stock for $5 more per share than you bought it at the $55 strike, plus keep the $1.50 per share premium. You would have made $6.50 profit per share, more than ten percent in this case. Selling options is the most sensible way to safely make extra money on stocks that you plan to hold on to for the longer term anyway.

Every time that your option that you sold expires worthless, you can always sell another one and collect another premium.

What Are Put Options on Stocks?

Put options are the opposite of call options. They give you the right to sell a hundred shares of a company stock for a given strike price until you reach the expiration date. The basic terms are all the same with call and put options on stocks.

While speculators purchase puts in the hopes that the strike price will fall to sell the option for a profit, hedgers who own the stock can use them to protect their investment. Look at our example of ABC stock again. You bought the shares at $50 per share and you want to make sure that you do not lose your principal on the investment.

You can buy a put option for the stock at $50 strike price to guarantee you the right to sell your shares for the $50 that you paid for them. This will cost you the premium upfront. Buying puts is often more affordable than buying calls, since the general belief is that the stock market goes up over time.

Buying a longer expiration date will make more sense than buying shorter ones more often. You might have to pay $3 per share for a two month option. A one year option might be $10 per share. So long as the put option is in effect, you will not lose money on the price of the stock, even if it fell to zero.

You may have realized that you do have expenses in paying these premiums. If the stock price does not eventually go up, you could lose money on your put insurance premium that you paid. One way to defray the cost of the put option that you buy is to sell the call option that you read about in the earlier paragraphs.

By doing this at the same time, you will generally be able to cancel out the costs of the put option or even come out ahead if you buy the right combination of call and put expiration contracts.

Why You Should Consider Dividends When You Buy Stocks

If you are like many investors, then you may think that the main reason to buy a stock is to hold it in hopes that its price will rise over time.

While there is nothing wrong with this idea, there is an easier and smarter way to make money on stocks that many savvy professional investors and other financial experts recommend.

You can take advantage of this by purchasing stocks that have an established history of paying consistent, high dividends on a quarterly basis.

What Are Dividends?

Dividends are actually cash payments that companies give to you their shareholders. You became a shareholder in a company when you purchase its stock. Companies most commonly pay out dividends four times per year. The greater number of shares that you own, the higher amount of dividends you will receive, since companies pay them on a per share basis. If you own one hundred shares of Pfizer stock, and it pays twenty cents every quarter, then you would be given $20 per quarter, or $80 per year in dividends.

Why Do Firms Pay Such Dividends?

Companies pay you dividends in order to share their profits with you as a stake holder. They take a certain amount of their profits that they make and allocate them to shareholders. They do this to offer you an incentive to remain an investor in their company. It is important to seek out companies that actually pay dividends, since not all companies do this.

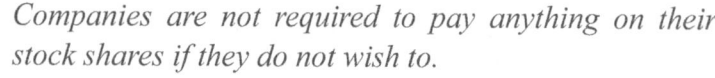

Companies are not required to pay anything on their stock shares if they do not wish to.

What Dividends Tell You About A Corporation

Dividends are a good indicator of the stability and strength of a company. Companies that are making money consistently feel confident paying out portions of the profits to the share holders. When you see a company that has a long history of paying dividends consistently, then this tells you that the company is in sound financial shape and is making money either every quarter or most every quarter. It is a good qualifying factor that you can use to separate out common from exceptional companies and stocks.

Dividend paying companies may not be the highest growth companies on the market. They are companies that are well established and have track records. They can afford to share the profits with their share holders. After a company begins paying out these dividends, it is likely to keep doing so if it can. This is because companies build up expectations of paying dividends.

If you see a company that typically provides $1.50 per share in quarterly dividends simply quit paying them after having offered them for some time, then it makes the company look bad or unhealthy. Investors will take this as a sign that the profits are declining or even gone. It could also mean that they company wishes to invest in additional expansion, so you have to watch a company's news to be certain.

Dividend Stocks Provide Cash Flow and Passive Income

You can never be sure that a stock price will appreciate sufficiently for you to sell it and realize a capital gain. But with companies that pay consistent dividends, you can reasonably count on receiving a quarterly check in the mail or a deposit to your investment account. With dividend payments, you are not required to sell your stock positions in order to bring in some money from your investments.

Dividends are both passive income and cash flow investments. They are passive income since they pay you regular earnings for not doing any work. Building up passive income is important in your preparation for retirement. They also represent cash flow investments, since dividends provide a steady stream of periodic income just for holding on to the investment.

Unlike with capital gains investments, which require you to sell the investment in order to realize a one time amount of money, these cash flow dividend investments will continue paying you quarterly without you having to part with the investment.

Dividend stocks are actually the best of both capital gains and cash flow investment worlds. While they provide you with the passive income and cash flow returns that you need to build, they also offer you the ability to realize a capital gain through price appreciation. You might collect dividends for many quarters or even years. One day, the company stock will hopefully have risen to a level considerably higher than at which you bought it. At this point, you can sell the investment and realize your capital gain as well.

This is why you should always consider dividends to be a primary factor when you decide in which companies to buy shares of stock. You may not see significant capital gains in any given year or several years with a certain stock. When add in the returns of the dividend yield, or percentage that the stock is paying you to hold it, then the returns will likely be substantially more impressive.

Dividends Allow for Reinvestment Into the Company

Another advantage of dividend stocks is that most of these companies will allow you to reinvest your dividends into the company stock if you so desire. This is simply taking the dividend payments and utilizing them to purchase additional shares in the corporation.

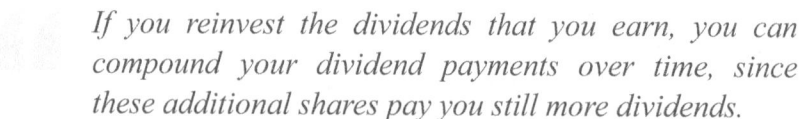

If you reinvest the dividends that you earn, you can compound your dividend payments over time, since these additional shares pay you still more dividends.

You can set your dividends to be automatically reinvested in the stocks that you own. This will eliminate you having to spend time managing the process. A popular and direct way to do this is using a DRIP, or dividend reinvestment program.

You sign up for DRIP with the company that you own the stock in directly. You can find these companies and the applications for the program on the firm's website.

Another way to accomplish the same result is using a brokerage account. A great number of the online brokerage accounts will easily allow this. All that you have to do is to request that they reinvest part or all of your dividends. You will receive the other dividends in cash deposited to your brokerage account. Dividend reinvestment also offers you the advantage of not spending your returns.

Dividends Help You To Stay Ahead of Inflation

Another great advantage in dividend paying stocks is that dividends provide you with an investment return that usually outperforms inflation. This is because most companies that pay dividends will increase them over time. Since they anticipate that their sales and profits will grow along with higher prices, they are able to pass it along in the profits that they share out with you as dividends.

Contrast this with low interest rate paying bonds, certificates of deposit, and Treasuries. Not only do they pay yields of only a few percentage points, but these rates do not go up with inflation at all.

Dividend Stocks Outperform Other Stocks

There are so many reasons why you should choose high paying dividend stocks over stocks without dividends. High quality stocks can pay as much as four to eight or nine percent dividend yields.

Even though there are never guarantees on a stock price appreciating, history shows that the prices of stocks that pay dividends usually outperform the prices of stocks that do not pay dividends.

The 3 Crucial Investment Steps to Create Passive Income

Wherever you look in reading about investment opportunities and the most advantageous ways to make money, you will see the phrase passive income used. Passive income can cover a variety of definitions.

According to the Internal Revenue Service, it is money made on an endeavor where you are not involved directly. Other definitions would include any income that you do not work to make.

The most frequent examples given for passive income include any forms of rents and income streams from limited partnerships. Many experts deem that money made from financial investments like coupon payments and dividends are also passive income. Financial professionals will tell you that a great means of getting ahead in your finances is to create some form of passive income. You can do this through following the three steps that are explained in the subsequent paragraphs.

Why Passive Income is Superior to Income That You Earn

Passive income is in many ways superior to income that you earn through labor. For one thing, it is like a multiplication of your efforts, since you do not have to work more, but you obtain a second income stream as if you were working a second job.

Passive income also receives tax advantages, as the IRS treats it differently than regular forms of income.

For people in most tax brackets, the tax rates on passive income will prove to be significantly lower than the tax rates on income that you earn through traditional means.

3 Steps You Must Take to Create Passive Income

Passive income does not just happen to you, as the name might imply. It is a form of income that you must first set up before you can benefit from it on a continuous basis. Once you go through the efforts to discover and establish some reliable form of passive income, there is no time limit to how long you can benefit from it.

Step 1 - Get into the Habit of Paying Yourself First

In order to set up your passive income stream, you will likely need to build up some investment capital with which to purchase the passive investment. This is true whether you are looking at a real estate rental property, a limited partnership, or a portfolio of high dividend and coupon paying investments. Naturally, coming up with this initial investment capital is easier said than done.

There is a practice that you can do to make it easier to first create your investment pool. This is to learn the habit when payday comes of paying yourself before you pay for everything else. It is a well known law of the universe that if you pay all of your expenses and bills first, then there will not be much of anything left to save and invest when you are done.

Since your needs will always expand to take up the available amount of money in your account, you have to remove your savings from the equation up front.

The simplest way to make sure that you are paid first is to simply set up an automatic transfer of part of your income with your payroll company through your employer. Most employers and payroll companies offer this courtesy at no charge and with little trouble to establish. You simply tell them a dollar or percentage amount from each pay check to take out, and they deposit this to another account that you set up.

This way when you receive your payroll in your normal checking account, then the savings and investment money will already have been taken out and you will not miss it much, if at all. You should make ten percent of your income your goal, and then it will not take long for this money to grow into a significant enough amount for you to begin seriously pursuing some passive investments.

Step 2 - Save 10% of your Income into an Investment Fund

Now, once you have made the effort to pay yourself first, it is important that you do not fall into the trap of simply building up the money into this low interest yielding savings account. There is no reason to settle for returns of a percent or two, or even less. This is not the passive income that you are seeking, although technically savings account interest is also a form of low paying passive income.

Instead, while you are waiting to achieve a certain minimum level for your significant passive income investments, you can start with the passive income generated from an investment fund.

This might be a mutual fund that invests in high paying dividend stocks or coupon paying bonds. Funds like these can easily pay eight to ten percent or higher returns.

It could also be a Canadian oil and gas investment trust. Such trusts pay monthly royalties from the sales of their oil and natural gas that they produce and market throughout North America and the world. There can be special tax incentives for investing in oil and gas producing properties such as these as well. When oil and natural gas prices are high, the returns can be considerable, exceeding typical dividend returns.

Alternatively, you might put all or part of your investment income that you are saving up into an REIT, or Real Estate Investment Trust fund. There are REIT's that invest in residential, commercial, and even industrial rental properties. They pay a share of the monthly rental or lease fees to you as an investor. Again, depending on the type of REIT, there can be special tax benefits that you realize with these kinds of investments.

There is no reason that you could not divide your investment fund money into all three of the categories above. This would provide you with a better diversification and offer you exposure to quality stock earnings, oil prices, and real estate activities all at once. This is because you can easily buy into these various types of investment funds commonly with as little as a thousand dollars or even less.

Step 3 - Research the Best Investment Possibilities

While you are building up your savings and seeing nice returns on the money in your one or more investment funds, you can be using the time interval to research the best investment possibilities for your passive income investments. You should expect to do some reading. There are entire books on passive income investing available from your local library or area bookstore. These will be written by successful and wealthy passive investors who have already walked down the road on which you are setting out.

There are also magazine articles that you can read in print or online. The Internet is an excellent resource for materials on current passive income opportunities. Make sure that you consider the source when you are looking at information. A site that is a reputable investment publication is naturally more reliable than an individual's personal website promoting his own passive investment possibilities.

You can also attend seminars on passive investments. These are fantastic opportunities to learn about not only the mechanics of passive investing, but also the current landscape of best opportunities. You should be prepared to pay some sort of participation fee to attend these seminars. You can look for them in your area newspaper or on the Internet.

Don't rely on advice from other people without your own research, and never invest in anything you do not understand. Conduct your own research and come to your own conclusion. Following blindly what others are doing is irresponsible and not far away from gambling with your investment money.

Three Mistakes to Avoid With Your Investments in 2011

As you listen to suggestions for what you should do with your investments and money in the new year of 2011, it is interesting to note that the majority of the talking heads and people that you know are only making suggestions for what you should do.

But while you are making those New Year's Resolution goals, it is also important for you not to forget that there are also some things that you should not do in the new year.

Three of these important mistakes to avoid are covered in the subsequent paragraphs.

Mistake To Avoid #1 - Do Not Sell Your Precious Metals Yet

The bull market for gold and silver has now completed its tenth year. If you have been enjoying the ride higher in both precious metals for a few years, then you may be tempted to cash out. This is especially the case for those of you who have been paying too much attention to the various anchors on the financial channels who have been against gold and silver for years.

Practically every year of the two metals' bull market run, these so called financial experts have suggested or outright declared their disdain for what they see as relic investments. They continuously state that especially gold has moved up as high as it will.

Now that silver has gained in excess of seventy-five percent in value this year, you can be sure that they will attack it with a passion also.

The weapon that you must use to defend yourself against these assaults is knowledge. Bull market runs in commodities commonly average from eighteen to twenty year periods. The shortest one on record ran for fifteen years. Either way, this gives gold and silver at least four to five more good years, and probably as many as eight to ten years more, of solid performance and consistent annual gains.

Besides this, it is especially true nowadays that uncertainty and fear of the still ongoing financial crisis are still very much evident. The latest phase of it is the sovereign debt crisis plaguing countries around the world, especially Greece, Ireland, Spain, Belgium, Portugal, and even Dubai. The problems in the world financial system that still continue highly support both gold and silver prices. Their roles as safe haven assets in times of trouble and difficulty are as important today as they have ever been before.

Do not allow the talking heads on the financial channels to convince you that anything is different in this respect. The year 2011 should be another banner year for both gold and silver. The move up will go far higher still. Do not waver and sell your precious metals yet. This is the biggest mistake that you can avoid in the new year.

Mistake To Avoid #2 - Do Not Settle For Low Interest Rate Returns

One of the easiest things to do in the world with your investments is to simply park them in a low interest bearing savings account, money market account, or U.S. government Treasuries. These are not bad investments inherently. The problem with them is that with interest rates at historic lows, these investments simply do not pay much of anything. Interest rates of a percent or two do not even allow your money to grow at the rate of inflation. When you receive these low yields, then your money will actually decline in value over time.

You can simply avoid this dangerous pitfall, and it does not even have to require much work on your part. There are so many investment funds on the market that pay five to ten percent returns on your investments fairly consistently. This should not come as a shock to you since the historical average gain for American stock markets like the S&P 500 is eight percent.

With a little more time and research, you can learn about the many different kinds of passive income investments out there. All of them also pay better than the low interest rate return investments that you saw outlined above. Whether you put your hard earned investment money into high yield dividend stocks, Real Estate Investment Trusts that can invest in industrial, commercial, or residential rental properties, or Canadian Oil and Natural Gas Trusts, you can count on monthly or quarterly checks in the mail just for holding them.

The real beauty of these investments is that they also have the potential to rise in value. This can give you capital gains as their share prices rise when you choose to sell the investment. Even in these difficult economic times of doubt and fear, there is no reason to accept sub-standard investment returns of one to two percent. Find a better place to put your money to work. In 2011, do not settle for low interest rate returns. It will only hurt your efforts to save for the future and your eventual retirement.

Mistake To Avoid #3 - Do Not Neglect Diversification to Protect Yourself from Inflation

One of the main concerns for the future of the United States' economy especially is that of potentially severe inflation that may begin to show up this very year in 2011. The U.S. government has pursued a dangerous course of expanding the monetary base since 2007 and 2008. In that amount of time, they have literally more than tripled the supply of American dollars in circulation around the world. This is not only scary to think about, but it will certainly have negative consequences in the near future.

Inflation is always a monetary event. As the supply of money that is available massively increases, while the amount of goods for this money to chase remains basically the same, the prices of goods will definitely rise. Many leading economists and investors have added their voices to the rising chorus that fears significant inflation. At this point, the question is how high will it be in a given single year and several year period.

This represents the greatest threat to the value of your savings and investments in the New Year. When you follow a path of diversification into inflation proof investments, then you can be certain that you will not be wiped out by high double digit inflation, or possibly even hyperinflation, as it strikes.

There are several different investments that outperform when inflation is a persistent problem. Commodities such as gold, silver, and oil are the champions of this category. Since many economists and advisers already recommend gold and silver as investment vehicles that should continue to rise this year, this represents a very good place to start.

In the past, you have seen real estate gain in times of high and rising inflation. If you choose to go this route with some of your money, just be careful. Professor Case of the Case Shiller Home Prices Index believes that residential real estate prices could fall another ten percent or more in value.

The best thing about diversifying your portfolio is that it allows you to spread your money and investments around to several different categories. The idea is that while one area in the portfolio may struggle, others will do well, so that they offset one another and still leave you with positive gains. Do not neglect to diversify yourself to protect against inflation in 2011.

The #1 Investment Strategy to Conquer Inflation in 2011

You are probably aware of the ongoing predictions of many economists and financial experts that significant inflation will show up in the near future.

This will result from all of the reckless money printing and runaway spending that the U.S. government is still wantonly pursuing. Because of this eventual threat to your financial prospects and retirement security, you need to be looking for ways to beat inflation in 2011.

While many people and analysts are focused on gold as the best commodity to overcome inflation this next year, silver will outperform gold again in the New Year as it did this year in 2010. There are five good reasons for why this is the case.

How Did Silver Perform Relative to Gold in 2010?

As of mid-December in 2010, gold had risen by around twenty-five percent for the year. It had set multiple new highs, reaching even into the fourteen hundred and thirty dollars per ounce range in November. Silver, on the other hand, had risen by over seventy percent, marking its best year by far this decade. It had climbed to over thirty dollars per ounce, and it looked on track to close near that amount at year's end, even as gold had pulled back from its new high.

Investors Are Becoming More Aware of Silver

As silver has managed to significantly outperform gold this year, investors are taking notice. The gray metal has mostly languished in the shadows of its big brother gold over the past decade. Now, the word is out that silver is back in the driver's seat. This will only draw more investors to silver in the coming year and for possibly several years to come.

Silver Is More Volatile Than Gold

When gold is going up, silver usually goes up along with it. The majority of analysts are predicting that gold prices will continue to rise in 2011. Silver is an inherently more volatile precious metal. This has to do with its limited supply and relatively high demand. When it moves, it can be both sudden and dramatic. This is another reason that though both metals are projected to move higher, silver should go higher still.

Silver Stocks Are Much Less Available Than Gold Stocks

You may not be aware of this fact, but the extremely limited available stocks of silver make it actually rarer than gold. There are anywhere from four to five billion physical ounces of gold above ground in the world today. This is the case mostly because gold is not consumed or used up. Ninety-five percent of all gold that has ever been brought to light is still available in the world today.

Available silver stocks on the other hand, are in a state of constantly going down. There were billions of ounces of silver available for use at the conclusion of World War II. Early this decade, this number had fallen to six hundred and seventy one million ounces, as of the 2004 World Silver Survey.

By the conclusion of 2009, available silver stocks had dropped dramatically to a shocking only twenty million ounces.

Remember that in the 1940's, the government alone kept several billion ounces of silver in its own vaults. Now the government is forced to go on the open market to buy silver in order to mint its popular one ounce Silver Eagles. This current world supply represents not only a low level from an investment point of view, but a dangerously low level period. There simply is not enough silver to match up with all of the rising demand.

Silver Is In Much Greater Demand Than Gold

Part of the reason that silver is anticipated to outperform gold in 2011 is because it continues to be in far higher demand than is gold. The investment demand for gold may so far be higher than it is for silver, but the industrial demands for silver are massively higher than they are for gold. This is because silver is useful for an enormous range of applications, ranging from jewelry and coins, to photography and silverware, to industrial applications.

When it is used, the metal is lost at the rate of ninety percent and then stored in garbage landfills. In light of all of these factors, it should not come as a surprise to you that silver has existed in a state of deficit concerning its supply and demand for more than sixty-three years now.

Silver's demand is only projected to continue rising in industrial utilization too. Silver counts electronics, wireless RIFF, and hospital uses among its applications. Because it is the best electrical conductor, it will only be used in greater amounts in the new national electrical grid that will be rolled out in stages over the coming years.

The metal is heavily used in catalysts, batteries, bearings, and brazing and soldering as well. It is essential in the process of making some fabrics like polyester, and in making formaldehyde and methanol. Nuclear reactors use silver in their control rods manufacturing. While there are presently thousands of important uses for silver now, there are additional applications for it discovered almost every day.

Supply and demand always adjust themselves in the price of a commodity. The supply of silver is fairly constant. It just can not keep up with demand, as it has not been able to since the 1940's. This will continue to drive prices substantially higher year in and year out.

Silver is Still Way Below Its All Time High

Gold and silver have been making several year highs in the past couple of years. The difference between them is that gold is making new all time highs, while silver is still significantly below its all time high set in the early 1980's.

Gold blew away its previous eight hundred and fifty dollar high from the 1980's back a few years ago. Silver has only managed to surpass thirty dollars per ounce this last year. Its all time high from the 1980's lies back at over fifty dollars per ounce. This means that even at thirty dollars per ounce, silver is only at sixty percent of its all time high. To reach this high, it still has to go up by more than two thirds.

These prices do not even take into account the inflation adjusted high for silver, which in today's dollars would translate to more than one hundred and fifty dollars per ounce. For silver to rise to the inflation adjusted high levels, it still needs to gain by greater than four hundred percent. These price comparison factors gives silver substantially more historical room to move higher than gold still possesses at this point.

2011 Is The Year of Precious Metals

The coming year of 2011 should be good for precious metals in general. There is so much fear and uncertainty in the world regarding the ongoing sovereign debt crisis, the fiat paper money currency crisis, and runaway government money printing and spending. These various factors should continue to lend support to all of the precious metals in the New Year.

The difference between silver and gold is simply that silver has more reasons to move higher than will gold this coming year, just as it did this past year. I was able to lock in a 173% return on my investment in 2010 by using some of the simple leverage strategies that are outlined in detail in my free Silver Fortune Formula report.

M I N D S E T

"Changing Habits, Attitudes and Intentions"

The 3 Money Habits That Prevent You From Passive Income

You will find that there are some bad habits that keep most people from gaining passive incomes through investments.

The arguments of not having enough money to begin investing, not understanding how to invest properly, and being afraid to lose your money are only holding you back.

Each of these bad mentalities leads to negative outcomes, but they can be overcome, and even changed into habits that support investing for passive income.

Bad Habit #1 - You Think You Do Not Have Sufficient Money To Begin Investing

If you are struggling with this bad habit, then you are not alone. Tens of millions of Americans are held back by the habitual attitude that says you do not have sufficient money to begin investing.

The outcome of this attitude is obvious. If you feel that you do not have enough money to invest in anything, then you will most likely never start investing at all. Worse than this, feeling like you lack enough funds to invest becomes a self fulfilling prophecy. Since you believe that you do not have the money to invest, you will likely start to think that you will never have enough money to invest and that you can never have enough to begin.

Once this bad habitual attitude sets in, you will not even try to make any efforts of saving towards investing. It will likely keep you from even saving money at all.

Overcoming this habit is a matter of changing your attitude and taking some actions as well. You have to begin by saying to yourself that I can invest with even a little bit of money. Encourage yourself to save up money towards an investing pool of money. This is most easily done by reducing your monthly expenses.

It may require cutting back on spending a little bit, like going out to dinner one night a week less in favor of a picnic or a pizza, or skipping the movie theater and popcorn for a move night in. Another way of saving money is to take on a part time second job, or to see if you can pick up some extra hours at work.

You might also start a little side business or work over the Internet, like online tutoring, making and selling crafts, writing articles for the various informational websites, or taking pictures to sell to stock photography websites.

By increasing your income, you will find that there is plenty of extra money to put towards investing in passive income. And, since passive income investments create additional cash flow, it will become a virtuous cycle once you get started investing in passive income investments.

You can use this passive income money that comes in exclusively towards additional investing if you like. When you turn this habitual attitude of not having enough income to invest into a motivating factor to increase your income or reduce your expenses, it can become a good habit instead of a negative one.

Bad Habit #2 - You Belief You Do Not Know How to Invest

This is another common habitual attitude that plagues countless Americans. The truth is that it is a more legitimate excuse than the argument that you do not have enough money to invest. Most people really do not know how to invest.

Just because this may be true now though, does not mean that it always has to be the case. Once upon a time, to learn about investing, you had to go down to the public library and browse through huge collections of books and magazines that dealt with the subject of investing.

The problem with this lay in the fact that many of the resource materials were out of date, or not current enough, to help you with the particulars of investing in the markets of that day and time. Besides this, you might not have possessed access to a really good library with a broad enough selection of materials from which to learn investing.

The difficulties of getting a good investing education in the past allowed you to feed this bad habit. Feeling like you did not know how to invest became the sincere conviction that you would never lean how to properly invest, and eventually that you could not learn how. This bad habit kept you from even trying to find ways around your lack of access to good investing resource materials.

Learning to invest is easier than ever now thanks to the rise of the Internet. Now, there are countless seminars and courses for investing offered online. You can peruse through many different kinds of investing instructional guides, videos, and e-books all from the convenience of your own home.

A few ideas are even offered for free, or on a free trial basis while you make sure that they will actually teach you what you need to know about properly investing in passive income investments. Using this understanding of how little you know about investing to motivate you to change the situation is the best possible outcome of this bad habitual attitude. With a little work, study, and time, your financial education will improve until you are prepared to do good passive investing.

Bad Habit #3 - You Feel Afraid to Lose Your Money

On the surface, this habitual attitude of being afraid to lose your money is at least somewhat sensible. The financial collapse, house market pullback, and Great Recession have shown many people that they did not have enough healthy fear of potential investment losses. But when this habit of fear stops you from investing at all, then it is a very bad thing.

If you fear that you will lose your money in investing, then you will be paralyzed with indecision. Even the best of intentions to invest will have a struggle to effectively do it around this habitual attitude. Worse still, fearing that you will lose your money can actually lead you to making poor choices that will cause you to lose your money in a reinforcing negative attitude effect.

Getting around this bad habit is difficult, but not impossible. The first key is education. Start by reading some success stories of investors who overcame their fears and limitations to become not just good investors, but great investors.

You should next begin to learn as much as you can about the investments that you are considering in advance of jumping into them.

Diversifying your investment money into several different investments is another sensible way to begin to overcome the fear of losing your money. While one investment could perform poorly or even possibly fail, a variety of different types of investments are less likely to.

Having a habitual attitude of fear of losing your money can be turned to your advantage. You can use this healthy fear to motivate you to carefully consider all of your opportunities before plunging into them head first.

Any bad habit that teaches you the importance of choosing your passive income investments wisely and carefully will only benefit you when you turn it around for good. Like this, you will be well aware of what you are getting yourself, and your investment dollars, into before you commit to it.

Use The 13 Virtues of Benjamin Franklin to Become Wealthy

Benjamin Franklin is one of the more interesting of the original founding fathers of this country.

The man who created numerous inventions that are still with us, such as bi-focals; who wrote practical and informative books, like Poor Richard's Almanac; and who became a great statesman and diplomat started his accomplished career by writing down thirteen personal and social virtues.

These virtues were his important guides for living a productive and meaningful life. They are still as relevant to you today as they were to Americans almost three hundred years ago. These thirteen virtues can be used to help create wealth.

1. The Personal Virtues

These thirteen virtues of Ben Franklin's can be effectively broken down into two main categories. These are personal and social virtues. All of them are practical in your daily life. The eight personal virtues are explained first.

The Personal Virtue of Order

Order proved to be a very important starting point for Franklin. With the virtue of order, he meant for everything in your life to have its place. Each element of your business is supposed to have its place and time. Your priorities must be managed and kept in order.

This means that when it is time to focus on work and your business, then focus on it wholeheartedly. When it is time for family activities or taking care of your life and health, you should not neglect this either. Only a person who has the proper balance between these various activities will find it easy to work effectively towards obtaining wealth.

The Personal Virtue of Temperance

Ben Franklin was big on keeping your mind sharp. You should be too. The founding father who accomplished so much suggested that you do not drink to elevation or eat to dullness. In other words, avoid the extremes in life. He is also suggesting that you compromise in personal and business affairs. Being able to find common, middle ground is a cornerstone of effective business practice and negotiation.

The Personal Virtue of Frugality

Benjamin held himself to the standard of using things wisely and well. His mantra of "waste nothing" is a mainstay in the philosophy of the truly wealthy. To put it another way, how many people do you know who got rich living lavishly through constant waste of resources?

Instead, make it a point to live within your means.

Saving and then investing money through frugal living will help you to build and achieve lasting wealth. Remember too that being frugal does not mean being stingy, only being smart with your resources.

The Personal Virtue of Resolution

Your word was your bond in early America. When Ben said to make it your resolve to do what you should and to do without failure what you resolve to do, he was talking about keeping your promises. This applies to all of your relationships in life, including family, friends, bosses, and business colleagues.

You should do for them what you said that you will do. Building wealth is a function of carrying out your goals and promises that you made to yourself. When you let yourself down, you are reducing your chances of achieving these personal goals. Make it a point to make good on any promise whenever you possibly can. If you fail, resolve to do better the next time.

The Personal Virtue of Moderation

No doubt you have heard the cliche "everything in moderation" many times. Ben Franklin proved to be a big proponent of this admirable quality. Moderation refers to simply avoiding extremes in anything. Franklin also meant it as a guideline to not hold grudges against other people. Both of these are sound principles to live by.

Avoiding extremes will allow you to focus on your family and business in the proper proportions, and help you to keep a balance between your work and personal life. Building wealth is good, but losing your family and loved ones along the way is a terrible price to pay. By forgiving all injuries done to you, and maintaining a balance in your life, you will be much happier too.

The Personal Virtue of Industry

Industry refers to not wasting time. Ben felt that you should always be busy doing something that was useful. Wasteful and unnecessary actions should be eliminated as much as possible. This is a golden rule to live by for making money and building wealth. When you are working, work hard and with dedication.

Do not sit around and think of ways to waste time and make the workday pass quickly by. Your goal should be to accomplish as much as you realistically can. In this way, your work will be more appreciated, leading to possibilities for advancement. If you have a business, it will flourish when you pursue it with passion and industry.

The Personal Virtue of Tranquility

Tranquility refers to more than simply peaceful living. It centers around not being upset and distracted by little things that are unavoidable or commonplace. When you are a tranquil person, you can be better focused on your work and business ventures too. Being upset and distracted by the unavoidable occurrences and setbacks in life will affect every aspect of your life, including your ability to work towards and build up wealth.

The Personal Virtue of Cleanliness

Cleanliness proves to be more important now than it did in Ben Franklin's time. You can not succeed in life or business these days if you are not a well groomed and reasonably dressed person. The greatest and most successful business people and wealthy people know the value of looking their best and dressing their best. Cleanliness gives great confidence too, which is essential in building up wealth in your life.

2. The Social Virtues

Benjamin Franklin also advocated five virtues that embodied social interaction. These virtues are especially useful in dealing with your acquaintances and business associates. When you practice them, other will want to engage in business with you.

The Social Virtue of Sincerity

You should live and deal with others as Franklin endeavored to do. He was careful not to trick, deceive or lie to people. When you tell the truth and speak honestly to people, you will have more friends and people who want to work with you. In today's scandal ridden business world, sincerity is more important than ever to help you succeed. "Honesty is always the best policy" still applies to all areas of life.

The Social Virtue of Silence

Ben counseled himself and you to only say things that build up and edify someone. Meaningless and idle conversation does not get you anywhere.

In business, knowing when to keep your mouth shut can be critical. The proverb "even a fool is considered wise when he keeps silent" is many times the best way to carry yourself.

The Social Virtue of Justice

By justice, Ben did not just mean not treating someone else unfairly. He also referred to performing the duties that are your responsibility. Treating other people fairly will get you far in business and life in general. Building up wealth gives you greater responsibilities to help out your unfortunate fellow man as well.

The Social Virtue of Humility

Being humble to Ben meant following the example of Jesus and Socrates. Neither of them were ever proud in their accomplishments. No one likes to be around you when you are always talking about yourself and all that you have done. If you instead focus on others' accomplishments and deeds, then you will have more friends and business associates.

The Social Virtue of Chastity

Benjamin advised that you live a pure life. This will help you to have a better marriage and family for starters. In the end, other people, whether personal or business associates, will always respect you for living a pure and admirable life.

The Devastating Effect of our Education System on Wealth

You have heard the criticisms against the American school system for many years now. The system does not motivate and inspire most students to enjoy learning and excel at school.

It will probably stun you to learn that the American educational system was designed with a limiting and restrictive basis to it in the first place. In the following paragraphs, you will come to understand how an education system came to be created in the United States that maintains and reinforces the status quo.

The Prussian System of Education Comes to the United States
In the 1700's and 1800's the German Kingdom of Prussia began instituting a new type of education that came to be the basis for the United States and Japan. This system of eight years of primary education had the name of Volksschule.

Provided for by tax based public funds, it offered the basic training that instilled in children a foundation of skills for the early industrialized world. These included reading, writing, and arithmetic. Besides this, it taught duty, ethics, obedience, and discipline, according to the Lutheran and Calvinist points of Christian world views.

Several key elements of the Prussian system of education found their way to America. You are well acquainted with the concepts of specialized teacher training, mandatory attendance in school, a curriculum set for every grade, compulsory kindergarten, and nationally administered testing for every student. These concepts proved to be revolutionary at the time, though they were not necessarily the most ideal premises for education in today's high technology and knowledge requiring world.

John D. Rockefeller and the General Education Board
Another major influence on the American school system turned out to be the philanthropic trust created by John D Rockefeller along with Frederick Gates back in 1902. This General Education Board began with their grant of one hundred and eighty million dollars, a vast and almost unimaginable fortune at the time.

This trust intended to mostly encourage and influence higher education throughout the South and the United States. It similarly promoted medical schools around the U.S. and encouraged better farming techniques throughout the South.

These all sound like noble goals, you are likely thinking. The problem with this foundation that had a major impact on public secondary education in its formative years lay in its early philosophy that underpinned all of their considerable efforts and influence on high schools and secondary education.

The 1906 statement of this Education Board claimed that it was not attempting to turn students or people in the communities into learned men of science or philosophy. It did not wish to create and train educators, authors, scholars, or poets from the people.

It also did not look for artists, musicians, painters, doctors, lawyers, politicians, or statesmen to train and nurture, claiming that the country had these in sufficient numbers. Instead, its goal lay in organizing children, and showing them how to do the same work that their parents performed imperfectly in a more perfect way.

In other words, this incredibly powerful educational organization set out to maintain and reinforce the status quo, rather than to teach students to aspire to greater goals and lives for themselves than their parents had. Rather than improve on children and their background in school, it only wanted to keep them at the same level as their parents and their social and economic standing from which they came.

The Resulting American Educational System

The educational system that you and your contemporaries have been left with is one that teaches people to follow orders without questioning them. The school system works to create blue collar workers and servers of the wealthy.

Rather than instill in the children a love of learning and thirst for knowledge of such critical topics as financial education, it suppresses learning of such elitist pursuits. In this way, generations of children are graduated who are trained and ready to work on behalf of the rich and not truly for themselves.

The Educator who Opposed The Education System

Not every teacher and educator approves of the American educational system that you see all around you today.

A long time educator of around thirty years named John Taylor Gatto has penned several books in protest of the system and the harm that it does to American children. Gatto has written his revolutionary and controversial book "Dumbing Us Down" in which he sets out the problems with the modern day American school system.

Problems in the American Educational System

The problems that are evident in the educational system that he sets out are several. First, the American education system leads to confused children. Rather than teaching them practical information, it offers them instead an incoherent collection of information that children have to commit to memory in order to keep up with the program. The tests only teach the children to learn something long enough to pass the exam, then to promptly forget it again. In this way it is much like television for children.

The system also teaches American children not to fight their class affiliation into which they are born. In doing this, the existing system similarly shows them how to be indifferent to their situation. The current system also teaches children to be emotionally dependent.

America's school system engenders a self confidence and self esteem that has to be reaffirmed by authorities and experts all of the time. This creates a self esteem that is provisional on approval. Finally, the system shows children that however hard they may run, they can not hide. This is because the children are always being watched over and supervised. They learn that doing creative study on their own to better themselves is not rewarded, but discouraged by the system that teaches the children to do the least with which they can get away.

Gatto has instead suggested that the kind of schooling that teaches children what they should know is based on home schooling. Here, a child's individual interests in learning can be encouraged and promoted. The necessary skills of learning and thinking independently can be instilled. To this effect, Gatto is presently creating a three part documentary on the failed system of compulsory education called The Fourth Purpose.

What the School System is Not Teaching

The school system is definitely not teaching children how to think for themselves. Similarly, it does not encourage nor reward self taught extra learning, which is critical for a person to grow and improve. Financial education is almost completely ignored, even though this is required if students are to learn how to better themselves financially.

Building wealth is a function of learning how to train, to study, to think, and finally to work for yourself. If these critical skills are not only taught, but discouraged, by a school system, then the effect of wealth creation can not be realized by the majority of people in the society. As you have seen in the previous paragraphs, this has not happened by accident.

Rather, the wealthy contributors to the education system, like John D. Rockefeller, perpetrated it on purpose. They had no interest in the common citizens rising up and bettering themselves. Instead, they wanted to raise up citizens who were well equipped to do what they were told, and to work better on behalf of the wealthy class that runs American quietly from behind the scenes.

Gatto's Disturbing Theories About Your Financial Education

A new book has recently come out on the education system that you may have heard of but not yet read. This is the John Taylor Gatto book, Weapons of Mass Instruction. At only 214 pages long, Weapons of Mass Instruction proves to be a highly readable explanation for how the education system works and what it is actually doing to children. The following paragraphs consider the author and his latest work.

About the Author John Taylor Gatto

If you are not familiar with John Taylor Gatto, he is an interesting individual. Having taught for almost thirty years in the American school system classrooms, he speaks about education practices and effects with a great deal of authority. After seeing the system from the inside out, he became an intense critic of it and activist against the present system of compulsory education.

He has written a number of books on education in America. His last book turned out to be the The Underground History of American Education. This long and overwhelming book covered the whole scheme of the education system and its intentions in America. His latest book, Weapons of Mass Instruction, has been called his best and most readable work yet by critics that like his writings and philosophy.

John Taylor Gatto's Basic Premise

Gatto stands apart from much of the American educating set. While most of them have some positive things to say about education in the United States today, he proves to be completely against the system. In all of his writings and discourse, Gatto claims that mandatory schooling was actually put into place in order for the government to obtain both social and political control.

He says that whatever terrible stories that you may have heard regarding the inability of schools to accomplish anything, the American school system does perform its primary objective quite effectively. The result of their mission, per the author Gatto, is a society that does what it is told and is kept intellectually simple. This produces a population and society that effectively cooperates with the requirements of both the large corporations and the government.

Gatto claims that the side effect of this educational system is the great damage that is done to society as a whole, as well as to families and individuals. The author leads a crusade of sorts to rally resistance against this compulsory schooling that he hopes will turn into an outright rejection of the present educational system. He accomplishes this through demonstrating to people the ways in which you have been tricked into faith and confidence in the essential nature of mandatory schooling that the government actually runs.

Sources for Weapons of Mass Instruction

John Taylor Gatto has a wide range of sources from which to gather his information for this latest book. He selects from the great quantities of research and reading that he has engaged in during his many years in education.

In the book, his own letters, speeches, and articles are incorporated and supporting of his constant theme.

Along the way, Gatto relates some very interesting lessons of history that serve to reinforce his thesis as cases of important things that you were not taught in school. The reason for this, Gatto claims, is that they could disturb your compliance with the way that things are in America today.

Gatto's Examples of the Failure of the School System

Gatto demonstrates his ability as a story teller in the Weapons of Mass Instruction. He uses this to tell the stories of actual individuals who abandoned the school system and went on to great success and accomplishments.

They did all of this despite the conventional wisdom that tells you that without a set of credentials, degrees, or diplomas, you will not do well in life. Gatto brings all of this together in his point that traditional schooling destroys individuals' abilities to be creative, forward thinking, and independent. These are all the characteristics of most wildly successful individuals.

For example, Gatto is not kind to even the Ivy League institutions of higher learning. He lays this out in his chapter entitled A Letter to My Granddaughter About Dartmouth. Here he relates his unfavorable opinion of Ivy League schools. Gatto tells you that America's education does not get significantly better at the majority of universities and colleges than it turned out to be in primary and secondary schools. This is an especially interesting chapter for someone who is undergoing the college application and selection process now.

Gatto's Government Stories that Make His Case

Some of you may be skeptical about John Taylor Gatto's thesis regarding government conspiracies centered around the educational system. Gatto will lay many of your doubts to rest with his final chapter. Here he discusses government intervention and relates three different stories about it to strengthen the case of his argument.

In one such story, Gatto tells his own tale from his days as an educator. At one point, he had a high school lecture interrupted and stopped in the middle of it by a full squadron of police. The superintendent of the school did not like the history lessons being taught; they were considered to be too disturbing.

Gatto's Afterword Call to Action

The Weapons of Mass Instruction concludes with an Afterword. In this final section John Taylor Gatto calls you to action to join The Bartleby Project. In this project, Gatto is suggesting that you and your children should begin peaceful protests against the education system by politely refusing to take the standardized tests.

He claims that such standardized testing is the critical component of the system upon which it depends. It would take a great amount of courage for a student to refuse to take these tests. Still, Gatto says that stronger attacks on the system are needed. He would like to see you take your children out of the school system and stalwartly reject the use of both curriculum and tests that are enforced.

Whether you agree with his entire premise or just think that perhaps a problem exists with conventional schooling, you will likely not encounter a superior treatment of the problem that John Taylor Gatto's Weapons of Mass Instruction.

Implications of Gatto's Theories for Financial Education

Gatto's disturbing theories have significant relevance to financial education and investing in this country. If he is right, then the establishment is attempting to discourage you from learning to take control of your own finances and invest for yourself. The fact that Social Security has grown to be such a crutch for Americans to lean on does support his argument.

The government does not go out of its way to encourage you to teach yourself all about managing your retirement accounts to take control of your own investments. Certainly the major brokerage firms and money managers are not in favor of you reaching the point that you can cut them out of the equation.

Whether Gatto is entirely correct in his assessment of the conspiracy to keep you ignorant and compliant or not, you should take away the lesson of how important it is to think, learn, and invest for yourself. No one will have your best interests at heart more than you do in the end.

Counting on Entitlement Programs Gives Away Your Power

The entitlement mentality has taken over the nation. Evidence of this abounds.

The social safety net, as it is euphemistically called, now commands more than one and a half trillion dollars in budget funding every year to cover the rising costs and benefits of Social Security, Medicare, and Medicaid.

While these programs actually started out as good emergency safety nets for the very poorest, they have come to represent this sense of entitlement that has infested American society like a plague. Such entitlement mentalities will not ever get you ahead, but instead only conspire to keep you poor.

Definition of Entitlements

Entitlements have two meanings in this context. On the one hand, they refer to the rights and benefits that Congress has enacted into law using legislation. Such entitlements stem from social beliefs and moral principles that claim these benefits are necessary provisions that must become legally required within the country. The goal is to provide social equality to a certain degree.

More conversationally, this word entitlement pertains to the idea that you deserve to have some specific benefit or reward. This concept of feeling entitled only began with life, liberty, and the pursuit of happiness in America. It has changed and evolved into an expected guaranteed high standard of life and promised happiness in recent years. The easiest way to understand this sense of entitlement is to see it as the concept that you should get something for nothing.

Background and Problems With Social Security Entitlement
The original goal of such entitlements lay in providing you with some basic minimum benefits. This proved to be a noble goal for the very poorest and hardest hit by economic depressions in society. The problem is that such entitlements like Social Security have turned into gigantic monsters that are consuming themselves over time. Before 2020, Social Security benefit payouts will have started to be more than the incoming receipts. Around 2041, the whole retirement system will start to fail.

The idea that someone else is responsible for your life is a very dangerous belief. This is especially the case when that someone else proves to be the government and their entitlement programs like Social Security. When you begin to understand the fact that the social safety net is far from safe and secure, you start to comprehend the dangers inherent in trusting in the government to take care of you in the future.

With the social security entitlement, you may not be aware of how it actually works. This is critically important to understand, so that you and other people do not depend on it for your future.

With Social Security, there is no savings or investments in an account waiting to be paid out, as there would be with a checking account or mutual fund. Instead, it could be correctly called an enormous Ponzi Scheme, even the biggest one in history.

This is because the government takes your money now to pay off their earlier investors into the program, today's retirees. They give you their word that they will do this same thing for you one day by soliciting contributions from future investors, or tax payers, to pay off your benefits.

Unbeknown to most Americans out there, with Social Security, there is no actual account that has your name on it. Truthfully, no one has an account with their name on it in the Social Security scheme; it is only one large account that is collecting taxes from today's workers to have benefits to pay out to current retirees. The disturbing truth is that the Supreme Court does not even consider that Social Security is your right to receive.

They have ruled that the law does not require any Social Security benefits to be paid out. This mean in practice that Congress can cut or modify these benefits whenever it suits them or the situation requires. In fact, they have done this in more than a dozen instances since the inception of the program. It will probably shock you to learn that the tax rate for Social Security only started out at two percent when the program started in 1935.

It has only been increased since that point to today's nearly eight percent rate. The Social Security trustees claim that this payroll tax will have to continue to rise in order to save the program, with the rate needing to climb to sixteen percent by the year 2041 just to continue to pay out today's level of benefits. If life expectancies keep rising, then the rates will have to go higher.

Problems with Medicare Entitlement

It is not only the entitlement of Social Security that you can not have confidence in providing for your future. Medicare is similarly in funding trouble down the road. Future Medicare obligations have skyrocketed to such an astronomical level that even if all of the residential properties and real estate in America were sold, presently valued at nearly $12 trillion, this would still not be enough to make up the shortfall.

This scenario will not be unique to Social Security and Medicare either. In all areas where you depend on the government to provide for your future needs, including health care, insurance, or housing, you will witness this same choice of either collapse or crushingly higher taxes present itself. Taking the money away from the people who have worked hard, saved, invested, and made it to give it to those who feel entitled but have not done these things, simply does not work out as a viable system on a long term basis.

Where the Entitlement Mentality Leads

When you attempt to redistribute the wealth from the rich to the middle class and the poor, you do not end up with a secure country where everyone lives well. What you instead end up with is a victim state that is known the world over as a welfare state.

This is exactly what the current President intended when he ran on the platform of the government being ultimately responsible for your daily life. One of his favorite phrases is that you are your brothers' keeper. This is good Biblical philosophy and motivation for generosity and charity towards the less fortunate.

Still, it was not intended to become the basis of a state that tells its citizens that you have to help out anyone who is less well off than you are, since we will make you do this with legislation.

This entitlement mentality really is a strong candidate for the guilty party that is keeping you poor, or at the very least from becoming wealthy. All incentive to work and improve your own personal financial state is quickly removed when you start to believe that everything that you require will simply be handed to you as your birthright or due reward.

Similarly, the motivation to work hard and build wealth becomes diminished once you understand that if you do reach a certain level of wealth, the government will talk most of it away in taxes to give to those who are entitled and less well off. Hard work and intelligent investing are the surer ways to wealth, not relying on the government to take care of you. Counting on entitlement programs to take care of you only gives away your power to do it for yourself.

The Seven Reasons Why People Fail to Become Wealthy

You may be wondering why you are not well along the track to becoming wealthy. The truth is that there are actually seven different reasons involved.

With most people, it is not simply one of them that is stopping them from growing rich over time, but a combination of many of them. Identify any that are holding you back in the following paragraphs so that you can work to eliminate them from yourself.

A Lack of Courage

Maybe the most common reason for you not becoming wealthy lies in a lack of courage. Lacking courage is nothing to be ashamed of, but it will keep you from pursuing your ideas and taking the necessary risks to grow wealthy.

A person who is afraid will not invest the money that he or she saves for fear of losing some or all of it. People without courage will never be able to launch out on their own to start a business for fear of failure either. Timidity is not a trait of the wealthy. Because of this, it is one that will have to be overcome if you are ever to accomplish your goals of growing rich.

Bad Habits

For many people, their own bad habits are holding them back from achieving wealth. Many bad habits can hold you back. One of the worst of them is undoubtedly the habit of spending all of the money that you make.

Another is the habit of putting any savings that you do realize into a low or no interest bearing account at the bank instead of investing the money for higher returns. You are never going to attain wealth without some good habits instead. Good habits such as hard work, thriftiness, and proper investing are all necessary in order to get ahead financially.

Laziness

Laziness is one negative character trait that is sure to lead to ruin over time if you can not purge it. The old Proverb that tells you to consider the ant, you lazy person, is one to bear in mind. Ants are constantly busy storing up food. When the winter time comes, they are well provided for as a result of their hard work.

Similarly, you will never see a lazy rich person, unless they obtained their riches from the lottery or some other game of chance. Laziness has to be replaced with hard work if you are to become wealthy. Investing is not easy, and requires study, additional reading, and practice to do well. Working for yourself is similarly the hardest work that you may ever do, although its rewards can be far greater financially than simply trying to get by working for someone else.

No Focus

A lack of focus, or total absence of it, is another sure way to stay poor. One thing that you can say about practically all wealthy people is that they are concentrated and focused on their dreams, goals, and plans. The only way to accomplish anything consistently productive and meaningful is to be sharply focused on both what you are doing and what the desired end result will be.

Only when you are working with direction towards such goals of improving your financial condition will you take any meaningful steps towards them. Gaining focus is not an easy thing to do. It will require putting aside distractions and motivating yourself on a daily basis. The old adage about getting up in the morning, looking in the mirror, and telling yourself positive, uplifting things has value. When you do this, remind yourself of what your immediate and long term focus is so that you will be more concentrated on your goals throughout the day.

No Financial Education

You may be like countless Americans and lack a good financial education. The school system throughout the United States certainly does not encourage nor offer such an education to the vast majority of its students. Financial education is something that you will have to work to acquire personally.

Without good financial education, you will lack basic understanding of things like making budgets, finding extra money from your income to save and invest with, and most of all, how to properly invest for higher and better returns.

Finding a remedy for no financial education will take some time investment and probably financial investment as well. You can start with no cost basics found in investments for beginners books at your area library.

There are good informational websites about budgeting and saving available online at no charge as well. Sooner or later though, you will reach the point of needing more advanced instructions and help. At this point, you will need to be willing to pay for membership fees of financial courses online, or at an area community college or university.

Helpful seminars will come to town teaching specific investment techniques, such as real estate investing or stock market investing. The more education that you can get regarding your finances and investing, the better off you will be in most areas of your life. Without such a financial education, you will never be good at managing either your money or your investments. It is difficult, if not impossible, to grow rich without effective money management and investing techniques. You can obtain these through some hard work, time, and money invested in your financial education.

Stuck In the Past

Another factor that keeps you from becoming wealthy is a burden of the past. There are many reasons that you could be held back by your past. One of the main things that limit people out of their past are investment failures that haunt them.

Something to keep in mind if you are one of these people is that many wealthy individuals suffered from one or more financial failures along their path to success.

Donald Trump is one such example. He has suffered from complete financial bankruptcy and yet come back to be more successful than ever before. You have not seen him stuck in the past for even a few minutes.

Similarly, you must not allow your past disappointments and failures to keep you from future prospects and successes. They certainly can not be allowed to prevent you from trying again. Escaping from your past can be done more effectively by studying the cases of those who failed in their endeavors, only to succeed on a grand scale later. There are many such investor profiles that you can read about to encourage and build you up.

Bad Influence from Friends and Family

There is a saying that you can tell how a person will turn out by looking at the friends with whom they spend their time. It is also true that your family can either serve as a great encouragement or a terrible detriment to your success. You may not be able to change your family and their influences on your prospects, but you can certainly pick out the friends with which you surround yourself.

Negative friends and family who always tell you that you can not succeed at something or better yourself are only holding you back by putting such thoughts in your head. Instead, you must surround yourself with positive influences who are on the track to success and mentors who have already achieved success in some areas of their lives.

The Impact of Collective Beliefs on the Financial Markets

There have been various reasons given for why the present depression, already referred to as the Great Recession, has happened.

Among the ones that you have heard are that assets became too highly valued in a series of real estate and stock bubbles, that banks made irresponsible and reckless loans, and that policy makers failed to raise interest rates to more normal levels and instead left them artificially low for extended periods of time.

All of these excuses for the present economic malaise have some validity and are true to a point. One reason that you may not have heard for why the economic crisis began and is still ongoing is that it is simply an idea that became a collective belief. The reasons for why this is a viable explanation for the Great Recession and financial crisis are examined in the following paragraphs.

How Fear Led to the Housing Crisis and Aggravated the Sub Prime Loans Crisis

If you stop and think it over a few minutes, you will be surprised how a person's fears can quickly spread and become the collective belief that brings down an economic expansion.

The financial crisis and great recession began with housing and sub prime loans.

But what preceded these elements were individuals' fears. Some-one somewhere, and probably many people about the same time, started looking at the greatly elevated prices for housing and de-cided that they were just not justifiable anymore. They had risen too far too fast. Surely they were due to correct to more historically normal levels versus people's income levels. This idea sparked and then spread as a wildfire would through a forest.

What might have been a simple downturn in housing and the over-all economy became aggravated by another idea that someone had around the same time. It began to be whispered that way too many dangerous sub-prime loans had been made. Surely they would de-fault, as the people who received them were taking on terms and payments greater than they could possibly afford.

When these loans started to actually go bad, the seed of fear had already been spread around to many Americans via the rumors about the loans on the financial channels. Once again, investors went into panic mode and started selling off stocks and assets in an attempt to get out before things headed towards a bottom.

The two kick off events that began the financial collapse and re-sulting Great Recession were ultimately based in the ideas spawned by fear. They then went on to become vicious self fulfill-ing prophecies. This actually happens at the outset of many eco-nomic downturns in the United States, especially the ones that are sparked by panic, such as this present one proved to be.

The Role That Sentiment and Confidence Play in Modern Economic Events

If you are still unconvinced by the idea that the collective beliefs of fear and crumbling confidence contribute substantially to economic setbacks and downturns, then consider some of the most closely watched economic indicators in the world today.

These are consumer and business confidences. Consumer confidence is literally what it says, a measure of how confident consumers feel about the overall economy, their job, and their imminent and future prospects. When it is revealed every month, this index has a significant immediate impact on economic outlook and forecasts, as well as how the stock market performs, another bell weather economic indicator.

Consumer confidence is directly tied to another closely scrutinized piece of economic news, consumer spending. This number can move all of the markets all by itself. The reason for this is simple. More than two-thirds of the United States economy is based directly on the amount of spending pursued by consumers.

When consumer spending falls, you can be sure that a chain reaction begins. Factory output is intentionally lowered as businesses realize that there simply will not be enough demand to support their current production of goods and services. Businesses take a defensive posture, and begin laying employees off.

The vicious cycle down begins, as fewer working employees means even less spending, and leads to lower tax roles. Even the country's various state and local governments are forced to cut back on spending when the tax base is significantly down long enough.

Lower business confidence is another thing that results from falling consumer confidence and consumer spending. This link in the chain reaction is not only a symptom of the problem, it becomes part of the economic downturn. Business confidence, like consumer confidence, bears a heavy influence on business spending.

While not as overwhelmingly large as consumer spending is to the entire American economy, business spending is definitely the next biggest category. So fear that started with consumers, translating into falling consumer confidence and leading to declining consumer spending, next infects business confidence and business spending, once again leading to fewer jobs and less economic output.

9/11 Example of Collective Belief Leading to Economic Downturn
You can look at 9/11 and the terrorist attacks principally in New York City as a concrete and fairly recent example of this phenomenon of collective belief leading to economic downturns. As terrible as they were in human tragedy terms and loss of life, the 9/11 attacks did not materially directly affect the economic production or industrial capacity of the United States. Yet, they did lead to a brief economic recession in 2001-2002.

In case you are wondering why this resulted, look no further than the collective belief idea. Consumer confidence took a massive hit from the terrorist attacks. That is the purpose of such attacks ultimately, and in that regard they were supremely effective. With falling consumer confidence went consumer spending.

You might argue that only the aggressive and immediate intervention of the Fed severely cutting interest rates, along with the administration's confidence bolstering retaliatory measures in Afghanistan and Iraq, prevented a major economic downturn over this event that, where infrastructure is concerned, only took down two skyscrapers in one city. The power of collective belief impacting the U.S. and even world economies simply can not be overstated.

Economic Facts That Have Not Changed Materially in the Great Recession

There are many key economic components that did not change in the wake of the Great Recession, further strengthening the argument that collective belief is behind the present depression in America. Consider the underlying economic fundamentals that remain unaltered. People's ingenuity and creative contributions to the economy have not disappeared. Commodities, real estate, and economic resources have not simply vanished or diminished.

What has changed tangibly is the value of the currency.

The dollar continues its steady decline that has only been made worse by the economic and financial collapses. Measured in terms of gold, the dollar has dropped from around $700 per ounce to $1,400 per ounce in only the four years since the economic collapse began.

That represents a staggering fifty percent decline against the historically accepted and unimpaired real asset of gold. Even the value of the dollar is largely based on the collective confidence of users and investors in it. The demand for it rises and falls with these groups' belief in what it is actually worth. The dollar too bears out the argument about collective belief having the largest impact on economic events like the present depression.

John Blake's Wealthy Guide Makes Use of Magical Powers

If you are the kind of person who prefers learning your financial lessons while enjoying an interesting story, then you should check out Mark Fisher's latest book "The Millionaire's Secrets: Life Lessons in Wisdom and Wealth." This is not your typical tome on ways to be smarter with your money.

It is the fictional story of an everyman kind of character who learns and teaches useful lessons about life and finance as he makes his journey through life. In subsequent paragraphs, you will see why this author and his new book deserve your attention.

About the Author Mark Fisher

Mark Fisher has been publishing books about finance, investing, and economic topics for more than a decade now. Among his recent past endeavors are such insightful books as "How to Think Like a Millionaire", "Capitalist Realism: Is there no alternative?", and "The Instant Millionaire" His current book "Secrets: Life Lessons in Wisdom and Wealth" is the sequel to "The Instant Millionaire" and represents a departure from many of his past works of non fiction.

The Style of Secrets: Life Lessons in Wisdom and Wealth

Mark Fisher set out to write a different kind of financial advice and life self help book in his latest solo effort. The author of the motivational standard "The Instant Millionaire" creates a moving and meaningful parable for the days that you live in with this work "Secrets: Life Lessons in Wisdom and Wealth."

While you may be the type of individual who tears through drier, more step by step how to advice on your finances, you are more likely to be a person who would rather read an animated tale about leading a fulfilling, meaningful life and achieving financial success. This parable style of teaching is not only more interesting than your typical financial guidance book, it is effective for the average reader.

The book takes its readers through a number of interesting and thought provoking short parables that read like a fiction work. Asking many deep questions that demand responses, it leads you along the road to wealth and sensibility.

Story of Secrets: Life Lessons in Wisdom and Wealth

The main character is John Blake, who turns out to be a still young thirty-two year old star advertising man. His work may earn him accolades in his role at this small town publication, but it certainly does not fulfill him. His life takes a dramatic turn and undergoes a major change when John encounters a mysterious millionaire.

This millionaire decides to share with him his proven methods for financial success. These include a variety of practical advice, such as prioritizing in life, concentrating on only one goal at a time, working around distractions, and learning to possess audacity as well as faith. Beneath the surface of all of these important lessons, you pick up the author's emphasis regarding the potent effects of positive thinking in your life, as stated in the line, "Day by day, in every way, I am getting better and better."

It also features a positive fatalistic view on life, as evidenced with "everything that happens is for the best." This turns out to be the case for the hero John Blake, who becomes a wealthy success and also succeeds in landing his dream girl.

You will find a few strange elements in the story of "Secrets: Life Lessons in Wisdom and Wealth." While the author Fisher is steering you along the road to financial success, he takes some bizarre turns with the main character John Blake. Blake has an interest in metaphysical ideas, and is in fact an ardent believer in the concept of reincarnation. It may be that the author is intent on suggesting to you that if you do not achieve the success that you dream of early in life, then you may get other chances at such success in future points.

Themes Highlighted in Secrets: Life Lessons in Wisdom and Wealth

The self help and business book disguised by its parable and fiction format offers many good lessons to anyone who is struggling with dissatisfaction in his or her chosen career and as of yet unfulfilled dreams. The themes related are both practical and uplifting.

The power of your mind is chief among these, and the parables suggest that by believing in something you can really achieve it. Improving your powers of concentration will build up your will power and help you to accomplish important and big results.

It further highlights the benefits of creating intensely specific goals that even come with amounts in dollars and deadlines for reaching them.

Mark Fisher the author warns against allowing fear to ruin your chances and obscure your real talents. He suggests that both audacity and faith in your self and your goals are necessary to reach success and attain the dreams that you really desire.

In this book, you are taught and reminded that you can learn how to succeed by paying constant attention to the important details and imitating the success of others. It also relates how a mind that is focused on only one concrete goal is capable of observing things that those who are not focused or who do not have the necessary motivation will miss.

The Twist of Secrets: Life Lessons in Wisdom and Wealth

On his way to becoming a great screenwriter, John Blake must learn all of the secrets guarded by the eccentric millionaire. As he learns them, he teaches you all about the importance of not only setting tangible goals, but also about persistence and taking risks.

This millionaire turns out to be the main character from the author's previous book, the "Instant Millionaire." The wealthy guide has magical powers that he uses to help John Blake make it on his particular path. By paralyzing Blake, the millionaire creates an environment where John has no choice but to concentrate solely on penning his screenplay.

Without this magical intervention, John Blake would likely not have reached his success and found his happiness. This mystical help can distract the reader from the core concepts that Mark Fisher is revealing and imparting, but it is necessary for the story to reach its intended result.

Final Verdict of Secrets: Life Lessons in Wisdom and Wealth
The final verdict of "Secrets: Life Lessons in Wisdom and Wealth" remains that it is a recommended story imparting financial truths. Mark Fisher's writing style in "Secrets" has been likened to that of famed, award winning author O. Henry.

In his interesting narrated story, author Mark Fisher reveals many hidden secrets of effective strategies for reaching success. He does this through the truths shared by the book's mentor in the form of the millionaire's secrets. The story is one of truths that stand for the ages. Since the subtitle claims that it is Life Lessons in Wisdom and Wealth, not only success in making money is detailed and promoted, but also wisdom for life.

Whatever cynicism you may have for this type of tale, Mark Fisher does a compelling job of eliminating it through the authenticity of the main character and his convincing supporting characters the strange millionaire and the true love interest. Yet the pearls of the book are not the characters nor the story telling, but instead the truths that are not limited to a particular time or place.

The sequel to "The Millionaire's Secrets: Life Lessons in Wisdom and Wealth" is sure to help the reader in his or her quest of the best that life has to offer.

The Five Stages of Grief About Your Financial Situation

No doubt you have heard about the five stages of grief that you experience when you lose someone who is dear to you. When you grieve over your loss and what might have been, this is a normal, healthy part of life.

You may never have considered before how this same five step process of denial and isolation, anger, bargaining, depression, and acceptance relates to your financial condition.

You may be like the many people, somewhere in the grieving process about your devastated investments and financial future, especially when you live in the United States.

This grieving represents the first steps of your doing something about the very real problem.

Stage One - You Engage in Denial and Isolation over Your Financial Future

The classic first stage involves extreme denial and isolation. You do not want to come to grips with your terribly set back financial future and discouraging situation after the financial crisis. When you consider your retirement prospects and the trouble that Social Security will be in over the next twenty to thirty years, no one can blame you for not wanting to face the future.

By ignoring it, you do feel better about your grief and problem. The difficulty results from this not solving or even addressing the financial problem that you face.

In the financial crisis, the government found itself in denial as things for the overall American economy began to fall apart. Chairman of the Federal Reserve Ben Bernake continued to opine for half a year or more that the country's financial situation was not so bad, and that things would not develop into a full blown crisis.

Finally the country's leaders acknowledged the many economic problems and began taking steps. In the same way, you may not want to face your financial future where retirement is concerned, but you will have to sooner or later. You will be far better off if you do it now instead of in five to ten years down the road.

Stage Two - You Experience Anger over Your Financial Future

In the grieving process of coming to grips with your now disadvantaged retirement prospects and financial future, anger is the normal next step that you will encounter. You may be angry at anyone else who you believe to be at fault.

You will likely find yourself looking to assign blame, if you can not find someone off of the top of your head. This will likely be the government. If they had not mismanaged the economy, then your investment portfolio would not have crashed and burned. If they had not robbed the Social Security trust fund, then perhaps the benefits would be in danger of failing before your retire, or while you are retired.

You might also blame your employer. You could find yourself saying that if he or she was more generous, then your matching 401K benefit would not have been canceled last year. Maybe you are a more realistic person, who understands that you share the blame for your declining financial condition. In this case, you will likely be angry at yourself as well, even if you could not reasonably have prevented your stricken financial situation.

Anger can be a useful emotion, especially if you allow it to motivate you to make the changes that you desperately need. What you have to avoid is prolonged anger at the government, your employer, or yourself that takes up all of your time and energy to keep you from focusing on doing something proactive and positive about your deteriorated financial future.

Stage Three - You Attempt to Strike a Bargain over Your Financial Future

In the normal next stage of grieving, you attempt to strike a bargain. When you are grieving, you will probably wish to make the pain and the problem go away so badly that you may find yourself talking with God, even when you are not a particularly devout person.

You might offer to do something in exchange for Him helping you to restore your shattered retirement hopes and financial prospects. There is nothing wrong with praying for help, in particular when your situation warrants it. You should just be careful not to sit around and do nothing. While you are praying for assistance, it is better to be taking proactive steps to remedy your situation as well.

Stage Four - You Feel Depression about Your Financial Future

The typical fourth stage in grief proves to be depression. This stage is all too common when you are examining your shattered financial prospects and hope for retirement. You will likely look at the hopelessness of the picture and encounter feelings of numbness and sadness. You are probably still angry beneath it all too.

This might be the most dangerous stage of grief after denial where your finances are concerned. When you look at your prospects and give up hope, then you are truly in trouble. It is at this point that you have to fight to get out of this dangerous place, since nothing will paralyze you worse than despair and depression.

When you sit around and believe that you are at the bottom and that things will never improve for you, then this can quickly become a self fulfilling prophecy, if you let it. Maybe you are too down to do much about your financial situation when you are in this stage. That is why you must move on to the last stage of grief as fast as you possibly can.

Stage Five - You Come to Grips and Accept Your Loss

The final stage of grief is the one that finally offers you relief and release. Once you at last deal with your loss of financial security and retirement prospects, then you are able to move forward effectively.

At this point, your sadness, anger, and depression have faded away. You accept the reality of your present situation. Now you are not blaming any one else any longer, whether it is yourself, the government, your employer, or the greedy investors who have enriched themselves by selling short the markets while your portfolio and hopes burned down like a wild fire.

At last you are finally able to put aside your sense of loss and motivate yourself to move forward. Proactive steps are necessary to save your retirement once you have seen your best laid plans derailed. There is not much time to waste in grief and sorrow. If you are able to put your grief firmly behind you and to start taking proactive steps, then you will find that you begin to feel better as you improve your situation little by little.

When you are a more upbeat person again, then you can do the things that are necessary to meaningful improve your situation. You might work more hours to save extra money. You could think of creative ways to bring in additional revenues every month.

With the grief over your financial situation behind you, you might come up with a creative side business or Internet based business that will enable you to bring in extra cash flow.

Certainly you will absorb financial and investing education materials better once your grief is behind you. This is the only way that you will find your financial future and retirement hopes restored, by doing something, or more likely many things, to improve the situation.

Simple Actions to Reframe Your Mindset to Start Investing

If you have not yet begun investing money on your own, then there are likely several different reasons for why this is the case. It is so easy to rely on others for advice and management of your investments and retirement portfolio.

There are several problems with doing this over the long term. In the subsequent paragraphs, you will see the reasons that you need to learn to begin running your own investments, and the changes that you should make in your mentality in order to prepare yourself for it.

Reasons You Should Not Rely on Others With Your Investments

No one takes your investment well being more seriously than you do. This is because self interest is such a powerful motivating factor. A stock broker and his or her brokerage firm have a highest agenda of taking care of themselves. They will work to make the greatest commissions that they can for themselves and the organization. Their ultimate goal is to ensure that the firm continues to make money so that they have a lucrative job.

You have seen the evidence of this truth in the past when major brokerage firms engaged in the promoting of stocks and investments that they really believed were worthless.

When the internal emails came out about them pushing these lousy investments off on their unsuspecting investor clients, people were shocked. You should not be really surprised by this behavior, since these stock brokers and firms only practiced what is in their best interest when they encouraged the sales of investments that rewarded them handsomely.

The other reason that you should not rely on others to handle your investments is that you will have to pay them generously to do this. The media constantly reminds you of how much money that investment banks and Wall Street companies are making. They are not earning these fees by working for charity or minimum wage.

When you add up all of the fees, differences between buying and selling prices, commissions, and account costs that these brokers charge you to invest for you, it will shock you. The truth is that if you allow a brokerage house to manage your retirement portfolio over a twenty to thirty year period, then you will pay an average of over three hundred thousand dollars in expenses to the brokerage firm and your broker. This is an enormous reason to start learning to invest on your own.

Attitudes that Stop You From Investing On Your Own

Fear is the principal attitude that stands in your way when you contemplate investing for yourself and by yourself. You will probably be afraid of failing. Failing in investing means possibly losing some or even a large part of your money. It also means potentially not making the returns that you expect from the accounts that your broker manages. Fear is the worst emotion for you starting to invest on your own, since it will likely paralyze you.

When you invest on your own, it can be lonely. This mindset is discouraging to everyone. You may feel like you are the only person that you know who actively manages your own money. Successful people are often by themselves in their endeavors. This is why you hear the cliche that it is lonely at the top so often.

Laziness is another attitude that you will have to get past to handle your own investments. It is understandable if you are tired from your work or business day. You will have to put in some significant time in order to learn all that you need to know and to actually pick out your specific investments. This is necessary if you are going to get away from having another person handle your investment dollars on your behalf.

Actions that You Can Take to Change Your Investing Mindset

Attitudes of fear and loneliness can be overcome when you put significant amounts of time into educating yourself about investing. You can do this through a number of different ways, all of which are important and helpful.

Begin by reading minimally one book on investing each month. You might even work your way up to two books as you start to understand the concepts better and find that the reading gets easier and quicker. You should also routinely read financial magazines, either in print or online. Forbes, Barron's, and the Economist are a few of these that are good choices for you to consider.

Other helpful financial websites that summarize many investment trends and share news on events that impact investments are also good places to go. Bloomberg.com is an excellent choice in free websites that do not even require memberships.

It is a good idea to find some area of investing in which you can gradually grow into an expert. This will be a good place to start investing.

A great way to help yourself feel less lonely in your self investment plan is to attend investment seminars as often as you can. Here you will see many other people like yourself who are interested in taking charge of their finances and investments for themselves. You might even make a connection with some of the attendees and form an investing friendship of sorts. Having other people around you who are taking proactive steps with their investment futures is a great encouragement. You can share ideas and motivate each other in your otherwise lonely investing work.

The more that you get excited about learning how to take control of your investments personally, the easier it will be to drive yourself to overcome the lazy aspect of your mentality. Enthusiasm for investing is like a rolling snowball or avalanche. It starts out tiny and gradually grows into an unstoppable force with time.

Start Out with Simulation Accounts

Something that will help you to overcome all of these mindsets that you are allowing to hold you back is to set up a simulation account in your area of investments. Whatever types of investments that you choose to pursue, you can usually get one of these trial accounts with a new online investing account.

Many online brokers will give you access to such a trial account at no charge when you open up an account with them. This is true whether you decide to pursue stocks and bonds, options and commodities, or even currencies.

You may have to fund the account first before they will let you begin using the simulation or trial account, but that does not mean that you have to begin putting your real money to work.

These accounts usually will include a balance of pretend money that they will allow you to invest in securities with actual market prices. Take as much time with the simulation account as you can. Not only is this fun to play around with, but it also allows you to try out and refine your investment strategies that you are reading about as you educate yourself on investments.

Money that you lose in this account has not cost you anything. Once you find that you are happy with your results, then you can begin working with your real money in the fully operating account with a greater level of confidence and interest.

Top 10 Financial
New Year's Resolutions For 2011

It is time to make the infamous New Year's Resolutions again. Every year, you and most other people come up with some goals to work towards in the New Year. Over seventy-five percent of the time, people abandon these goals in total failure.

The key to making them stick is to come up with resolutions that you really want to do and then to make a plan to see them through. This year, there are ten financial goals that you can set in your New Year's Resolutions.

Don't believe the main media circus. The economy is in very bad shape and 2011 will be a very critical year for many people. Make 2011 the year you step into financial education so you will be able to navigate your life without dipping further into the depression issue.

Each of these 10 resolutions will help to make your financial and personal future stronger and more hopeful. See how many of these that you can stay with and make happen. You may surprise yourself if you put some real effort into this process.

1. Get Financially Educated - Understand How Money is Created

Financial education is so very important to your financial future. No one will take the time to give you such an education if you do not make the first critical steps and start reading some good books. "Rich Dad, Poor Dad" and "The Wealthy Code" are two excellent places to start.

You should also set yourself a goal of attending at least one financial topic seminar this year. This might be on the basics of investing, on passive income ideas, on how to get involved with precious metals, or on how to hunt for bargains in real estate.

Seminars are good because you learn critical concepts from an accomplished speaker who boasts a wealth of experience. They will sometimes allow for you to pose questions to the host of the seminar as well. This is a very strong learning environment to help you in your quest to get financially educated in 2011.

While you are at this learning, pick up and read some articles about the ways that the American government is able to create money. It will shock you to learn how easily and slyly that they have been able to even triple the money base in the last three years alone. If you are going to protect your money from inflation, or rising prices, in the near future, then you must understand how the government is debasing the currency this year. Do not let this wait.

2. Understand Leverage and Good Versus Bad Debt

Leverage is a powerful tool that can multiply your investment gains and help you to build up your wealth at a rapid pace. To use leverage, you take out a loan for an investment. This means that you only have to put down a portion of the total investment cost, such as from five to fifty percent.

When only five percent of the investment cost comes from your money, then you have a twenty to one leverage. If you are covering half of the investment cost, then you gain a two to one leverage. Leverage is often used for buying houses, businesses, precious metals, or stocks on margin.

Good debts are the ones that allow you to make investments in assets that offer capital gains returns or provide passive income. Bad debts are the ones that you charge up in order to buy consumable goods that you simply use up. In 2011, you should learn to understand the difference between the two types of debt, and how to use leverage to increase the returns on your investments. This will make huge differences in your investment results and financial future.

3. Set a Financial Goal That You Would Like to Achieve

You should also set a financial goal that you wish to reach in 2011. This will be different for every person. You might decide to pay down your debt in 2011. You might look to establish an emergency fund with a certain percent of your income in it. Alternatively, you could decide to save and invest a certain percentage of your take home income.

Whatever your personal financial goal for the New Year is, make it one that is realistic for you to accomplish. Setting too high a goal that you have no hope to realistically achieve will only leave you discouraged and frustrated. It is far better to set a smaller personal financial goal and be able to reach it than to aim to high and be disappointed by the results. In other words, use good sense in setting this financial goal, and then take steps to actually accomplish it.

4. Start Investing in Silver

Silver and gold are the hottest investments from 2010 and for the entire first decade of the new century. Silver prices are rising and making new multi-year highs. Silver is up over seventy percent this past year alone. But the bull market in silver and gold has only just reached its first half.

This is the time for you to establish your position in silver, so that you will not miss out on the enormous profits that you can still make. Even at today's nearly $30 an ounce, silver still has not neared its all time high of over $50 per ounce. This means that there are significant gains still left to be realized in the gray metal. Resolve to get involved with silver ounces as soon as you possibly can in the New Year. It will not stay at these prices much longer. Start with reading my free Silver Fortune Report.

5. Focus on More Income Instead of on Saving Money

Saving money is a noble goal. While there is nothing wrong with saving money, it is far more productive to make a greater amount of income. Your financial picture will benefit more from the higher cash flow than from some savings. You should look for ways to increase your income in 2011.

If you are able to establish one or more streams of passive income in the New Year, this will be even better. This might involve you purchasing some high yield dividend stocks or funds, obtaining a real estate rental property, starting a business, or getting involved in an oil trust fund or Real Estate Investment Trust.

6. What Are Your Talents? Find Out How You Can Serve Others With It

You have different talents and abilities from any other person. A terrific goal for the New Year is to learn what these are and to find ways to help other people by using them. You might be a great organizer, a good manager of money, an excellent cook, or any number of other things. You will be amazed at how good serving others makes you feel inside.

7. Create a Plan for Starting Your Own Business

The painful truth is that almost no one ever gets rich by working for someone else. This is because most of the rewards for your contributions and hard work go to benefit the owners of the business for which you labor. Look at any wealthy person example and you will see that they started a business on the road to riches.

You should come up with a plan to start your own business this New Year. It does not have to be an enormous enterprise. This might even be a small Internet based home business that you start and run. If you really want to get ahead financially, this is an important New Year's Resolution for you to make.

8. Quit Watching TV and Reading the News and Read a Financial Book Instead

There is nothing inherently wrong with watching television from time to time, or in reading about what is happening in the world in the news. If you want to improve your financial status, then you will need to cut way back on these activities and pick up a good financial book instead.

A financial book will help to further your financial education and prepare you to take charge of your personal finances in a meaningful and proactive way. If you read just one financial book each month in 2011, then you will be a far more financially savvy person by the end of the year than you are now. You will also feel better equipped to manage your own investments, which is a critical step.

9. Start Investing Even with Less than $10 per Month

You are probably like many people who feel that if you do not have thousands of dollars to invest, then you should not even bother with the effort. This is totally the wrong mindset. With even $10 per month or less, you can begin investing. You can buy shares in quality stocks or some mutual funds that pay dividends for even these low prices.

If you go to many of these companies' websites, you will see that they will allow you to purchase only one share at a time. Like this, you will build up some investments and be taking the right steps towards securing your financial future. Remember that every little step forward is progress over time.

10. Get a Financial Mentor

A financial mentor is a person who is successful with their finances and investments. When you find someone like this who is willing to give you good practical and personalized advice, then you will learn ideas that have worked well for them in the past. You may never have considered the concepts that made them successful.

They will be able to act as a capable sounding board for any ideas that you are thinking to try out in your own financial endeavors as well. There are many places that you can find a financial mentor. You might look around under the topic in your local newspaper or on a mentor site that has a chapter in your area.

R E T I R E M E N T

"Planing for Financial Freedom"

Retirement

Gold Roth IRA - The Better Retirement Investment Vehicle

Among the various retirement investment vehicles available to you are traditional IRA's, Roth IRA's, and Roth Gold IRA's. All of these forms of retirement accounts have their supporters and detractors.

You should know the differences between them and the ways that they work, as well as their advantages and disadvantages, to make the best possible choices for your particular views and scenario.

Traditional IRA's

Traditional IRA's are retirement vehicles that permit individuals to make as much as $5,000 per year in contributions to these accounts towards retirement. If you are age fifty or greater and want to make additional contributions, $1,000 extra per year is permitted in so called catch up contributions. With traditional IRA's, you are able to deduct the money put into the plan from your current income for taxes. There are some particular requirements that you have to meet for this.

Traditional IRA's also have additional limitations. These include an age limit after which you are not allowed to make contributions. This age restriction is at age seventy and a half with these IRA's. They also suffer from a required minimum distribution.

In the year that you turn seventy and a half, you have to start drawing down the account value by April 1st of the following year. The balance must go down little by little, with the proceeds adding on to your current income. It is not important whether or not you need these funds.

Traditional IRA's have some benefits. They do not limit how much money that you can make and still contribute to them every year. Their tax treatment situation may work better for you, if you are like most people. For example, most of these funds become ordinary income when taken out. This means that they are considered for income tax purposes at the point when you withdraw them. This is to most people's advantage, since their tax rates will generally be lower in retirement than they are now.

There are some other downsides to traditional IRA's. Chief among these is the early distribution penalty. Any amount taken out before a minimum retirement age given out at a penalty, if it is withdrawn before the age of fifty-nine and a half.

Roth IRA's

Roth IRA's have some significant differences from traditional IRA's, although there are a few similarities. One of these similarities that you will see is that their annual contribution maximum amount is the same. In 2010, you can deposit as much as $5,000 to either type of IRA account. The same $1,000 catch up deposit applies as well.

This is mostly where the similarities end. Roth IRA's can never be funded from after tax dollars, as can most IRA's. This is because Roth IRA's pay out tax free monies when they are withdrawn at retirement.

For you readers who feel like having tax free dollars in retirement will be a substantial benefit to you, this may be the way to go.

Roth IRA's have a number of other advantages over traditional forms of IRA's. There is never an age limit for contributions with Roth IRA's. This is especially helpful for people who do not plan to stop working around age seventy. There are also no required minimum distributions with Roth IRA's. This means that you only have to start drawing down funds from these accounts when you need them.

Roth IRA's do have their own downsides when compared to traditional IRA's. There are income limitations for Roth IRA's. Single tax filers must make less than $120,000 in adjusted gross income per year. Married filers must make under $176,000 in adjusted gross income per year together in order to make a contribution. For large income earners, opening and contributing to new Roth IRA's are simply not permitted. The limitations and income rules are not a factor with the traditional IRA's.

Once again, Roth IRA's main benefits lie in the fact that they are both penalty and tax free monies. You can even withdraw them before retirement without these penalties should you wish to purchase a first time home or become disabled. If your life is cut short, your beneficiary may also access these funds at no penalty at your demise.

If you feel that your tax rates in retirement will likely be higher than what you pay now, then you should seriously think about a Roth IRA. The Roth IRA main advantage remains that you can pay the taxes now. This allows you to have truly tax free income distributions in retirement.

Gold IRA's

One other thing that you can do with an IRA is to turn it into a Gold IRA. Although you will find that the IRS closely regulates gold IRA's, they do permit investors to hold gold in these types of retirement accounts. A gold IRA is really an IRA that is held by a custodian in another party's vaults. The custodian must allow investments in precious metals, and not only gold.

There are a few limitations on what kinds of gold can be placed inside of a Gold IRA. The IRS will not allow you to gather collectible metals and coins. Minted coins, bullion, and bars are permitted though, and the range of them that are allowed is considerable.

One ounce, half ounce, quarter ounce, and tenth ounce gold coins are allowed if they are American Eagles or Buffaloes, Canadian Maple Leafs, Austrian Philharmonics, or Australian Nuggets. The only silver coins that are allowed are the one ounce varieties that were struck by the U.S. Treasury. Some types of other bullion are allowed. These include various forms of gold, platinum, silver, or palladium.

Setting up the Gold IRA Custodian Maintenance

You can not simply keep your IRA gold in your house or at your local bank in a safe deposit box. The IRS requires that it be held by a legitimate IRA custodian that keeps gold and precious metal types of investments. You will be required to locate your own custodian in setting up such an account. Your gold will be stored at a third party depository.

Funding Your Gold IRA

All gold IRA deposits have to come in the form of cash. Once the as much as $5,000 deposit per year or rollover from another IRA is made, the custodian will wait for your instructions on which coins or bullion to buy. You can never send in your own acquired coins to the custodian to be stored on your behalf.

Different custodians have various rules and limitations. As an example, there are custodians who will allow you to have both gold and stocks in the IRA account together. This permits better diversification within the single IRA account. It is never a bad idea to find such a custodian when you are setting up your gold IRA.

Gold IRA's have a few other limitations. The biggest ones relate to selling the precious metals in the account. These become taxable when they are sold, unless they are quickly transferred to another IRA and reinvested, so you should treat them as a long term investment until retirement, and not as an account in which to trade gold or other precious metals. Also, Gold IRA accounts can not be set up in a company or LLC designation. They must be in the custodian's name and held on your behalf.

The advantages to putting your retirement money into gold are several. Chief among them is the fact that gold has always kept pace with and generally outperformed inflation over a given period of time. If you believe that severe inflation will eat up your retirement monies in the future unless you do something to protect it, then a Gold IRA is a sensible way to go.

What Baby Boomers Should Do To Secure Their Retirement

Baby Boomers are getting closer and closer to retirement. Some of them have already reached it. Over the next five to fifteen years, the majority of them will approach the retirement accounts' and Social Security Administration's permitted retirement ages of from sixty-two to sixty-seven.

For all of you baby boomers who are nearing and entering retirement, there are several things that you should start doing now and as you enter retirement. These include doing things that you love for work, investing in things that you care about, and hiring a financial coach or a mentor. The following paragraphs explore why it is never too late to engage in these rewarding and beneficial activities.

Begin Doing Something that You Love for Work

If you are like the majority of American workers, then all of your life you have worked in jobs that you did not necessarily love and care deeply about. This likely resulted from financial necessity, as you had to provide a decent living for yourself and your family.

Quite possibly you feared the financial ramifications of abandoning more financially lucrative jobs in order to pursue something that you were passionate about but that probably did not pay a salary on which you felt you could live. It is still not too late to change this and begin a new career in something that you love.

Employment experts have suggested again and again that most people are capable of having two to three, or even more, different viable careers within their working life. It may not be until you reach that third career that you get to do a job that really matters to you.

As you approach and near retirement, this can certainly change. If you are a person who has invested wisely and planned well for retirement, it may mean that you do not really have to work in your golden years. This does not have to stop you from doing something that you love as a part time job. Keeping yourself occupied is a good way to ensure that your health and vigor stay with you long into your retirement years as well.

When you do not desperately need the high stress and high paying job any longer, this is the most ideal time to make the switch over to another field that you have always had an interest in and wanted to try. Even if you find that you still need to or want to work full time, likely your financial picture at retirement will permit you to branch out in to something that pays less well but fulfills you.

It may be that this is simply another field than what you have worked at in the past. It could be that you have always wanted to start up a certain small business. Perhaps you wanted to write a book.

Whatever your hope was for work when you were young and idealistic, do not miss the opportunity presented by retirement or near retirement age and the accompanying financial scenario to pursue this. Late in life job fulfillment is far better than a life lived without any fulfillment in your work at all.

Begin Investing In Things That You Care About

Baby boomers are at the point in life where they should be able to make some investments in things that they care about as well. It may be that you have been enthralled with the ideas and technologies surrounding renewable energies, such as windmills, solar panels, and wave generated energy. Perhaps you always feared to get involved in such newer technologies, or found that you had too much going on to take the time to properly research the companies investing in areas that you love.

Maybe you are a person who respects and admires socially responsible companies. You might have always wanted to invest in them, but feared that they would simply be charity cases that lost you money. In fact, this is not necessarily the case. Canada has an index called the Jantzi Social Index. It follows a balanced basket of sixty different Canadian firms that have been chosen for their ethical and socially responsible trading practices.

It may surprise you to learn that this index actually performs better than does the traditional Canadian exchange benchmark, per statistics gathered by the Social Investment Organization. A large enough group of socially responsible companies exists for you to pick out organizations that you care about and still put together an investment portfolio that turns out to be well balanced.

Now that you are at or nearing retirement, this is not the time to settle for the same types of investments that you have always pursued but never been excited about. Instead, you are at last reaching the point in your life when you will have time to really sit down and properly think about the types of investments about which you feel passionately. Take advantage of this extra time to make sure that your heart, and not just your head, is involved with your financial decisions in investing.

Retirement time is also a good point to start thinking about investing for the people that you care about. You may want to be sure that you are able to leave a significant amount of money or an income stream for your children after you are gone. There are ways to ensure that this dream of yours does not go neglected. If this is where your heart is, annuities are investment opportunities that you should investigate.

Many of them allow you to make a one time lump sum or series of payments into the account that will guarantee that a minimum numbers of years of payouts to you are generated. These can be arranged so that your heirs continue to receive them after you are gone, or so that they pay out a lump sum to them at one time. Retirement age is definitely the time for you as baby boomers to think about investing in the things and people that you care about the most.

Begin Visiting With a Financial Coach or Mentor

The worst decision that baby boomers can make as you approach and enter retirement is that there is nothing new for you to learn, or no way to improve yourself. Just because your principal working years are behind you does not mean that you should stop growing as a person.

Learning and sharing experiences not only helps you to feel more fulfilled and maintain a sense of purpose, but it is also good for keeping your mind sharp and focused. Engaging a financial coach or mentor is a great way to do this as you prepare for your retirement years.

One thing that a mentor or financial coach will be able to help you with is coming up with ideas for ways to improve your resources and activities for retirement. They may have many ideas from experience that you have not yet considered. These could involve different ways of investing, living economically on a retirement budget, or new careers or part time jobs that you might pursue in retirement.

Working with a mentor gives you as a baby boomer fresh perspective on life. This should be pursued, regardless of whether you are nearing the end of your primary career and full time working schedule or simply contemplating a shift to a different job and field.

<u>ECONOMY</u>

"Managing Resources for Prosperity"

Why Deflation Is A Normal Process in a Healthy Economy

Deflation is a term that you do not hear too much of in the news. This is because the government leads everyone to believe that the costs of living, and of goods and services, should always be rising over time.

But contrary to this official line, deflation is actually a natural process that occurs from time to time, and it is beneficial for savers and investors.

What Is Deflation?

The official economic definition of deflation is a lowering in the costs of goods and services. Deflation can happen if the yearly inflation rate drops to lower than zero percent, thereby creating a negative inflation rate.

The result of such deflation is an actual gain in the purchasing power of your money. This means that a same quantity of dollars will purchase a greater number of such goods and services than it did previously. It is accurate to say that deflation actually increases your money's real value in the national economy.

To put it simply, when there is the presence of deflation, your money will buy more, your wealth increases, and you might not have to work as many hours to pay your bills.

Types of Deflation

There are several different types of deflation that can occur. Some of them are natural processes that do not involve any government interference. Among these are demand side and supply side reasons for deflation.

Demand side deflation includes growth deflation and cash hoarding deflation. Growth deflation proves to be a growth in the supply of goods on the market. As the supply increases but the demand does not keep pace, this leads to a natural drop in prices. It shows up as a decline in the CPI inflation index.

Cash Hoarding deflation, conversely, refers to an increase in cash savings. It leads to a slow down in the speed of money moving through the economy. As the demand for money increases, but no additional supply is provided by the country's central bank, then the value of the money rises.

Supply side deflation is the other cause of deflation. Bank credit deflation is the principal type of such deflation. It occurs as a result of a diminishing supply of bank credit. This happens as a result of a contraction in the overall money supply, or through a number of bankruptcies of financial institutions. Either cause of deflation leads to the same end results of a greater value for money than existed previously.

Deflation can be a good thing as it is often seen as part of a healing process. After an economic contraction, deflation is often in evidence. The event results from and also leads to higher savings than in the past, which is also good for the citizens of a national economy over the longer run. If you believe that your money will be more valuable tomorrow than it is today, then you will be more inclined to save it and watch it grow in value, courtesy of deflation.

What Is Inflation?

In stark contrast to deflation, inflation is the rising of the prices for goods and services over a given period of time. Inflation means that your money is losing in value all of the time. It is what is commonly seen in most typical years in the United States and in fact around the world.

While deflation is good for savers, since your money and wealth is increasing in value over time, inflation is just the opposite. Since your savings and investments are actually decreasing in value over time, inflation is positive for spenders and borrowers. You know with inflation that your money next year will purchase less, so you choose to spend it now. Similarly, as a borrower, you know with inflation that the debt that you have to repay will be worth less in a few years, making the repayment amount in effect cheaper.

Inflation happens when demand for goods outpaces their supply. This usually happens as a result of the government printing more money, since inflation is primarily a currency driven event. More money in the system creates more demand for a limited supply of goods and services. Inflation is the normal that you have come to expect, year in and year out, as a result of the government gradually growing the money supply. It actually makes you as an investor and a saver poorer, and it is especially bad if you are a person living on a fixed income, such as a retiree.

Why the Government Creates Inflation By Intervening

Why would the government be interested in there always being inflation every year, you may be wondering.

Should they not wish to reward savings and investment, rather than spending and borrowing? The answer to this question is not so complicated as you might believe.

The governments of the world actually need inflation for several reasons. First of all, if they have a target inflation rate of two to three percent per year, then it benefits them intrinsically. Because inflation occurs as a result of a greater amount of money being pushed into the system, this means that they are actually able to print an additional two to three percent of money per year.

Greater amounts of money for the government to spend means a bigger government that spends more money every year and over time. Practically all governments are machines that only want to get bigger. By setting an expectation of an annual inflation amount, they literally give themselves the excuse to print more money each year.

Another reason that governments want inflation is because they need inflation to be able to stay on top of their debts. When the United States government tells you that it has a $14 trillion dollar debt, this is a scary thing. It is probably now clear to you that this is an unmanageable amount that they will never be able to repay. Yet the government does not plan to repay this debt in today's valued dollars at all. They count on paying it back, if they ever do, in tomorrow's dollars, twenty or thirty years down the road.

At three percent inflation per year, for twenty to thirty years of time elapsed, this would mean that they would actually be repaying between sixty and ninety percent less in a fixed dollar amount. Another way of saying this is that twenty to thirty years from now, thanks mostly to the ravages of inflation, $14 trillion in debt will not seem like so much.

The constant expectation of steady inflation over the years not only helps governments to justify and manage their debt levels, but it gives them an implicit excuse to allow them to increase still more over time. So long as they can continue to propagate the idea that inflation will whittle down the true value of money that they have to repay, they can get away with this.

A final reason that your government really does like inflation is because they consider it to be a sign of a healthy and growing economy. Inflated dollars lead to higher consumer and business spending, which supports a greater economic growth and output. By encouraging spending, they boost the economy. Your government knows all too well that saving actually takes money away from growing the economy. That is the last thing that they want to encourage.

Arthur Laffer's Views on the Future of the U.S. Economy

Among the more influential economists in the last thirty years is Arthur Laffer. With a nationally prominent career stretching from the Reagen years into the Clinton years and beyond, his thought, policy, and works have had a profound impact on tax policy and understanding.

Arthur Laffer's contributions and view of the future economy are all discussed in the ensuing paragraphs.

Early Professional Years and Contributions

Arthur Laffer obtained his BA in economics back in 1962 from the Ivy League Yale University. He earned an MBA in 1965 from Stanford University. By 1971, he had obtained his PhD in Economics from Stanford University as well.

In the years that followed, Laffer became a tenured professor teaching at the Graduate School of Business in the University of Chicago. It was at this point that he had a critically important conversation with the President Nixon and President Ford officials concerning tax policy. During this meeting, he drew a diagram of a taxation curve on a napkin that came to be known as the Laffer Curve.

You should know that this Laffer Curve effectively makes the case for lower taxes. Although Laffer did not claim to have invented the idea behind the curve that bears his name, he was the one to present it to the influential policy makers of the day, including Donald Rumsefeld and Dick Cheney in 1974.

He claimed that the idea for it came from John Maynard Keynes and Ibn Khaldun. In this curve, Arthur explained how both zero percent and one hundred percent tax rates would yield zero tax revenues. He argued that on the lower side of the middle is the tax rate that optimizes total tax revenue. He pushed for a significantly lower tax rates than were presently in place in order to increase the government revenues to maximum.

Arthur successfully argued that by lowering the rates considerably, the revenues would rise, as the economy that could be taxed expanded at a substantially greater rate than when a higher tax rate discouraged expansion and investment. These ideas began to take hold and became especially important under President Ronald Regan.

Arthur Laffer and his California Years and Contributions

Following departure from the University of Chicago, Arthur became a tenured professor at the University of Southern California at their Marshall School of Business. While there, he proved to be among the main instigators for the Proposition 13 writing. This tax law put a property tax limit into effect on California property. In time, it encouraged an enormous number of these kinds of laws in different states throughout the U.S.

Arthur Laffer and his National Stage Spotlight

From 1981 to 1989, you will likely remember that President Ronald Reagan began his Regan revolution that spawned an unprecedented period of national economic growth and job expansion that lasted past the end of the century. As an important member of President Reagan's Economic Policy Advisory Board, he proved to be at the peak of his influence during these important years.

His ideas on tax policies were actually put into place not only on state levels, but also on the Federal level starting with this administration. He wrote what became his most famous work during this period, entitled Supply Side Economics: Financial Decision Making for the Eighties. At the time, the renowned economist wrote and co-wrote a number of other newspaper articles and books as well.

The balance of the 1980's saw Arthur Laffer teaching at Pepperdine University in Malibu. At this time, you saw Laffer throw his hat in the ring for the U.S. Senate from California. Although he lost the Republican primary, he continued to be active in national economic and political decision making. He called himself a stalwart conservative and libertarian.

Arthur Laffer and President Clinton

In the 1990's, Arthur Laffer threw his support behind President Bill Clinton. In both terms, Laffer encouraged President Clinton in his conservative fiscal policies. He again pointed to these policies as being among the main reasons that the U.S. economy continued to grow and expand at a record pace.

Arthur Laffer Since the Year 2000

Since the turn of the new century, Laffer has kept himself occupied as the Co chairman for policy for the Free Enterprise Fund, an influential think tank. He serves side by side with Larry Kudlow in this capacity. He continues to author numerous articles and works on economics.

In his latest economic and political tome that he co-authored in 2008 entitled "The End of Prosperity: How Higher Taxes Will Doom the Economy - If We Let It Happen," Laffer and the other authors made the case against Americans electing a left wing democrat.

He feared that you would see this kind of President raise taxes and abandon the successful economic policies of the past twenty-five years. Laffer would hold up the continuing economic malaise as being a result of President Obama's economically negative policies that he has pursued since he took office more than a year and a half ago.

Arthur Laffer's Present Views on the Future of the U.S. Economy Arthur has continued opining on the national economic situation since The End of Prosperity came out. He is most concerned that the terrible mistakes caused by high taxes in the Great Depression will be repeated.

Arthur tells you again and again that no government can tax its country back to prosperity. He sounds an ominous tone when he states that if the policy makers are listening, they should be aware that both state and federal American tax policies are back on the tragic crash course of the Great Depression. Laffer somberly points out that state tax net increases versus last year are up three point one percent, representing the greatest amount since 1991.

He also worries that the Bush tax cuts will be permitted to expire next year, an event that he sees as devastating to the national economy. Finally, Laffer references upcoming tax increases that he sees as necessary to pay for the new health care system and the vilified cap and trade ideas that are lurking in the not so distant future.

Laffer has also pointed to the intentional devaluation of the dollar back in 1933-1934 as having created major problems. He said that the money supply increased by more than sixty percent at that time, with monetary base being grown by in excess of thirty-five percent, while adjusted reserves were increased by around a hundred percent.

Arthur likens that period to what is going on today, with similar easy monetary policy filtering through the system. He reminds you that during that time, the CPI inflation index increased by fifteen percent even though double digit high unemployed persisted. Once again, he warns of parallels with today's national economic situation.

Laffer says that all of this goes to show you that inflation can happen during such a depression, as it clearly did then. Inflation is always a monetary phenomenon that results from devaluing the currency, much as is being done nowadays.

Arthur's last comment on the future situation is that he fears that the wrong lessons from the Great Depression have been learned. He says that blaming high unemployment numbers and the upfront dip in prices that was seen on tight money is leading the decision makers to massively expand the money supply. He also worries about their fighting rising budget deficits through raising taxes, which made the Great Depression so much worse than it should have been.

The Battle of the Currencies Will Destroy the Global Economy

In the aftermath of the terrible financial collapse of the last few years that led to a severe plummet in most country's economies and exports, you have witnessed a competition among different countries' central banks.

This competition has been to devalue their currency against those of rivaling nations.

The reasons that this has been happening, how it is happening, and the terrible results that can result from it are all explained in the subsequent paragraphs.

Floating Exchanges versus Fixed Exchanges

In a floating currency system, a country's currency is permitted to move up and down versus other currencies according to the wishes of the market. The daily exchange rate is set by supply and demand forces on the international exchange markets. A currency would not have to be fully convertible for this to be the case.

Fixed exchange systems involve currencies whose values are set by a central bank. These rates are announced from time to time and move only very slightly around a target rate with minute variations. China is the classic example of this form of currency regime.

The reality is that practically no countries really allow their currencies to float freely. In fact, their central banks intervene in the currency markets when their desired currency ranges are not maintained by the market. This is being increasingly seen in light of the violent currency swings following the terrible economic scenario of the past several years.

National Mechanisms for Dealing with Fluctuations in Exchange Rates

There are several ways that countries choose to deal with fluctuating exchange rates. Nations like Argentina operate currency boards. The currency board makes certain that all of the nation's currency circulating is backed up by a certain amount of foreign exchange reserves kept in the central banks vaults. This keeps them from printing more money, and forces all branches of the government to only spend money that they collect in taxes.

Still other countries choose to fix the value of their currencies to a currency basket or single currency. The idea behind the contents of the currency basket is that they are comprised of currencies with which the country trades. These countries generally opt to peg their currency in the end to reputable currencies, like the Euro and the U.S. Dollar. Bulgaria's currency the leva is pegged to the Euro at a fixed rate, while the Thai baht is set against the Dollar.

You will find other countries that utilize a crawling peg. A crawling peg proves to be a currency exchange that is affiliated with various other currencies but is allowed to change by a tiny amount each day. When this type of country devalues its currency, they set up the rate before hand and make it clear to the public and the markets.

A crawling band is a variation on this where a country permits an exchange rate to float freely withing a range that is set both below and above a centrally set currency peg.

The Reason that Central Banks Intervene on Behalf of their Currencies

Central banks have their reasons for intervening on behalf of their currencies. They might be interested in safeguarding the currency against rapid appreciation. They might alternatively be interested in moving them down to an exchange rate that they believe to be better for the country's exports.

As a currency's value falls against its trading partners' currencies, its exports become cheaper to citizens in the other countries. This boosts the country's exports and thus the resulting overall economy. This became especially important to countries after the economic catastrophe brought on by the Great Recession. Countries' primary goals became those of stimulating their economies back to health. Many of them chose to do this by playing with their currencies.

How Central Banks Intervene With Their Currencies

The easiest way for a country and its central bank to intervene in its currency is to talk the currency up or down. They do this by announcing that they are contemplating intervening in the international currency markets to support or drive down the value of their currency. The limitation with such a method lies in the fact that it only works once or twice. After the international markets decide that a central bank is only bluffing, then they will not take the central bank's threats seriously anymore.

A more effective way for a given central bank to impact its currency value is to literally make a foray into the international currency markets. If they wish to reduce the value of their currency, they will come into the market and sell their currency massively while buying the currency of their trading partners. This will cause their currency to fall as the supply of their currency greatly exceeds the available demand.

Examples of this manipulating of currency by intervening abound in the last several years. You have seen the Swiss take the lead in this form of currency intervention since the Great Recession. On three separate occasions, they have engaged in massive selling of their own Swiss Franc while at the same time buying Dollars and Euros with everything they had.

Each time that the Swiss Central bank does this, they increase its effectiveness by instructing their larger banks to similarly engage in the process. UBS and Credit Suisse have both been party to this currency manipulation.

In just the last month of September, the Japanese have practiced the same type of intervention. They did not want to see the Yen get any lower against the dollar. To counter this consistent drop of the Japanese Yen against the dollar, they intervened by massively selling dollars and buying Yen.

In both of these cases, the two governments and their respective central banks achieved their aims in the short term. The Swiss did see the Swiss Franc fall against the Euro and the Dollar for a brief period. With each intervention, the effectiveness has decreased. Rather than discourage the Swiss from continuing to practice currency intervention, it has only spurred them on to try it more aggressively.

The Japanese similarly saw a brief positive reaction to their intervention that lost its effectiveness later in the same month. Whether they will try additional manipulation or not remains to be seen, but they have threatened to if necessary to stop the sliding of the Yen.

Why the Competition of Countries to Devalue their Currencies is Dangerous

You are increasingly witnessing major economies and central banks choose to devalue their currencies in an effort to prop up their own failing economies at the expense of their neighbors' and trading partners' economies.

This is sometimes called an effort to beggar your neighbor in a violent race to the bottom. When countries begin manipulating their currencies through devaluation to make their own exports more attractive to foreigners, it sets off a series of violent competitions.

Other major economies then decide that they must do the same thing in order to prevent their exports from becoming too expensive to purchasers in foreign countries. Trade wars invariably end up erupting as each country becomes frustrated that they can not keep their currency down and their exports up in relation to those of their trading partners.

These kinds of actions in the Great Depression caused it to go from what might have been a fairly minor recession into a world wide economic collapse that took decades to end.

As currencies fluctuate more and more wildly, global trade starts to be affected. Finally, it begins to break down altogether. This is how a battle of the currencies ends up destroying the global economy.

How Interest Rates Create Cycles of Economic Depressions

Interest rates and interest charged for money loaned is a daily part of modern life anymore. Almost no one would think of loaning out money without charging interest.

It may surprise you to learn that this was far from the case throughout most of recorded history.

In a majority of history, interest charging proved to be at the very least a controversial matter and at most an illegal crime that could even be punished by death. The modern day manipulation of interest rates actually cause economic recessions and depressions.

The History of Interest and Usury

The fathers of modern civilization are generally regarded to be the Greeks. Yet, they were so against the concept of charging people interest for loans that they made the penalty a punishment by death.

Plato decried such usury, or interest, to be a vehicle for creating inequality of wealth that would ruin peace between citizens. The Romans permitted usury in the early days of their empire but placed a limit on what you could charge another person.

Usury as a concept came from the loaning out of cattle in the Roman Republic. If you lent out thirty cows to someone for a year, then you would require them to pay you back with a greater number of cows than only the original thirty. This is because some of the cows would have delivered calves.

Since the Romans decided that it was only fair to return a certain number of cows with their offspring back, they carried the thought process a step further, believing that other loans ought to have offspring too. Their typical interest rates ranged from four to twelve percent per year.

The three great religions of the Ancient Western world also forbade the charging of usury. Original Judaism, Christianity, and Islam all condemned it strongly, even though their modern day adherents allow it and collect it themselves. Judaism did not allow Jews to charge other Jews interest on loans.

Islam completely forbids the practice of interest. In Christianity, the First Council of Nicaea made it illegal for members of the clergy to charge usury nearly seventeen hundred years ago. Additional ecumenical councils extended these rules to non clergy members of society. By the Lateran III council, people charging interest were forbidden from having Christian burial or receiving any blessings of the church.

Pope Clement V made the crime of usury equivalent to heresy seven hundred years ago, overturning any secular law codes that permitted it in the process. Despite this fact, Lombard merchants, bankers, and pawnbrokers practiced their money lending trades along the pilgrim routes to the Holy Land following the crusades.

Interest finally started to be accepted as a legal practice again in the late middle ages in England. Permission was granted around five hundred years ago for individuals to charge interest on money that they loaned others. The 1545 Act Against Usury decreed by Henry VIII codified it into law and started the concept of interest as permissible and acceptable in the modern English speaking world.

Throughout the early modern age, loans made by merchants and goldsmiths began to rise in prominence. These were all given out with a contractually stated interest rate and repayment amount clearly stated and enforced.

These interest rates could run from twenty to thirty percent per year on short term loans. In and following the 1500's, as capital became more available, interest rates gradually declined to about nine to ten percent per year. As the rates became more reasonable, religious offense at the practice of charging usury gradually declined.

Economic Cycles of Expansion and Recession Are Created by Interest Rates

Today, the interest rates are officially set by the central banks of governments. Banks use these so called prime rates as a basis for the rates that they turn around and charge you, their customer.

These prime rates are not fixed and static at all. Instead, they are constantly being adjusted by the governing authorities in an attempt to keep the economy level. The unfortunate result of raising and lowering the interest rates is that economic cycles of recession are literally created.

In the United States, the NBER, or National Bureau of Economic Research, proves to be the trusted source for announcing when the economy is in an expansion or contraction period. Expansion is defined as when a few different economic data points, such as growth in the total economic output, or Gross Domestic Product, are occurring. Economic contraction happens as a result of a decline in these data points, particularly in terms of GDP. This organization does not attempt to explain how these expansion and contractions work, nor from what they result.

Interest Rates That Lead to Economic Recession and Depression
When the economy is expanding, the monetary authorities, namely the Fed, attempt to keep the economy from expanding too quickly and overheating. They become concerned that increased expansion is causing rising demand to chase goods too quickly. This leads to rising prices of most goods and services. The Fed steps in fearfully to prevent the rising prices from getting out of hand. They do this by raising the government interest rates in an effort to slow down the movement of money.

As banks follow suit and raise their interest rates that they charge businesses and consumers, borrowing and credit tends to become choked off. Businesses borrow less to invest as the repayment costs become higher. Consumers also decide to push off major purchases, such as cars and homes. The consumer and business spending levels begin to fall. This effect reverberates through the economy in a vicious cycle. Less consumer spending and falling consumer confidence leads to still lower borrowing and spending levels.

The same is true with businesses. Rising interest rates lead to business cut backs and contractions in production. Layoffs can result, which reinforce the entire downward spiral.

Businesses hiring fewer people and even letting people go means that there are still fewer payroll dollars to be spent keeping the economy growing and going. Finally, the big picture economic numbers begin to tell as a result. As the GDP ceases expanding with the growing unemployment, falling consumer spending, and diminishing consumer confidence, a downturn is officially declared. This is usually called a recession.

Definition of Recession

The definition of a recession is an economic downturn where real gross domestic product falls for at least two quarters in a row. A more revealing way of explaining recessions is to say that when business activity has passed its peak and begun to fall, all the way until such bottoming business activity has leveled out, this a recession. Similarly, when such economic activity begins rising once more, this is named an expansionary period. Recessions last about a year on average.

Recession Versus Depression

Severe recessions become depressions if they get bad enough. An easy to understand definition for you for a depression proves to be a recession that endures for longer than a year and involves a bigger business activity decline that in a typical recession.

Since the 1930's, the government has not officially named any recessions depressions, although the financial meltdown of 2007-2009 certainly had all the hallmarks of a depression. The term has become associated with such a negative connotation, that the government tries to avoid it altogether.

Blame the Keynsian Economic Model for the Financial Mess

If you are like many Americans, you probably wonder how the country got to the point of running such high deficits that the national debt could reach an almost inconceivable level of over $14 trillion.

A single economic model takes most of the credit, and also bears most of the blame, for the modern day economic system that underlies the majority of industrial, advanced economies and their enormous debt loads.

This is the Keynesian model of economics, which is explained for your benefit in the following paragraphs.

Background to Keynesian Economics

John Maynard Keynes is actually the father of the twentieth century economic thought that bears his name and has such a tremendous impact on the developed world's economies today. His ideas first became popular and put into practice during the throes of the Great Depression.

The theories that built the economic philosophy of Keynes concepts first appeared in his book that he published in 1936, entitled The General Theory of Employment, Interest, and Money. Keynes' ideas for solving the Great Depression revolved around a novel solution for the time of stimulating the economy.

The British born economist had two approaches for how this stimulation of the depressed economies might be accomplished. On the one hand, he argued that you could reduce interest rates, which he believed would cause individuals and businesses to start borrowing and spending money again.

On the other hand, he insisted that a government investment program in infrastructure was necessary to significantly step up spending for the overall economy. Such government spending would then lead to a greater level of production and investment that spiraled into still more income and spending. He believed that this first stimulation of the economy would begin a virtuous cycle that led to a final boost in economic activity levels that were multiple factors of the initial investment.

Central Theories of Keynesian Economics

A central tenet of Keynesian economics that you may recognize is that decisions made by the private sectors occasionally result in larger picture economic outcomes that are not efficient. Because of this, Keynesian economics strongly argues in favor of vigorous government policy responses to the private sector decisions.

This includes a full range of both monetary policies and steps taken by the Central Bank, as well as fiscal policies and steps taken by the government, in order to help stabilize and smooth out the economic output levels in business cycles.

Keynes also took issue with savings, not only on a government level, but also from businesses and consumers. According to his economic theories, savings that were in excess of planned investments represented a severe problem. It would lead to recession and even depression if carried out.

Too much savings would happen when investment fell, possibly as a result of declining consumer demand, negative business expectations, or too much investment in prior periods. Keynes argued that savings had to fall in lock step with investment in order to keep an economy from contracting.

Where government spending was concerned, you saw Keynesian economics take an opposite approach to previous economic thought. The classical economics argued for governments to balance their budgets, not run deficits, or build up excessive levels of debt.

Keynes and his economics insisted that governments actually following such policies only made the problem significantly worse. Spending and investment needed to be increased, not decreased, in order for a greater demand for labor to exist and its products to increase.

Another important interpretation of Keynesian economics revolves around the idea of international economic cooperation and even coordinating economic policies internationally. The Keynesian economics' system has been used to argue in favor of economic organizations and institutions that are international in nature.

By governments submitting to such close coordination and cooperation, massive disruptions in the world economy business expansion might be mitigated, and thereby peace might be promoted and war avoided.

Keynesian Economics Implemented

Keynes' thought had a major impact on President Franklin Roosevelt's belief that too little buying power had led to the Great Depression. Because of this, Roosevelt began implemented some of Keynesian economics late in the depression, particularly following 1937. This was not the true triumph of Keynesian economic thought yet.

The full triumph of Keynesian economics which led it to become a cornerstone of modern industrial economies took place after World War II. The spending by governments in the second world war caused the shaken world economy to be jump started. By the 1960's, Keynesian economic ideas had taken on an aura of practically official policy in both the United States and the newly forming social democratic Europe.

Although Keynesian theory declined in relative importance in the 1970's, it has seen a resurgence since the turn of the new millennium. The economic crisis of 2007, already referred to as the Great Recession, has caused economists and government leaders to return to Keynesian Economic ideas and policies.

You have seen the leaders of both Great Britain and the United States pursue his ideas aggressively once again, both in former British Prime Minister Gordon Brown and Presidents George W. Bush and Barrack Obama.

Elements of Keynesian Economics That Have Been Revived
Especially the Americans and British have gone back to several
Keynesian Economic ideas. The first one is that aggressive government policies are able to efficiently manage the economy. The
involvement of the Fed and Treasury in orchestrating mergers and
acquisitions of institutions deemed to be too large to fail is an example of this.

The second idea resurrected is that significantly unbalanced government budgets leading to deficits are not inherently bad or evil.
This Keynesian economics idea that counter-cyclical fiscal policies
had to be taken to attack the declining business cycle is evident
everywhere.

Using deficit spending to prop up the national economy and try to
tackle consistently high unemployment has become such a hall-
mark of government policy today that the government adds trillions to the national debt faster than ever believed possible in the
past.

Advantages and Disadvantages of Today's Keynesian Economics
The upsides to these recently pursued economic policies are fairly
obvious, since they are what you hear the administration trumpet-
ing all the time. While unemployment has not really improved, at
least it has not become any worse in the meanwhile.

The President will also hold up an economy that is growing again
as proof that the Keynesian ideas are working. He and his advisers
like Ben Bernake would likely point to the saved banks, entire
banking system, and car manufacturing companies as still more
evidence that the use of Keynesian economic ideas has again saved
the day. From one point of view, these are all valid points.

The downsides to the same policies are often the mirror image of the advantages to the Keynesian economic policies. Although huge amounts of government stimulus money have been spent, has the economy really been saved? Unemployment remains only slightly off of its Great Recession highs.

The economic growth that has been praised is slowing and talk of a double dip recession is growing. Companies that were saved are once again pursuing the same policies that practically ruined them only a year or two before. On top of this, now the government has an almost unmanageable debt load to finance both now and in the future.

Are We Too Irrational to Run a Rational Financial World?

John Lanchester is a British novelist who is famed for his award winning From Debt to Pleasure novel debut. He came across the unbelievable story of the worldwide economic crisis several years ago when he was engaging in back story research for one of his novels.

As he delved into the tragedy that wracked the world economy, he understood that he had run aground the most fascinating story that he had ever encountered.

As a result of this, the novel writer paid extremely close attention to the greatest financial crisis since the Great Depression. His research led him to pen the non fiction work entitled I.O.U.: Why Everyone Owes Everyone and No One Can Pay.

Characteristics of I.O.U.

It is more than fair to say that Lanchester truly brings the ready wit of a novelist to the project of his I.O.U. book. To this he adds great skills in narration and an understanding of the ridiculous nature of mankind in his retelling of the story of the still unfolding financial crisis.

The book proves to be a truthful and fact filled version of the story that is called so incredible that if it were made into a movie screen play or novel, the critics would ridicule it as so improbable as to be unrealistic.

For example, Lanchester goes into gory details of the economic crisis as though it were a car that you were driving recklessly down the highway before throwing it into reverse. Likely you understand what would happen if a person did this. The engine would blow up, the car would erupt into smoke and flames, and finally the car would wreck on to the side of the road causing massive injuries and probably death in the process.

Origins of the Economic Crisis

Lanchester tracks the greatest economic crisis in at least seventy years back to the attitude that ensued with the collapse of Communism in the late 1980's. He engages for the first section of the I.O.U. story in the retelling of the way that the country built up a financially based economy that proved to be totally out of control and only got faster and more reckless with every passing year. The author describes in brilliant and glowing terms the euphoria and insanity that enveloped the titans of Wall Street in the world following 1989.

Lanchester says that the financial centers began increasingly depending on such complicated mathematical tools as derivatives to share and spread around risk within the financial system. He calls this as a total breakdown of common sense and reason, a leaning towards obscure and abstract ideas, and concepts that no one could hope to explain in the common vernacular of the English language.

Ideas About Capitalism Turning On Itself

Maybe it is as a result of his ability as a novelist. Lanchester demonstrates an able skill for making the complicated financial economy fit into everyday English explanations. He says that following the fall of Communism, Capitalism needed a new foe to battle.

In the absence of any obvious ones, it chose to cannibalize itself. In colorful English, I.O.U. details the almost unbelievable tale of a global economy that was operated by cons and tricks, lying loans, and a variety of strange and deadly financial weapons of real mass destruction.

Ideas on The Origins of the Asset Bubbles

Though Alan Greenspan has vigorously defended himself and Central Bankers in general as not having caused the asset bubbles with artificially low interest rates, I.O.U. does not countenance this view.

The book points out that the asset bubbles were likely around ninety percent the fault of central bankers not paying attention to the perils of lower interest rates for extended period of time. The Europeans and British also managed to build up significant asset bubbles, and they too pursued the same lower interest rate policies as the Federal Reserve did.

Take on Leverage

I.O.U. has much to say about the perilous amounts of leverage that investment bankers pursued in the run up to the financial collapse. He points out that Barclay's of Great Britain possessed a 1/61th equity, or cash, to assets, or loans, ratio.

This was an inevitable recipe for disaster. He states clearly that the average amount of leverage employed in the United States proved to be 35:1 while in Europe it turned out to be even higher at 45:1.

This dangerous risk that the bankers put their companies and shareholders through yielded enormous profits during good years. Much of these found their way into the accounts of the executives as a result of self voted on generous bonuses. It was not that the banks were making so much money by being smarter or better, but that they were tacking on significantly riskier and larger bets at the roulette wheel.

I.O.U. shows you that the typical annual return for stocks in banks went from the long term average of two percent up to sixteen percent from 1986 to 2006. This resulted not from skill or intelligence, but instead from very risky gambles with the shareholders' money.

Why Things Are Not Really Getting Better

The banks have been charged with two mandates that are incompatible. The first is to reconstruct their shattered balance sheets so that they do not sit on the verge of bankruptcy. The second task is to continue to lend out money to businesses and individuals. They have been instructed to save money and continue spending it all at once.

Both goals are not possible together. Because of this, banks have mostly hoarded any penny that they could, in an effort to deleverage their balance sheets and build back up their capital as quickly as they might.

Take on the Inevitable Catastrophe

The work claims that the end game explosion and collapse could not be avoided in light of the unbelievable set up. The book tells you that when people without jobs who had no money to their name were empowered to purchase real estate that they could not possibly afford to own, then the collapse of the American based banking system proved to be inevitable.

I.O.U. reminds you that the $4.6165 trillion dollar costing government sponsored bailout turns out to be larger than the total expenses of the Louisiana Purchase, The Marshall Plan to rebuild Europe after World War II, all of the Apollo moon landing programs, the wars fought in both Korea, Vietnam, and Iraq, and the savings and loan crisis of the 1980's all combined.

In the conclusion, I.O.U. holds up the ludicrous nature of having a financial system that proved to be constructed by mathematicians who did not have a clue in what they were doing. It points out that man is too irrational to run a financial world based on the concepts of rationality. The book leaves you with the warning that the world must ban the use of dangerous and complicated investment tools such as derivatives that have led to the destruction of the world economy at the hands of the insatiably greedy investment bankers and their come what may attitude.

The book turns out to be a serious critique of the insatiable greed and reckless stupidity of today's financial power brokers. It is both deep and thought provoking while at the same time a funny and enjoyable experience.

How Long Will the Dollar Continue to Rule The World?

If you have followed the news closely during the Great Recession and in the wake of the United States led world wide financial collapse, then you have heard a number of countries' representatives call for an end to the U.S. Dollar as the world's reserve currency.

Perhaps you have scoffed at the suggestion, as have many American economists and pundits. This is no laughing matter though, as an end to the dollar based world currency situation is inevitable. In fact, its decline has been hastened by the serious and angry accusations of the U.S. having mismanaged the world economy.

The U.S. Position of Having the Dollar as the Reserve Currency Is Threatened

Nouriel Roubini is a highly respected and prescient national economist who saw the financial collapse of 2007-2009 coming. He has laid out the arguments for why the future of the American dollar as the world's reserve currency is in jeopardy.

The crux of the argument is that spending and borrowing beyond a country's means lead it to losing its status as world's reserve currency. This is particularly true when growth is based on credit and asset bubbles.

Only countries that prove to be long term net lenders and foreign creditors are able to maintain a world reserve currency status for long periods of time. The British empire is a terrific example of what can happen. In the 1800's and first half of the 1900's, the British Pound remained the envy of the world as the reserve currency of the globe. This status only became threatened as a result of the enormous debts racked up by Great Britain from World War II. These combined to bring down the Pound as the world's reserve currency for a hundred and fifty years.

The U.S. debt levels are approaching burdensome levels that were seen in the last days of the British Empire's pound reserve currency status. Unless real growth can be restored, and spending and debts controlled, then this envied position of the dollar as reserve currency of the world will similarly slip. After all, it has only existed in such a position since the years following the Second World War.

The Privilege and Benefits of Being the World's Reserve Currency
You have experienced many benefits indirectly in your life because the U.S. Dollar has been and remains the world's only reserve currency. For one, you are able to borrow money at lower rates than are the peoples of other countries, even those living under highly developed economies seen in Germany, Britain, France, and Japan.

Besides this, the government has been allowed to finance its increasingly bigger annual deficits for greater period of time and at considerably lower rates of interest. This permits the government to pursue spending that it could not otherwise afford year in and year out. A similar benefit lies in the fact that the U.S. has been capable of floating debts in its own currency because its currency is the reserve currency.

This translates to all risks associated with exchange rates being put on those who loan the country money. Lastly, since commodities have been priced in U.S. dollars, the steady decline of the dollar has not always translated to greater costs of energy and other imports.

The Results of Losing The Dollar's Status as World's Reserve Currency

Should the Dollar finally lose its coveted status as reserve currency of the world, then there would be a number of related penalties that both you and the country would feel almost immediately. For one, higher interest rates would afflict both the government on its enormous national debt and individuals like yourself on your personal debts.

The United States would be required to spend more money on imported goods. This would translate to higher prices for you at the gas station and on numerous other items like cars, electronics, luxury goods, and even clothes and toys. Perhaps most disturbingly, a greater cost of borrowing would weigh on the economy, causing lower consumption, slower growth, and lower levels of investment. Reduced spending by the government would likely be one of the ultimate results.

Central Banks and Foreign Treasuries Hold the Majority of their Assets in U.S. Dollars

The overwhelming majority of central banks and foreign treasuries keep most of their assets in U.S. Dollars or U.S. government debt.

One thing that will herald the eventual dropping of the dollar as reserve currency to the world will be when the dollar becomes less and less of a holding by these institutions. You have already begun to see this taking place in the last several years.

More and more central banks have sold some of their dollar holdings and replaced them with either Euros or gold.

Last year, central banks' holdings of the U.S. dollar dropped to a record low of sixty three percent of foreign reserves, the lowest point that it has been at since the dollar became the world's reserve currency more than fifty year ago. In the same time, allocations of central bank holdings to Euros, British Pounds, and the Japanese Yen all outpaced the dollar by more than ten to one each.

More than ten percent of all new foreign reserve allocations went into each of these alternative currencies, while closer to one percent went into dollars. This is a disturbing long term trend for the dollar. If it continues, it will eventually lead to the dollar being dropped as the world's reserve currency.

What Has to Happen For the Dollar To be Dropped As World Reserve Currency

For the dollar to be formally and officially de-listed as the reserve currency of the world, the Bretton Woods Agreement will have to be completely abandoned. Since President Nixon abandoned the tenets linking all currencies to gold in this agreement in 1971, it has been only the U.S. dollar that was accepted as a reserve currency, as arranged in this treaty.

Informally, the dollar could be gradually replaced as a reserve currency through several activities. One of these is the ending of settlements of foreign trade in dollars. The other one is the ending of pricing world commodities markets of gold and oil in dollars. Both of these actions have been threatened in the last few years, and in some cases, have already begun to happen.

In the last few years, the Chinese have begun signing currency swap agreements to settle trade with other countries in Chinese Renminbi. They have made deals like this with countries ranging from Argentina, to Indonesia, to Belarus. While these three countries together have economies that only represent a tenth of that of the United States, it is the increasingly common trend of countries choosing to settle trade in a currency other than the dollar that is the real concern.

Oil and other important commodities are still priced in dollars, but this could change too. Iran finds an increasingly more sympathetic panel of member states in OPEC every year when it nominates pricing oil in a basket of currencies based on the IMF's special drawing rights currency.

For the moment, Saudi Arabia manages to vote down this rebellion in the ranks, but one day, the majority may go with Iran. The day when oil is no longer priced in dollars will be the one remembered as the day the dollar ceased to be treated as the reserve currency of the world.

The Shadow Market - A Network of New Economic Masters

Various conspiracy theories have been advanced over the years. You may remember the Shadow Banking System one that claimed that a small group of people controlled banking from behind the scenes. This actually turned out to be mostly the case.

Another, more present conspiracy theory is explained to you in Erick J. Weiner's book The Shadow Market: How a Group of Wealthy Nations and Powerful Investors Secretly Dominate the World. This work proves to be well researched and argued, making it an imminently plausible and scary concept.

Premise of The Shadow Market

Eric J. Weiner the author is a lauded financial journalist. In his latest work The Shadow Market, he shares with you the new reality of the global economy. The old notion of the United States having everything under its thumb is a thing of the past, he argues.

Instead, a group of foreign countries and super wealthy private investors have begun to wrest control of the world economy out of the hands of the U.S. by means that the government is not able to effectively contest. Most American citizens understand little to nothing of this plot, the author contends, and yet it will have dramatic consequences for each and every American if it goes on unchecked.

Eric Weiner pulls back the secretive curtain of the world of international economy and finance and shows you the way that they impact geopolitical projections of power here. He argues quite effectively that the biggest power brokers in the world economy nowadays are neither the leaders of the seven richest industrialized nations, nor the Federal Reserve Bank, nor even the mighty multinational banking corporations. Instead, these new economic masters are a network that counts trillions of dollars in its assets and holdings.

This network is comprised of astonishingly wealthy, mostly unregulated, and secretive investment groups, especially foreign dominated sovereign wealth funds, private equity funds, government controlled mega corporations, and hedge funds. Weiner reveals to you that these shadowy groups are steadily purchasing all of the valuable resources and assets on earth, one piece at a time.

Understanding the World of the Shadow Market

Eric Weiner's story reveals the hidden facts on this shadowy market that is beginning to pull the strings. He tells you that there is no prominent literal center of operations such as London's City or Wall Street.

Besides this, there is no committee or board of directors formally leading the group. Neither do they have a common currency or stock index that tracks their progress. Instead, they are characterized by a constantly evolving global network that sees major money move in a projection of geopolitical influence, sometimes with astonishing speed.

The group is headed by countries that are loaded with cash, and includes such heavy weights as China, The United Arab Emirates, Kuwait, Saudi Arabia, Singapore, and Norway. This shadow market group is constantly engaging the smartest and best international financial minds that they can hire. Even as you read this article, they are busy putting together the simply enormous investment holdings that will become the basis of the center of power in the economy of tomorrow.

How the Shadow Market Players Have Furthered Their Objectives While the Great Recession raged and many businesses and financial leaders in the West were either preoccupied with the problems or running for cover, the players of the Shadow Market were out shopping for assets that you saw go suddenly on sale. They used the credit crunch and other liquidity problems in the West to bring out their enormous check books and make huge investments.

They dominated the capital markets and used this power to gain significant holdings in not only multinational corporations, but also great quantities of natural resources and enormous parcels of farmland all over the planet. This is not the limit of their ambitions, as the Shadow Market players have similarly engaged in political policies. These are now possible as a result of their enormous wealth. Such policies are putting them at aggressive odds with both the U.S. and various other governments.

Weiner the author continues making the case that the enormous groups of capital that is unregulated are increasingly dominating the planet's finances to the point that the U.S. has suffered the loss of a great amount of its economic power and influence.

He reminds you that they have accomplished this generally without our obvious knowledge. His most frightening example of Shadow Market players is obviously China. From Weiner's perspective, our seemingly benign but aggressively growing trade and finance rival in Asia now has the United States secured in a choke hold.

The Shadow Market really plays up this Chinese threat. You, like most Americans, are possibly unaware of China's shocking and rapid advances in just the last several years. China has poured billions of its dollars into private equity funds, as well as hedge funds. The most notable example of this investment is the Blackstone Group.

More than this, they have spent additional billions of dollars to secure or access strategically important natural resources found in Australia, Iran, and throughout the African continent. It is no secret anymore how much money the United States owes the Chinese through their near trillion dollars of Treasury holdings.

As far as their political power gained from all of this economic clout goes, you may remember how as President Obama and his Treasury Secretary Tim Geithner went to China, both of them were reprimanded for America's mismanagement of the world economy then sent home. Our debt to the Chinese dragon is allowing the Chinese to be capable of establishing the dialogue terms as the two powers sit down to talk.

Misnomer of the Word Secretly in the Shadow Market's Subtitle
The Shadow Market book uses the word secretly in its subtitle. This is not precisely the truth. The majority of author Weiner's examples given in the book do not turn out to be a great secret.

If you watch the news, then you will know that the United State has been mortgaged to the Chinese through their impressive holdings of Treasury debt. You will similarly be aware of the fact that private equity companies and hedge funds have developed into major players on the world's economic fronts.

You probably also know that as the U.S. is struggling along with a shattered housing market and major unemployment, the oil rich Arab sultanates and Chinese have gained positions of new found power and influence, as a result of the enormous amounts of money that they bring to the table.

He does convincingly argue what you may not know so well, that these entities are deciding to spend their piles of cash more and more here at home. This is because they smell a chance to gain not simply appealing investment returns, but also greater political power as a result of these financial investments.

In the end, Eric Weinter's book is a very scholarly and imminently current account of what is really going on behind the scenes in the world. He is ahead of the daily headline events that you will hear about in the news over the coming years. The accomplishment of this book lies in its changing the topic of conversation from friendly international competition on to true global financial warfare.

It remains a serious and pressing book for any person to read who cares about the future direction of the world economy, the U.S. place in that, and where you should put your money to take advantage of it. Commodities of all kinds are where he would have you invest to benefit from the resource grab underway.

Why Does The Case Shiller Home Prices Information Matter?

When you attempt to figure out where the country is in the ongoing economic and financial crisis, one indicator that you should watch closely is the Case Shiller Home Prices Index. This is because this leading indicator of housing sales price changes tells you how the real estate market is performing every month.

Since a majority of financial experts agree that the decline in the real estate market began the economic and financial crisis, the broad consensus is that the country's economy will not truly improve until the real estate market stabilizes and then improves.

The subsequent paragraphs explore the latest grim results from the Case Shiller Home Price Index and discuss the basics of the way that it works.

What Are the Latest Case Shiller Home Prices Index Results?

The September results for the Case Shiller Home Prices Index are the most recent. The company released them on November 30. You should know that analysts who are upbeat on the so called economic recovery expected the results to be about level to slightly down. The consensus of forecasters looked for down slightly by -.4%.

The actual information came out at down two times what the average analysts hoped to see, at -.8%. Besides this, the results for the previous month August were furthermore revised down, as were the results on a year on year basis. Standard and Poor's that publishes the Case Shiller Index also said that the drop in housing prices showed signs of getting faster and worse.

To give you an idea of how severe a drop this is versus what analysts expected, consider some of their reactions. HFE said that the report proved to be significantly weaker than anticipated. They predicted that prices might continue to decline nationally in the housing market for another couple of months.

Another respected analyst, Mizuho, took a more sobering assessment of the U.S. housing market as a result of the data. They stated that the home prices have fallen for three consecutive months. They said that the declines came across the country and impacted all of the measured twenty cities except for Washington D.C. the capital. Most telling, Mizuho pointed out that they believe that you will see housing prices fall by another shocking ten percent on a national average basis.

It should not come as a surprise to you that the stock market reacted negatively. The Dow Jones Industrial Average bell weather index fell by around a hundred points shortly after the open on the discouraging and unexpected news. This Case Shiller Home Price data is significant to more than just nervous stock investors though. In a very real sense, it impacts your own home's value. Because of this, it is worth you learning something about the Case Shiller Index and what it means.

What is the Case Shiller Home Prices Index?

While you have quite likely heard analysts or news commentators mention this index measurement before, you may not understand precisely what it means and how they figure it up every month. In fact, Standard and Poor's publishes the leading measures and indicators of the United States residential housing market with these Case Shiller Home Price Indices.

Specifically, the Case Shiller Indices track real changes in residential real estate values at a couple of different levels. They measure it on a national average scale. They also figure it in the top twenty and top ten leading metropolitan parts of the country. Analysts generally latch on to the top twenty markets as the more important piece of information to show how the home prices are really doing on a broad scale.

You can imagine that such an undertaking can not be performed over night. The data that they put out is always two months behind, to allow them time to compile and compare the housing prices for all of these major markets.

Every month, Standard and Poor's releases the information on the final Tuesday of the month at nine in the morning New York time.

How is the Case Shiller Home Prices Index Determined?

The national home price values are released on a quarterly basis. The leading real estate index prides itself on covering around seventy-five percent of all United States housing stock according to value. It includes the nine U.S. census divisions of the country.

This Case Shiller Home Prices quarterly national index is determined by working with a three month moving average of prices to give it more consistency and to reduce the impacts of any month that had irregular data because of things like holidays or bad weather that might influence sales.

In contrast to this, you see that the twenty metropolitan regions and ten metropolitan regions monthly indices deal with only the home price changes of the month in question.

The indices themselves use a well respected means of figuring up and comparing price changes. This proves to be the repeat sales methodology. This method actually tracks and quantifies the changes in the prices of single family homes through gathering up data on real single family home prices in the particular regions. The twenty regions include Seattle, Portland, San Francisco, Los Angeles, San Diego, Las Vegas, Phoenix, Denver, Dallas, Minneapolis, Chicago, Detroit, Cleveland, Boston, New York, Washington D.C., Charlotte, Atlanta, Tampa, and Miami.

As people sell their homes in these varying regions, you see the new sales price reported and then matched up to the earlier sales price. Case Shiller refers to these two points of information as a sale pair. They then compile every sale pair for a given region and average the changes between each pair into the single index.

The Case Shiller Index looks through the data cautiously to sift out any information pairs that might throw off the accuracy of the index. They have done this since 1987. With a more than twenty year track record, the Case Shiller Indices prove themselves to be the reliable way of measuring home price data that you can use for either investment purposes or research about your own house or one in an area to which you might move.

Where Does the Case Shiller Home Prices Index Get This Information?

You are probably wondering at this point where the people who work at Case Shiller get all of this information on sales data to compare. They use a collection agent to gather it for them. Fiserv provides information and technology services to act as the calculating agent for the Case Shiller Indices. They get sales information on prices from a variety of sources. They then go through a cross check of all information points with a methodology that they invented. Fiserv is so precise, that they have indices that even go down to a microscopic zip code level.

Why Does The Case Shiller Home Prices Information Matter?

For you personally, you might make investments that are sensitive to housing and real estate price changes. This is especially the case if you are a buyer of real estate investment or rental properties. Besides this, if you are considering relocating to a different part of the country, you will find it useful to know how the home prices are stacking up there compared to where you live now.

POLITICS

"Banking and Government Interventions"

Will The G20 Group Soon Take Over The World Economy?

If you keep a close eye on the news or financial channels, then you will undoubtedly hear about the G20 from time to time.

The following paragraphs go through the rudiments of what the G20 organization is all about so that you will have a better understanding of one of the more important groups in the world economically.

The G20 Explained

The organization of the G20, or Group of 20 Nations, came into being in 1999. This meeting of Central Bank Governors and Finance Ministers is set up in order to get the most important industrial and developing nations of the world together to talk about the most critical issues and problems in the world economy. The founding meeting of the G20 occurred on December 15-16, 1999 in Berlin. Here both the German and Canadian finance ministers hosted the first meeting of the group.

The G20's Mandate

You may be aware of an older, smaller, more select group of the G8 (or G7 plus Russia) great industrialized nations of the world.

The G20 has not replaced this elite group, but has actually super-seded it in importance over the last ten years. This is because the G20 has gradually turned into the more effective meeting place for the development of the world economy.

Its goal is to encourage transparent talks between the key industrial nations and the developing, emerging market countries pertaining to elements of key importance for the economic stability of the world. Ultimately, the G20 assists in supporting development and economic growth around the world. It does this through creating chances for cooperation of international power brokers and finan-cial institutions.

Nations of the G20

It is useful to know the players of the G20 to better understand its relevance in the world economy. Included are the nations that you would expect from the world's richest countries, comprised of The United States, The European Union, Japan, Germany, the United Kingdom, France, Italy, Canada, and Australia.

Also, there are the up and coming world economies, including China, Brazil, India, Argentina, Mexico, Indonesia, Russia, South Africa, Saudi Arabia, South Korea, and Turkey. Besides these na-tions, the World Bank is represented by its president, and the Inter-national Monetary Fund is represented by the Managing Director.

These countries together represent the vast majority of the world's economic activity. When all the members of the European Union are counted, the participants' economies cover ninety percent of world GDP, or Gross Domestic Product that is the sum of all goods and services produced.

Fully eighty percent of the global trade is represented, along with two third of the planet's population. It is this broad economic representation and international membership that lends the G20 its influence and respect in relation to the world economy and financial system management.

The G20 Origins

Because of the financial crises at the end of the 1990's, as well as the acknowledgment that a number of developing nations were becoming more important and yet were ignored in the international discussions of economic affairs and governance, the G20 arose. In advance of the first meeting of the G20, other groups had been convened by the G7 from time to time to help with the global economic challenges.

You saw the G22 forum held in both April and October of 1998. This forum took place to have other countries than the G7 involved in resolving the global aftermath of the then financial crisis, especially as it pertained to developing economies. After this, two more meetings of 33 nations were held at a G33 forum to talk about reforming the then world financial system and structures of the global economy.

Proposals that came out of these two sets of meetings demonstrated that regular consultation of the emerging market economies offered significant advantages as a routine meeting body. The next year saw the formal creation of the consistent group of participants that are still seen in the G20 today.

G20 Meeting Frequency

The main meeting of the Central Bank governors and finance ministers of the G20 happens only one time each year. The 2009 meeting took place in St. Andrews in the United Kingdom back on November 6-7 of 2009. The most recent such meeting occurred on October 22-23, 2010 in Gyeongju, South Korea, with the Republic of Korea acting as the host for the year. Besides this principal meeting of the economic decision makers, there are two other meetings of the officials' deputies held earlier each year.

These other sub meetings are intended to research and agree on topics to be tackled by the finance ministers and central bankers towards the year's end. Besides these meetings, a great amount of advance technical work is accomplished. It happens in the form of reports, workshops, and case studies on particular subjects of interest whose goal is to provide the central bank governors and finance ministers with insights and analysis of subjects of interest and relevance to the upcoming meetings.

G20 Accomplishments

Since their establishment in 1999, the G20 has handled a wide variety of economic issues. These include reducing abuses of the global financial system, agreeing on best growth policies, fighting the funding and financing of terrorists, and handling financial crises.

Besides this, the G20 member nations have set internationally acknowledged standards of fiscal policy transparency, anti terrorism funding, and fighting money laundering.

The year 2004 saw the nations agree on greater standards of information exchange and transparency on tax matters. They did this to cut down on such international scourges as tax evasion and financial system abuses.

The worldwide financial collapse and Great Recession demonstrated the willingness and ability of the G20 to effective work together to halt the spread of the financial malaise in 2008. Much of their meetings and actions since then have been centered on assisting the world in efficiently handling the aftermath of the crisis and its financial repercussions.

As an example of these steps that the G20 has taken, they have begun implementing historically unknown coordination of macroeconomic policies, like the previously unheard of fiscal expansion totaling five trillion US dollars, working with unusual instruments of monetary policy, expansion of financial regulations, and strengthening of the world's financial regulatory regime. The Financial Stability Board has been set up as a result of these emergency measures.

Controversy Surrounding the G20 Actions

Not everyone is in favor of all of these measures that the G20 has taken in light of the financial crisis. Some nations like Germany are particularly worried about the specter of runaway inflation that will be unleashed by the unprecedented $5 trillion expansion of U.S. dollars into the world financial system.

Other countries like the United States only reluctantly agreed to the supervisory powers of the Financial Stability Board that they fear will limit growth in the world through excessive regulation in the future.

Whether you are in favor or against some of the G20's decisions and resulting actions, their influence is certain to grow over the world economy in coming years.

The G20 leaders came together and unanimously voted to designate the group as the world's premier financial meeting forum for facilitating international economic cooperation.

Are Shadow Banks Financial Weapons of Mass Destruction?

In the last few years, you may have heard the phrase shadow banks and have wondered what the financial gurus were talking about.

Shadow banks differ from the traditional banking system in several key ways. Their nefarious sounding name may be justified, since they are capable of wrecking the financial system, as you will discover in the subsequent paragraphs.

What Are Shadow Banks?

Shadow banks turn out to be financial institutions that look like and behave like regular banks in a number of different ways. They are not exactly banks though because of some key differences in their operations.

One of these main divergences lies in the fact that traditional banks such as Bank of America, JP Morgan Chase, Wells Fargo, and Citibank all accept deposits and use these to fund their loans and other investment activities, while the shadow banks do not accept deposits. Shadow banks are sometimes called investment banks too.

Shadow banks seek to run themselves like regular banks, only more aggressively. Their principal difference is that they use cheap short term loans and investor capital in order to cover their daily operating costs and investments.

This practice of avoiding deposits allows shadow banks to escape from much of the strict regulation that typical banks deal with all of the time.

The Shadow Banking Industry Begins

The shadow banks and shadow banking system actually started in the form of money market funds back in the 1970's. These money market accounts work much like deposits that are held back by banks. The key difference in them is that money market funds do not fall under the same rigorous federal regulations as do the normal banks.

From these humble beginning as money market funds, shadow banks developed into investment banks that drastically expanded in scope and size following the year 2000. Since then, these institutions have carved out a constantly more important and larger niche as operating capital lenders to businesses. In June of the year 2008, the American shadow banks had reached the equivalent size of the regular deposit banking system.

Coincidentally at this point, a similar event to a run on traditional banks befell the shadow banking system starting in 2007 and especially during the summer of 2008. At this point, you saw investors curtail their funding to numerous organizations in the shadow banking industry. The disruption of this shadow banking system proves to be a central part of the continuing sub-prime mortgage crisis, in fact.

How Does The Shadow Banking System Operate?

These shadow banks actually grew up beside the regular banking industry. They utilized many current implements of modern finance, such as credit default swaps and interest rate swaps. This gave them the ability to transfer around risk and lock in future interest rates.

The idea was simply to bring down the cost of credit and to make it more readily accessible and available for the final borrowers. Besides this, they aimed to divide up the payment and credit systems so that they became separated from one another. Much of the routine banking business' regulations are on the payment system. This is to ensure that if you write checks off of your account, then the money will really be transferred to the payee's account.

Even though these shadow banks operate in the twilight, ironically, the regulators not only permitted their existence, but they actually encouraged them. The thinking went along the lines of wishing to get some of the balance sheet risks away from the regular banking system.

They also thought that it would not be a bad idea to take away credit risk and interest rate risk from the old established banking system. The way that finance began to work was under the premise that the old banks would originate and close loans. They would then package them up, securitize them, and finally sell them on to the shadow banks.

The shadow banks would come up with funds to buy them using money market funds, mutual funds, and even asset backed commercial paper that they sold.

Like this, they side stepped the regular banking system in raising funds and in avoiding entirely the regulation that actually protected and supported the old deposit based banking system.

The Impact of the Shadow Banks on the Financial and Economic System

These shadow banks then became the providers of capital for continuously offering mortgage products to consumers and operating capital to businesses. They give the traditional banking system a constant influx of funds so that these banks can turn around and loan them out again.

The problem is that the same risks that banks had with their questionable loans did not disappear in the transfer of assets, but only moved on to other unregulated parties in the shadow banks.

The risks of solvency and liquidity problems did not go away like this, they only migrated to these shadowy institutions. The shadow banks act as investment pools, gathering the investment dollars of many different individuals and sources to invest in securities that yield higher returns over longer time frames.

These collateralized debt obligations and other investments also created market risk, liquidity risk, and credit risk for the shadow banks. In the last few years, it has become apparent that the investment activities that the shadow banks pursued were so systemically dangerous that they were actually financial weapons of mass destruction. But with no regulation from the Feds that banks labored under, there was no one to limit their activities or question the investments that they were investing in and backing heavily.

The Shadow Banks' New Struggles

It is noteworthy to look back and think that before the bubbles in the real estate and credit markets burst, these shadow banks had the reputation of being among the most financially stable and reliable financial institutions in the entire world economy. Because of this perception that the shadow banks fostered, they had the ability to short term borrow funds at unbelievably low rates of interest.

The way that the shadow banks pay back their initial investors represents a lot of the problem and danger with them. Lenders and investors are paid off with still more money that the shadow banks borrow from new lenders. In other circles, this is known as a form of Ponzi scheme.

What happens when the shadow banks are no longer able to make the incredible returns that they generated before, such as has been an increasing problem for them since the financial crisis began? The danger escalates that they will no longer be able to access such unbelievably low cost funding with which to repay their earlier creditors.

As an example, if you are able to borrow money at only one percent rates, then you might pay off your first credit card balances with money advanced from your second credit card. You might do the same thing for your second credit cards using your third credit cards. This works out fantastically well for you until you reach the point that the credit is no longer so readily available to you, or until the creditors will no longer agree to loan you more money at only one percent.

As the markets are becoming less liquid, shadow banks are running into these same kinds of problems. Their rates of interest are rising, and the "creditors" are less willing to lend to them than before.

This is making the financing of their daily operations much more difficult.

It remains to be seen if and when this ticking time bomb of the shadow banks will go off, once again plunging the American banking system into serious and real crisis.

Why Government Stimulus Money Does Not Create New Jobs

There has been much debate in the last several years about how many new jobs can be created through government stimulus programs. Since the new administration took over, they have had several opportunities to pass spending bills that were supposed to create more jobs and bring the unemployment rate back down to a reasonable level.

The end result has been that the unemployment rate has barely budged, despite all of the hundreds of billions of dollars and even trillions of dollars that have been spent trying to create jobs. For a variety of reasons explained in the subsequent paragraphs, government stimulus money does not create jobs or wealth.

Government Stimulus Redistributes Money and Does Not Create Anything

The government has been attempting to create economic growth and jobs a number of times in the last century. In both the 1930's, 1960's, and 1970's, enormous increases in spending were tried to boost growth and job creation. All three of these attempts failed dismally. So far in the last few years, this has again proven to be the case. Why is this consistently so?

The reason that government spending does not actually increase economic growth lies in a simple truth. This is that every dollar that your Congress injects directly into the economy has to come out of the economy first. It is either first borrowed or taxed out. This means that government spending is really only redistributing income that already exists. It does not actually expand employment or productivity.

As a result, it is not creating other jobs or income. Some economic experts point out that it may even weaken the condition of the private sector, since it takes such resources away and steers them to uses and areas that are less productive. When this is the case, it is interfering with economic and job growth.

Taking Money from Savers and Giving it To Spenders Does Not Create Jobs

The reality is that Congress does not possess a vast bank vault of money that it can simply draw from and hand out. The money has to come from somewhere else. Congress obtains this money by taxing it or borrowing it from savers to give out to spenders. Additional spending power has not been created in this action. Instead, the money has only been redistributed from a certain group of investors and savers to other people.

The idea of taking money from savers and giving it to spenders does not create additional spending either. This is because savers' money is kept in the economy and used there. Most Americans who are saving are investing by buying financial instruments like bonds and stocks, or by entrusting it to banks who lend it out to spenders.

This finances business investments and spending and can lead to economic growth and job creation. Savers' money already impacts the economy, and usually in meaningful ways that contribute to growth and jobs. By taking this money away from the savers, you are removing it and all of its benefits from the economy. Giving it back to the spenders in some form or another is merely distributing it again, but to a less productive group of people.

Government can get this money by taxing the money away or borrowing it away from savers. When they take the money for stimulus through taxing it, they are only redistributing that money, not creating anything new. Were Congress to instead decide to borrow this money off of the domestic investors, they would be reducing the amount of money that the investors have to help the private economy to expand.

If instead Congress decides to borrow the stimulus money from foreign investors, they still have to repay it, and with interest on top of that. Plus, the money that the foreign investors would have probably put into the private domestic economy anyway has simply been transferred to the government instead.

You must remember that all stimulus money spent has to come from some place. Usually you see it taken from the more productive sectors and spent in the less productive ones instead. The sad truth is that when government spends these borrowed debt funds to attempt to create economic growth, it does not cause the true net creation of any jobs as a result.

What it does instead is to simply take away wealth from private or foreign citizens who would have invested it here anyway. This money is then utilized to provide for government planned jobs that the economy does not typically benefit from or really need in the first place.

In the end, since these jobs are not efficient and useful, when the government stimulus money has been spent, then such jobs will probably go away. No net positive increase in long term jobs will result, and yet the money will have been redistributed and spent anyway.

Stimulus Money Often Goes to Large Corporations to Buy Smaller Ones

Another problem with the idea that government stimulus money creates jobs is that much of the stimulus money ends up with larger corporations who do not really use it to hire people. Instead, they take this grant money or subsidy money and use it to acquire smaller companies.

The problem with this lies in the fact that as soon as a larger company announces that it has bought another company, you hear them similarly announce the accompanying thousands or even tens of thousands of layoffs that will be used to increase efficiency. The net effect is that more jobs are lost as a result, and this is actually happening all of the time with money that the government had earmarked to be used to create more jobs.

Instead of economic growth and jobs being created, companies tout their productivity gains and returns on investment that they realize with these acquisitions.

Stimulus money going to larger corporations is actually not helping to create more jobs, but is instead working counter produc-
tively and often times reducing jobs instead.

Ways that Economic Growth and Jobs Can Be Created in America
There are effective ways that the government can encourage economic growth and job creation in the United States. These do not
revolve around stimulus money spending, as you have already
seen. Quite the contrary, the government is most effective in expanding the economy when they do just the opposite of spending
extra money.

It is not coincidence that as the size of the U.S. Federal government was being reduced by twenty percent in the decades of the
1980's and 1990's, that the national economy experienced its largest rate of expansion in history. Job growth and wealth creation
were unparalleled. You saw this as a result of less government
spending, and not more.

Another supporting piece of evidence for this lies in the fact that
your government actually spends considerably less money than do
all fifteen of the European Union countries that were members before 2004. Despite this, the U.S. benefits from a fifty percent more
rapid pace of economic growth, a GDP that is forty percent larger,
and unemployment rates that prove to be significantly lower.

As governments shrink down, take less money from you, and allow
you to invest it in productive growth of the economy, the overall
economy grows and more jobs are created along the way.

How Wall Street Is Running the U.S. And Global Economy

As the national economy and financial system stood on the brink of collapse, the elites in Washington spent a huge amount of time and resources saving Wall Street and the bankers rather than throwing a life line to the common working American.

A new book is out suggesting that all of the Presidents since Ronald Reagan have put Wall Street ahead of Main Street.

This interesting and increasingly held view is covered in the book Capital Offense, How Washington's Wise Men Turned America's Future Over to Wall Street.

The Premise of Capital Offense

Michael Hirsh engages in a full blown, interesting account of the time period that he refers to as the Age of Capital in his new book Capital Offense. He makes the work more attention grabbing by relating the story from the point of view of its major players, including President Ronald Reagan, Milton Friedman, Timothy Geithner and Larry Summers.

He begins by going through the history of the last several decades. Michael Hirsh tells you that Washington came to the position of believing that by keeping the investors happy, you could manage to have an economy that was not simply growing, but continuously booming.

In the course of the work, he relates how these policies led to a full blown economic crisis centered in Asia, suffering and struggling in South and Central America, and finally a traumatic Great Recession in both Europe and the United States.

The author asks a series of interesting and pertinent questions that the book sets out to answer. How did the smartest decision makers of or day and age permit this to occur? Is is possible that these terrible setbacks did absolutely nothing to shift the free market ideology of the Washington elites? Michael Hirsh sets out to prove that ideology proved to be responsible for this, and not lobbyists.

Key Elements of Capital Offense

Michael Hirsh brings up a number of important elements in his Capital Offense. His research and reporting are both first class, as he is the Senior editor for Newsweek Magazine. He leads you to listen in on important and previously closed door conversations held between administration officials and high level advisers to the White House, like Alan Greenspan, Paul O'Neill, and Robert Rubin.

In the work, Hirsh brings to life the important characters and their sometimes exciting clashes of personality, such as the ones that occurred between Joe Stiglitz, the economist who won the Nobel Prize, and Larry Summers.

Besides this, the author provides important insights for the reasons that President Obama waited such a long amount of time to address the economy and the reasons that he is not doing enough.

By doing a review of the mistakes made in fully three decades of reckless regulatory, fiscal, and financial policies, the author recounts tragedies like the Savings and Loan disaster, the undoing of the Glass-Steagall Act, the handling of Enron, and the entire subprime mortgage collapse. Capital Offense draws an interesting conclusion from the aftermath of the financial crisis. This is that Wall Street will keep dominating the world's economy.

Capital Offense's Three Decades of Washington History

Capital offense and its author believe that the last three decades of history in Washington are critically important to how we got to the Wall Street elites running the U.S. and global economy. Hirsh tells you that it all started with the Reagan Revolution that began in 1981. This movement created a deregulation process that detached a great deal of the economy from the historical antitrust rules and regulatory oversight. This gave birth to the rollicking financial age that you have lived through since then.

This enormous failure of the system that resulted proved to be a product of both major parties. Hirsch passes the blame around. He claims that President Clinton and his people share as much responsibility for the problems that resulted as does President George W. Bush's administration. Over a twenty five year period in American history, the conventional wisdom remained that markets may go up and come back down, but whatever they do, they act more intelligently than governments.

In the 1980's, deregulation created a booming era. The 1990's fed on this, along with the Cold War's end, to make the entire euphoria that much greater. The absolutism of the free markets evolved from being a concept that had been dismissed as idealistic into a secular religion of the country. It gained hold of the collective national imagination and policy making to turn the economic debate massively toward the right of the ideological spectrum.

As a result, once liberal democrats became known as Eisenhower Republicans, while Republicans latched on to the idea of small government fanatically. In the light of this unstoppable ideology, Wall Street proved to be capable of doing almost anything with no one to stop it.

It is a good point the author makes for you in saying that the financial weapons of mass destruction, which became household names following the subprime mortgage meltdown, did not magically appear from thin air. These collateralized debt obligations first had to be created, nurtured, and expanded to levels of complexity.

This took place for two entire decades. Even though the market would suffer from catastrophes on an fairly routine basis, no changes to address the situation were enacted besides still more deregulation of the markets. The collateralized debt obligations represented a long standing idea, that of taking questionable assets and turning them into attractive packaged securities as the central bankers and regulators ignored the entire dangerous process.

Capital Offense's Take on Where Obama Failed

Michael Hirsh does more than simply point out how the system failed you and all Americans. The author states that much more needs to be done than President Obama has enacted so far.

Capital Offense claims that President Obama let slip a once in a lifetime opportunity to reshape the entire American economy, Wall Street, and the world economy in the mix.

Though many saw him as a reincarnation of President Franklin Roosevelt, he chose to delegate the economic agenda to Timothy Geithner and Larry Summers, who instead took a conservative type of approach to reform and economic stimulus. Meanwhile, the President allowed himself to be occupied with issues that were not so urgent, such as nuclear disarmament and health care.

Rather than take on Wall Street, Obama's point men on the economy chose to leave the engine room of the entire economy unmolested. They counseled Obama not to break up the large financial institutions, and he made the critical decision not to engage in such radical reform of the system. In the end, Obama agreed with Geithner and Summers that the crisis had not been caused by the size of organizations that were too big too fail.

Because of this lack of change, too little confidence was given back to the financial system, which was truly necessary to witness a complete recovery. An insufficient number of jobs have thus been created. Hirsch says it looks increasingly likely that you will see high unemployment numbers and poor growth dogging the President as the time for reelection approach in 2012.

He claims that only with a second enormous fiscal stimulus could the President hope to jump start the economy and get people back to work, and this looks less likely everyday.

Social Security - A Problem That Still Needs To Be Solved

You may not know that Social Security is the largest single expenditure of the national budget.

Consuming 20.8%, it proves to be even slightly larger than defense and Medicare with Medicaid. As such, it is the biggest social retirement program in the whole world, measured by dollars spent.

Today, Social Security is believed to prevent fully forty percent of every retirement aged American over sixty four years old from being in poverty. The program has become so vital for retirees that it is hard to imagine an America without it, yet Social Security only dates back to the 1930's.

The financial problems surrounding Social Security are a result of the program not really addressing the root of the issue of from where money for retirement should come.

The Founding of Social Security

President Franklin Roosevelt enacted a great deal of legislation during the dark years of the Great Depression, as part of his New Deal Social welfare. In 1935, Social Security became a cornerstone of the programs.

When it was first established, Social Security proved to be quite different from the version that exists today. For one thing, it included unemployment insurance then, and not only today's four categories of retirement, survivorship, disability, and death.

Besides this, the majority of minorities and women were intentionally left out of the programs of both pensions for old age and unemployment insurance in the original version. You saw this accomplished by the exclusion of labor in such fields as agriculture and domestic service, as well as intermittent workers.

The original program also left out government employees and most nurses, teachers, librarians, hospital workers, and even social workers. Minorities and women held the vast majority of such positions, with women comprising fully ninety percent of all domestic labor in 1940 and two thirds of black women also working in this field.

Agriculture proved to be dominated by black men at the time. As a result of such discrimination, two thirds of all African Americans and more than fifty percent of all women employed in the work force did not qualify for Social Security.

President Franklin Roosevelt turned out to be the first American President concerned with protecting the elderly.

The Social Security program actually came into being as a means of helping out senior citizens. Their poverty rates proved to be higher than fifty percent during the 1930's and the Great Depression. Besides addressing the problems of old age, social security targeted unemployment, general poverty, and the struggles of widows and orphans.

Social Security Today

Over time, the program has grown, expanded, and improved to include all members of society. Three years ago in 2008, Social Security paid out over $615 billion in benefits for the single year. As it has grown to cover all people entering retirement age and Americans have begun living longer than when the program was fashioned, the ability of present workers to support present retirees has become increasingly strained.

Because of this, the government is periodically forced to raise the age at which full retirement benefits will be paid out. This is now up to sixty-seven years of age. This still has not addressed the revenue shortfall, which will cause Social Security to be incapable of supporting all estimated retirement benefits in the coming twenty to thirty years time.

The Social Security Administration claims that by 2041 this will be a major problem. The Congressional Budget Office says that by 2052, the Social Security Trust Fund will exhaust its final loans to the general budget that were built up in the many years of surplus revenues taken in over benefits paid out. At this point, only seventy-four to seventy-eight percent of the promised benefits will be available, unless payroll taxes are significantly raised.

Attempts to Reform Social Security Through Privatization
You are probably wondering why no one has done anything to try to fix the Social Security problems that have become increasingly evident in the past. In the last thirty five years, various efforts to address Social Security's growing funding problems have been attempted.

Presidents Ford, Carter, Reagan, George H. W. Bush, Clinton, and George W. Bush have all tried to privatize social security. In one form or another, they have wanted in vain to put the burdens of retirement provision back in the hands of the private sector, where our capitalist system believes that it belongs.

You have seen these efforts at reform continuously opposed and stymied each time, as the retirees have a powerful lobby and feel that they stand to lose the most by the substantial altering of the Social Security retirement program.

Former President George W. Bush went so far as to outline a way whereby you would have control over your own Social Security Retirement account, much as you do with your IRA or 401K retirement accounts. He believed that greater amounts of retirement money could be generated by you managing your own retirement monies, as has mostly proven to be the case with the other forms of retirement accounts.

These valiant attempts to place retirement planning back in the hands of private individuals, where it ultimately belongs, were torn to shreds by critics and opponents.

The Real Problem with Social Security

The truth is that the country simply can not support the major portion of retirement for such a long living and large segment of the population indefinitely. To do so, Social Security taxes would have to rise to more than thirty percent of all payrolls in coming years.

Solving the problem with government money has been tried and simply does not work. What needs to happen is to address the real problem, like President George W. Bush started to do with his major reform proposals.

This real problem is the fact that people have come to believe that their government should provide for their retirement.

Although this has become a true mentality of practically the entire nation, it is not a facet of capitalism that the country so cherishes. Nor is it anything that the founding fathers ever intended for the country. Instead, you should be made to take charge of your own financial future in retirement.

The idea of letting you manage your own retirement dollars that you personally contributed in your payroll taxes is a good start. It has been proven time and again that you are capable of managing your own money far better than the government is.

Solution to the Problem with Social Security

A transition has to be made off of government retirement reliance and on to personal preparation for retirement. Obviously, the retirees currently on the program can not simply be dumped in the midst of such retirement. Nor maybe can workers about to retire be expected to suddenly be deprived of their retirement plan. But gradually, Americans have to be given much greater incentives to take their own retirement planning in their own hands.

If there is going to be a social security tax levied on payrolls, then it should increasingly go into individually owned and controlled retirement accounts that operate like IRA's and 401K's.

You and all Americans need a great deal more financial education to be capable of understanding both the need and means of effectively managing retirement dollars.

Only when you, and all Americans, are empowered and enabled to save for your own retirement will the problem of relying on a gradually failing Social Security program be solved.

The Potential Fallout of the Next Quantitative Easing Round

Everywhere that you look, you hear the financial talking heads and news reporters discussing the imminent to start Quantitative Easing II program, somewhat affectionately referred to as QE2.

The latest $600 billion that the Fed is about to start printing and flushing into the economy is creating an even bigger stir among investors and financial experts than the last and bigger round of quantitative easing did.

In the subsequent paragraphs, you will see the shocking fallout for the U.S. dollar, American economy, and prices of gold that well respected, mainstream, nationally known figures are predicting.

Background on the Newest Quantitative Easing

In case you are unfamiliar with this latest economic salvo from the Federal Reserve, they announced in October that they would soon start printing another massive quantity of cash, this time to the amount of $600 billion.

They plan to use this money for a seemingly innocent purpose of buying government bonds. This is Fed speak for transferring the created money electronically into banks' accounts in exchange for paper government investments.

This way, they inject more money into the banks and overall economy in an attempt to lower interest rates further, since bond interest rates fall as their prices rise from the additional buying.

They hope yet again that this will encourage people to borrow more money from banks and spend it on propping up the economy and housing. Their dream is to lower unemployment as an end result of these efforts.

Unfortunately, all of this money printing that the Federal Reserve and Treasury have been engaging in since 2007 are not without consequences. The latest $600 billion ensures that between them they have more than tripled the worldwide supply of U.S. dollars in existence. You are soon to see the terrible repercussions of all of this irresponsible expansion of the United States' money supply.

How Will This Effect The Dollar?

A number of financial and investing experts have now lined up on the side of a steeply falling dollar as the first of the consequences for runaway money printing. Confidence in the dollar is already shaky. This quantitative easing is likely to prove to be the proverbial straw that broke the camel's back.

Bill Gross is the founder and managing partner of PIMCO, the world's largest bond fund. As such, financial insiders consider him to be among the greatest and foremost experts on bonds in the entire world. His response to the quantitative easing two announcement lay in a single comment. He claimed that this new Federal Reserve policy will cause a twenty percent devaluation of the U.S. dollar. For those of you who do not trade or closely follow currencies, a twenty percent drop in a currency is shocking and even catastrophic.

Bill Gross is not alone is his sentiments regarding an imminent severe decline in the dollar. Economist and best selling book "Aftershock" author Robert Wiedemer has declared similar warnings. He says that if Ben Bernake, the Chairman of the Federal Reserve, actually carries out this latest round of quantitative easing, and President Obama's misguided economic policies do not soon become reversed, then we could soon see the dollar completely collapse.

Best selling book "The Great Super Cycle" author and investor David Skarica sees the same future in store for the dollar as a result of QE2. He was recently queried about what lies in the dollar's future at a crisis investing summit. Skarica's prediction is for an incredible fifty percent decline in the dollar's value over the next several years.

In light of all of these informed and professional opinions on the dollar's fate in the wake of the presently ongoing money printing spree, it is no great stretch to suggest that not only your dollar denominated investments like stocks, bonds, and mutual funds, but also your currency's cherished purchasing power, are all in great and perhaps imminent danger.

How Will This Effect Inflation?

The dollar value is not the only major economic casualty that financial experts and investors are predicting. Inflation is another specter that is increasingly forecast by credible national economic figures.

Warren Buffet is widely hailed as the greatest living investor, and as a candidate for the greatest investor in the modern age. He said last year, before the second round of quantitative easing even began, that the government politicians would take the easy solution to the many problems facing the country's economy and future now.

He claimed that they will simply inflate away the currency in order to be able to meet the unfunded obligations like social security and medicare, as well as to pay down the enormous debts and deficits.

The reason that they would choose to pursue this inflationary policy, ruining many fixed income people and investors in the process, is that they just do not have the revenues to cover their obligations while servicing the unsustainable debt. With a lower valued dollar, debt is simpler to pay down.

Billionaire investor John Paulson is the founder and manager of one of the largest hedge funds on earth. When he talks about investments and the economy, people listen carefully. He has said in September and October that inflation will soon skyrocket from all of the money printing that the Fed is practicing. He expects to see low double digit inflation per year no later than 2012. He predicts that this will destroy the bond market and strengthen stocks and equities in the process.

Resulting Predictions for Gold and Silver

John Paulson has some incredible predictions for gold along with his inflation forecasts. He looks back to the way that gold rose in 1980 at greater than one hundred percent more than the money printing that the Fed pursued.

Based on the monetary expansion that is going on, he sees gold rising to minimally $2,400 per ounce between now and 2013, and more likely to as high a level as $4,000 for every ounce, if gold overshoots targets like it did back in 1980. Paulson is not simply talking about gold; he has put his money up on the yellow metal as well. He freely admits that eighty percent of his assets are now in gold.

Paulson almost never shares his opinions on gold prices and inflation except through his research reports, so this speech that he gave is telling of his strong opinions on the near to medium term future of gold.

If you have a hard time believing that gold can rise to the $2,400 to $4,00 range in such a short amount of time, then consider this. The $850 per ounce former high of gold reached in 1980 represented an inflation adjusted high of more than $2,500 per ounce in today's dollars. Gold is scarce, and there simply is not enough of it to go around when more and more investors see it as the only safe place of putting their money. Silver has even more leverage and will over time outperform gold.

Something to think about is that Paulson is not on the high end of the predictions for gold prices in the coming years. There are experts who believe that it will reach even $8,000 per ounce. Before you shake your head at this dizzying price prediction of gold, remember that the total value of all gold Exchange Traded Funds in the U.S. today is about $80 billion, lower than the market capitalization for only McDonald's.

What Extending the Bush Tax Cuts Mean For Your Finances

For a number of months now, you have heard debate and speculation as to whether or not President Obama would push for extending the Bush tax cuts that President Bush passed early in his first term.

Economists have been greatly concerned that if President Obama did not manage to prolong them, then it would hit the economy with a de facto tax increase at a time when the economy proves to be particularly weak.

In a press conference that the President gave the second week of December, he announced that he will work in a major compromise with the Republicans in Congress to pass a bill that both keeps the tax cuts in place and offers other help for all Americans who are still struggling with the economic fallout created by the Financial Crisis and Great Recession.

What Is The Opposition to the Tax Cuts About?

Not everyone is happy about the announcement that the President will compromise to extend the tax cuts for another two years. In the past, President Obama himself argued vehemently against these tax cuts, especially during the election campaign against Senator John McCain.

Many democrats are angry that he has stated his decision to work to get the tax cuts passed. The liberals especially feel betrayed by this.

The reason for this sentiment is that democrats believe that the tax cuts favor the wealthy more than they do the working poor. There have been mixed arguments on this issue for years. Republicans maintain that only with tax cuts will the rich feel comfortable in hiring more workers and expanding their businesses to grow the economy.

They also insist that since the rich already pay the majority of the taxes, they should get a larger tax break. The democrats do not want to hear any of this. They feel that the poor need more tax breaks exactly because they are poor. To them, it does not matter who pays the majority of the taxes, so long as the working class and the poor are helped to survive.

What Are the Particulars of the Agreement on Extending the Tax Cuts?

The President has agreed on a number of important points besides the tax cuts. The center piece of the deal is that the Bush era tax cuts will be extended across all income levels and tax brackets. This means that the wealthy will continue to enjoy their tax breaks at the same time as the middle class keep their tax cuts.

The President admits that he does not agree with many of the points in the deal. He claims that it is necessary to compromise with the Republicans in order to secure the tax extension for all Americans who are middle class.

In exchange for the President consenting to keep the middle class tax breaks, the Republicans agreed to provide significant help to middle income and lower income workers, along with the unemployed.

In this agreement, besides them extending the Bush tax cuts, you will see another tax reduction with this package. The payroll tax on social security presently levied at 6.2 percent for every working person will go down. They will reduce it for one year by the amount of two percentage points. This will be effective with every pay check, so that workers do not have to wait until the following year to realize a tax refund.

If you are a worker who makes fifty thousand dollars annually, then this will give you a tax savings of a thousand dollars over the year. If instead you are a worker that has to pay the larger maximum social security tax of $6,621.60 on an annual salary of $106,800 or higher, then your tax break will give you a $2,136 savings. This tax break would take the place of the low income and middle income tax cut that existed in the economic stimulus package last year.

How Much Will the Tax Cuts Cost?

There is always a cost to cutting down your taxes. This is especially the case when it is applied to all income levels of American workers. This new tax extension will cost the country around nine hundred billion dollars during the next two years. You are probably wondering how the country will pay for it. The answer is exactly as you may have guessed.

The government will completely finance the tax breaks by increasing the already massive fourteen trillion dollar national debt by another nearly trillion dollars. This is an interesting way for them to pay for it, as both Republicans and Democrats claim to be interested in dealing with the country's long term problems with imbalances in the budget.

Other Aid That The Government Will Offer in the Agreement

The President's deal that he reached with Republicans will include more benefits than simply tax cuts. Besides the government prolonging the Bush tax cuts by another two years and increasing the one year social security tax break, they will also offer more assistance for unemployed people and give out incentives to help out all businesses and many families. They hope that this will enable Americans that are struggling with unemployment and underemployment to get back on their feet.

Anyone who you know who is still unemployed will benefit from the government extending the jobless aid by another thirteen months. This will be affected to help out those people who have become the long term unemployed. The government knows that unemployment benefits are already running out for some individuals. If this extension on unemployment benefits is not passed, then up to seven million people would lose the assistance that they so desperately need.

Besides this, there will be other tax credits that aid working class families. The earned income tax credit that actually gives tax money to families whose incomes are below a certain level will be broadened to include more families. Some families will see their special tax credits for college tuition continue.

Businesses and investors will receive benefits from the tax compromise also. Companies will be allowed to buy particular pieces of equipment and then to write off these costs of them. Investors who have enjoyed the maximum tax on dividends and capital gains at only fifteen percent will continue to receive this rate for the next two years.

A last area where you might benefit from the compromise that will extend the tax cuts from the days of President Bush involves the alternative minimum tax. This alternative minimum tax is a tax that focuses on people who own homes in high income states. The original intention of the tax lay in making sure that wealthy people who avoided taxes altogether because of their deductions would still have to pay a certain minimum amount.

The problem with this alternative minimum tax is that because of changes made to the tax code in the days of President Reagan, even twenty-five percent of the country's tax payers are now required to pay it when they file. Even if you only earn thirty thousand dollars to fifty thousand dollars per year, you can be forced to pay it.

Thanks to the deal that has been reached as a part of this Presidential and Republican law maker brokered compromise, the alternative minimum tax will be changed to exclude up to twenty-one million families who would be impacted by it.

Monetizing the Debt Could Push the Gold Price Over $53,000

Monetization is a word that you do not hear so often, but it is very important in any case. The government uses it in the creation of money and to pay for the national debt.

It is also a process that could one day take gold to astronomical levels that you can hardly imagine from $1,400 to over $53,000 per ounce one day.

The subsequent paragraphs go through all that you need to know about debt monetization with gold so that you can understand how it is possible for gold to vault to such extreme levels as nationally known and respected economist Martin Armstrong predicts.

What Actually Is Monetization?

Monetization first refers to the procedure involved in creating a currency. It works by a government central bank establishing an item that will be used as the nation's legal tender. These days, you almost exclusively see bills and bank notes that central banks print used in the monetization process. Things that have no intrinsic value themselves, like these paper bills, are able to be monetized.

The only requirement for it to work is that these bills or other items that function as money must be hard to create or obtain. Governments can also monetize valuable objects like gold, silver, and diamonds. Throughout most of history, monetizing actually involved using precious metals instead of bills. Part of the problem with today's government debt crisis has resulted from paper bills replacing items of actual value like gold and silver.

Modern governments have given their central banks the power to monetize currency exclusively. In the United States, the Federal Reserve does this. They claim that they do not print new money to pay their bills. They are supposed to only pay debts using money that they have monetized and placed into circulation. Otherwise, they can choose to sell bonds to the public to raise more money.

What Means Monetizing the Debt?

Today's governments have a bad habit of not living within their means. This is why they are required to create and issue bonds that they exchange with investors for more money. By making these bonds and offering them for cash, governments are creating money too. They finance the government spending that is beyond their tax revenues by monetizing the debt. Such monetizing of the debt works through a two part procedure.

First the government will issue this debt that they create so that they can finance their spending. They will next sell it to investors and the public. This way, they have extra money to spend. The downside is that governments have been able to create incredibly large and scary debts through this process of monetizing the debt.

How High Are the Government's Debts Now?

Through the process of monetizing the debt, the U.S. government has been able to amass an amazing fourteen trillion dollars of money that it owes to both foreign investors and its own citizens. Foreign countries such as China, Japan, Great Britain, and the oil rich Arab Gulf States mostly hold this debt. They do this through sovereign wealth funds that invest their country's money in such government debt. Banks and investors in these other countries also participate in purchasing American and other countries debts.

Can The Government Ever Repay Its Debt?

The speculation is growing that the United States will never be able to repay its debts that have grown to be an incredible amount greater than anyone has ever seen before in history. This means that investors would not ever be able to get their money back all at once.

If even just the Chinese wanted to cash out their American debt as it came due and not reinvest in it, the United States would not be able to give them paper bills back unless they printed more of them en masse. This leaves the country with three choices, all of which would increase the prices of gold.

The government might choose to default on the debt or to restructure it. This would crush the economy and destroy the value of bonds and related investments all over the world. For a major Western country to default on its debt is considered a terrible tragedy and risk to the entire world economy.

Just take a look at Greece and Ireland in their situations. They are not even considered major economies and yet the International Monetary Fund and European Monetary Union decided that it is better to make enormous loans to them than to see them default on their debt.

How the Government Could Inflate Away the Debt

Another way that the nation could choose to pay off its debt that would be less painful is in inflating the debt away. They would do this by simply printing extra bills to cash out investors in the Treasuries as their due dates arrived.

Creating trillions of dollars in new bills all at one time would cause massive inflation that you would quickly see turn into hyperinflation. This means that prices would rise incredibly fast on everything from food to energy to consumer goods. People living on fixed incomes, such as retirees, would be wiped out. Inflating away the debt is less serious than defaulting on it, but it still comes with very painful and negative consequences that would wreak havoc on the economy to a greater or lesser extent.

Monetizing the Debt Using Gold and the Gold Standard

Martin Armstrong is a well respected American economist who has been given awards as the national economist of the year in the past. He argues that the United States has another way that it might both pay off its debt and back its currency up with tangible value. This is in using its considerable gold reserves to restore it to fiscal responsibility.

Until 1971, the U.S. actually operated on a gold standard where money could only be created as they mined or obtained more gold through trade. Now the U.S. gold reserves prove to be the largest in the world at two hundred and fifty-two million ounces.

Martin Armstrong says that if the U.S. were to announce that it is backing all dollars in existence, including the debt, by gold once again, then this would create a gold price of over $53,000 per ounce.

More than fourteen trillion dollars divided by the U.S. gold reserves gives you this number. Even the amount of all the gold in the official world reserves would still require a price tag of over fifteen thousand dollars per ounce to cover the U.S. debt that exists presently.

This sounds like an incredibly drastic step for the government to take. Turning gold into an astronomical store of value to instantly cover the debt and restore value to the paper dollar currency would be less severe than defaulting on the debt or choosing to allow sky high inflation to reduce it over time.

Whether or not you will see the government choose to resort to such a measure, these theoretical gold prices demonstrate the reason why gold that costs $1,400 per ounce is actually not such a high price after all.

H I S T O R Y

"Events That Shaped Our Present"

The History and Consequences of The Dutch Tulip Bubble

Numerous bubbles have risen and burst in just the last ten to twenty years. You may think that bubbles are a product of the recent post World War economy, but in fact they actually go back at least more than four hundred years to early modern Europe.

The Dutch Tulip Bubble is an interesting case study of how bubbles can start from seemingly ridiculous things and go on to cause major economic catastrophes.

Origins of the Dutch Tulip Bubble

It is ironic to think that the tulip that has become a national symbol of the Netherlands is not even a native species to the country. It only came to the low country as a botanist named Carolus Clusius brought it with him from Constantinople in 1593. This botanist planted a little garden for the purposes of using the tulip in research for its possible medical uses.

The whole Dutch Tulip Bubble developed as a result of Clusius' neighbors, who entered his garden by night and took a few of his tulip bulbs, thinking to sell them for some quick florins, the country's currency of the day. Their action led to the Dutch bulb trade.

The Dutch Tulip Bubble Takes Off

In just a few decades, owning tulips in the Netherlands developed into a wealthy person's fashionable trend. As more of the rich demanded tulips, the prices for tulip bulbs started to rise. Before long, regular bulbs began selling at irregular prices. Bulbs that proved to be truly rare sold for inordinate sums of money.

As an example, one Viceroy tulip bulb had a sales price of the equivalent of today's $1,250. Rarer bulbs like the Semper Augustus tulip bulb sold for even twice as high a premium. You can still read the records of the many goods exchanged for a single bulb. The exchange bills cover a number of items, including a suit of clothes, a bed, and fully a thousand pounds of cheese, all for one tulip.

At the peak of the crazy bubble, these tulip bulbs had become so valuable that no one wanted to take the chance of planting them after buying them. Showing off bulbs that were not even grown became the commonplace trend. There is a story of how such a plan went horribly wrong as a sailor in port thought that a displayed bulb was actually an onion and simply ate it as his breakfast.

Peak of the Dutch Tulip Bubble

This Dutch Tulip bubble went on and on for some time. The peak of the bubble itself did not actually occur until the winter of 1636-1637. At this point, you could accurately say that tulip traders were earning, and sometimes losing, whole fortunes all the time.

A skillful tulip trader might hope to earn as much as 60,000 florins in only a month, representing a whopping $61,710 when converted into present day U.S. dollars.

As you can imagine, with so much money being made, there was literally nothing that local governments might try to do in order to call off the rabid pace of trading.

The Collapse of the Dutch Tulip Bubble

It will surprise you to learn what brought down the Dutch Tulip Bubble. A day came in Haarlem, the Netherlands, where a tulip buyer did not appear in order to hand over the money for the bulb that he had purchased.

A panic started and ran like wildfire all over the entire country. The panic led to a complete rout in the tulip bulb market. In what surely ranks as one of the most spectacular bubble collapses in all of history, it only needed a few days for tulip bulbs to be back to trading at a shocking one hundredth of their prices only days before. The tulip bubble had burst massively, and no doubt a good many tulip traders had to run for their lives in order to avoid debtor's prison.

The Dutch Tulip Bubble In Retrospect

It is all too easy for you to hear this story and laugh. Pointing fingers at the Dutch and calling them simpletons for being willing to pay astronomical prices for mere tulip bulbs misses the point. Economic bubbles are not new now, and they did not prove to be new even back in those days. And before you judge the Dutch too harshly, consider your own behavior.

We continue to do the same silly things today. If you doubt this, think back to the dot com bubble at the turn of the century. How many of you paid an obscene amount of money for a single share of tech company stock in which the company had no more chance of ever turning a profit than it did of going to the moon?

These bubbles all begin the same way. They start with an irrational inflating of an asset price. In time, the price gets so high that any objective third party who is outside of the system would be able to point to it and laugh. One day, somebody blinks and the whole thing comes crashing down on you. People engage in this behavior time and time again as they want to have something that is rare and wonderful and difficult to obtain. The trend behavior of everyone is doing it also influences them.

Recent Bubbles in the U.S. Economy

There have been many recent major bubbles in the U.S. economy that you have seen collapse in just the last few years. The housing market and real estate bubble was one. You probably remember just a few years ago how it seemed like housing prices had only one way to go forever and that was up. We are still living with the effects of that collapse.

The stock market proved to be another overinflated bubble. With the Dow at fourteen thousand, pundits started asking how much longer it would be until the revered index reached twenty thousand points. A year later it stood at just over six thousand points.

Consumer credit turned out to be another such bubble. You likely recall the days of cheap and easy money from credit cards and banks.

It seemed like there would never come a day and time where the credit card limits and low interest rates came to a screeching halt. Those days are but a distant memory now for most Americans and even many sound businesses.

Current Bubbles in the U.S. Economy

The runaway level of U.S. government debt has been called an ultimate bubble by some watching economists. It has not been so long since one congressman famously remarked that with a billion here and a billion there, soon you are talking about real money.

Now the government debt ceiling is over fourteen trillion with a "t." Most people can not even fathom how large a number a trillion really is. Telling them that it is a thousand billions is also meaningless. And yet, despite this incredible level of national government debt, the interest rates on it are the lowest in American history. Surely this is a bubble whose time of expanding is coming to an end soon.

Another bubble that is often pointed to is the U.S. dollar. Despite the United States running the most enormous such literal deficits and debts in history, the dollar continues to hold a significant value that is greater than most currencies in the world. As it is the reserve currency of the world still, you had better watch out when this one pops one day.

How Nations And Societies Are Following The Tytler Cycle

Anyone who is a student of liberty and fan of freedom will be interested in a theory called the Tytler Cycle. The Tytler Cycle describes the ways that a society departs from enslavement and finally arrives at the point of freedom and prosperity.

The cycle works in a continuous circle, eventually leading back to enslavement. In the subsequent paragraphs, you will see why some Americans are suggesting that the US has neared the end of the prosperity and freedom part of the cycle and is a step away from the alarming enslavement point again.

About Alexander Tytler

You may not be familiar with the name Alexander Tytler. Tytler proved to be a Scottish historian. What makes him interesting is that he lived, researched, and wrote in the same years as the Founding Fathers of America.

Tytler created a theory that detailed a cycle that constantly repeated itself throughout history. He claimed to have learned that all different democratic societies evolved through this identical cycle time and time again. Tytler had many examples of this cycle from different nations throughout history. Unfortunately, practically all of his work became lost.

The Tytler Cycle Explained

The good news is that enough of Alexander Tytler's work survived to understand his insightful and sobering theory. Tytler started out with the premise that all democracies go around in a circular cycle. This idea eventually became name for him. In each complete cycle, about two hundred years of time elapsed. A nation and society would start out in enslavement, or bondage as he called it.

The society and people who began in bondage would have little to no freedoms in the beginning. As the people lived in very difficult circumstances, they would finally turn towards religious or spiritual faith to help sustain them.

As a result of their belief in God and heaven as a comforting part of the afterlife, they would find the necessary courage to struggle for and finally attain their freedom. From freedom and its many inspiring benefits, the people and nation would obtain a great level of abundance in material possessions and wealth.

At this point, the positive side of the cycle would end and the negative side of the cycle would begin. In time, selfishness arose out of the material abundance. As people began to expect and to demand more for themselves and to focus less on the good of the whole country, they also became complacent and lazy. Laziness would lead to apathy and eventually dependence on others as a result. Finally, the dependent people would end up back in slavery and bondage.

The Tytler Cycle ran in the following order:

- Bondage
- Spiritual Faith
- Courage
- Liberty
- Abundance
- Selfishness
- Complacency
- Apathy
- Dependence
- Then starting over with Bondage

The Periods in American History as they Relate to the Tytler Cycle
A look at the United States' history would draw uncomfortable parallels with the Tytler Cycle. The country went from bondage and grew into spiritual faith in the 1760's with the formation of the Sons of Liberty. From 1770 to 1783, it developed from this spiritual faith to admirable courage during the Revolutionary War.

The country achieved a long period of liberty that you saw climax from 1784 to 1865 with the end of the Civil War and freeing of the American slaves. The greatest period of national prosperity showed in the advance from this liberty to abundance phase that took place from 1866 to 1969. By many measurements, things in the United States have been in a static or declining state since the nineteen seventies began.

As one example, the government abandoned the dollar's historic link to gold then. The nation has since witnessed a shocking decline of the dollar's purchasing value against gold of from only $35 for an ounce in 1970 to over $1,400 for an ounce in 2010.

The Relevance of the Tytler Cycle to Present Day America

Some writers and observers in American society have become convinced that America is in the negative side of the cycle now, somewhere between selfishness and dependence. The evidence of this is all around you. How many more Americans right now are engaged in working the national system in order to get a free ride out of it than are trying to build up the country?

Alexander Tytler has sober words that could be applied to America today all too well. He said that democracies are temporary by nature. He did not believe that they would ever survive as enduring forms of government.

They could only exist until the point that the citizens discovered that they had the power to vote generous benefits to be given to themselves out of the public coffers and revenue. At that point, the voters would be certain to select the candidate that guaranteed the highest level of financial benefits from the treasury.

Tytler said that because of this, each and every democracy would eventually fall apart because of poor financial policy and weakened finances. Dictatorship and enslavement would always result after this.

This is an alarming assessment when it is applied to the present day situation in America. Americans have constantly voted for themselves bigger and better benefits over the last forty years.

These have been financed by the Federal Reserve's electronic printing press.

This works to support the country's Ponzi schemes, such as Social Security and Medicare, where the early investors, or payers into the system, are paid off today with new contributions from you the worker. You are also promised that you will get the same payoff from tomorrow's workers in the future.

The debt levels have risen to unsustainable levels of higher than fourteen trillion dollars and are not projected to be paid back or paid down at any foreseeable point. The country's future has been mortgaged to keep the whole benefits system going, as one day the bill will come due for you and your children.

A Closer Examination of America's Present Place in the Cycle

You may have been among the numerous Americans who have accused the present administration under President Obama and Congressional leaders Harry Reid and Nancy Pelosi of engaging in a never before seen in American history usurping of power. They have achieved this by spreading their socialistic political and world views throughout America against the majority's will and by boosting the government's spending drastically.

Today's democratic party in power is by far and away the most radically socialist that you have seen run the country. Among their policies pursued before the mid term elections was to undo the welfare reform established in the 1990's. This reform had been an attempt to reign in the runaway benefits that the citizens had voted for themselves in the past.

Besides this, Americans are consenting to more and more of their daily lives being taken over by the Federal government. This makes you more dependent on them with each passing day.

The Federal government handles a greater and greater share of individual Americans' responsibilities now than ever before.

There is hope that the cycle of decline can be reversed or maybe postponed. The recent mid term elections have at least given the country a more balanced government where the House is controlled by the opposition Republicans. This will finally prevent the citizens and leadership from voting themselves more bankrupting financial benefits, for now anyway.

Will We See Another Gold Seizure Act in the Near Future?

If you have ever looked into buying gold coins as investments before, then you are probably aware of the fact that there are two main divisions in gold coins.

These are bullion gold coins, valued only for their precious metal content, and collectible gold coins, valued for gold content and presumably for rarity or historical factors.

Many coin dealers will encourage you to buy the collectible gold coins because the government actually seized all gold bullion coins during the Great Depression. This creates a fear that the government may issue another such gold seizure act to protect the falling dollar in the future.

The subsequent paragraphs investigate the history behind the gold seizure act and examine whether it is likely to happen again in the near future.

Background of the Gold Seizure Act

The good times and easy stock market wealth creation of the roaring twenties came to a screeching halt in the Black Tuesday market crash of 1929.

Far from being an isolated event, you saw the crash begin a long, painful, drawn out decline in the stock market that finally caused the world wide Great Depression.

Then President Franklin D. Roosevelt took a series of measures in an attempt to jump start the country out of this demoralizing economic crisis that saw unemployment at twenty-five percent and GDP down by as much as fifty percent.

The Reason Behind the Gold Seizure Act

Among his dramatic measures that he pursued was an Executive Order confiscating gold in 1933. The reasons behind President Franklin's draconian measures lay in his desire to boost the value of the dollar significantly as a means of fighting off the growing depression.

President Roosevelt knew that if all American turned in their gold for dollars, it would provide two advantages for the currency and economy. On the one hand, it would dramatically increase demand for dollars, as all gold holdings had to be used to purchase dollars. At the same time, it would significantly boost the government's holdings of gold, making the paper dollar currency that was still backed up by gold appear stronger.

Specifics of the Gold Seizure Act

To carry out this executive order effectively, President Roosevelt made it as stern as possible. The hoarding of gold had to stop, and he hoped that people would choose to spend their dollars once they had received them in lieu of their gold. Roosevelt's order threatened fines or even imprisonment for those who chose not to turn in their gold.

An interesting exception to the rule has become the basis for promoting the sale of collectible gold coins to this day. The main exemption in the gold confiscation order turned out to be collectible gold coins. The executive order actually stated that Americans would be permitted to possess gold coins that had a recognized special value to those who collected unusual and rare coins.

After President Roosevelt completed his confiscation of all the gold bullion coins, he moved on to the next step in his master plan with gold. In the next year of 1934, he devalued the dollar substantially against gold, raising the value of gold by almost seventy-five percent, and thus decreasing the dollar's value by a drastic margin as well.

As far as the fate of the bullion gold coins of the day, a great number of them were later on melted down after having been seized, while others were sent to Europe when the countries wanted to redeem dollars for gold.

The Benefits for Collectible Gold Coin Holders After the Act

The people who held collectible, or rare and unusual, gold coins following the act profited handsomely in their holdings for two reasons.

Their coins first increased in value substantially since gold rose from $20 each ounce to $35 each ounce in the wake of President Roosevelt's devaluing the dollar.

Secondly, the melting down of seized gold coins created a greater rarity for the coins that had not been confiscated. These events of the 1930's cemented the point of purchasing and holding gold coins that are collectibles.

The Possibilities of Another Gold Confiscation Today

Coin dealers, including large national coin dealerships, have argued that you might see another gold seizure act in the near future. It is true that conditions in the U.S. and world economies have been eerily similar to those seen in the 1930's over the past three to four years.

Real unemployment is the highest it has been since the Great Depression. Economic growth and trade has taken a severe setback. Banks have failed in numbers not seen since World War II.

Still, even though the U.S. dollar is once again in trouble and the American economy has taken severe hits in the past several years, several things are different now than in the 1930's. For one thing, President Franklin Roosevelt's executive order is actually not in effect anymore.

On December 31 of 1974, President Gerald Ford issued Executive Order 11825, repealing President Franklin's executive order of 1933. In fact on the very same day, Congress passed a law restoring the rights of all Americans to possess bullion gold again. While this does not make it impossible for gold to be confiscated again, it makes it less likely.

The law that makes gold confiscation far less likely to occur again today came into existence in 1977. That year you saw Congress take away the authority of the President to regulate the transactions of gold in any time of national emergency besides war time. Once again, this makes it very difficult for a sitting President to justify taking American's gold bullion holdings away from them these days.

The Confiscation Proof Nature of Collectible Gold Coins

Even if the government did choose to change or ignore the law of 1977 preventing Presidential meddling in the physical gold market except during war, you should carefully examine the idea that collectible gold coins would be exempted from such a recall.

The truth is that there is neither a Treasury department regulation or national law that makes these kinds of collectible gold coins confiscation proof in case of another gold seizure. Just because President Roosevelt chose to allow these types of non bullion coins to be held even after confiscation does not mean that a current President would allow the same exemption.

Another thing to remember is that Roosevelt's order no longer has any legal binding, since President Ford repealed it. Any future confiscation of gold coins would stand alone, and not be bound by legal precedent.

On top of this, even if the President at the time of such an order chose to honor the spirit of President Roosevelt's executive order, his order referenced "rare and unusual coins," not collectible coins. It is worth nothing that a vast majority of coins being sold as collectible types of coins today are neither unusual nor rare, as there are many millions of them in existence.

Old U.S. gold coins are a case in point. Twenty Dollar Liberty's and $20 St. Gaudens' coins are actually fairly common, unless then come certified in a high grade from one of the two coin grading agencies, PCGS and NGC.

The fact of the matter is that conditions today make it less likely for the government to decide to seize gold coins today than in the past. Still, assuming that owning collectible gold coins would protect your investment from such an executive order or Congressional act does not have a basis in current reality. Unless you buy truly rare gold coins, you would not have an argument on which to stand anyway.

Money

<u>MONEY</u>

"Understanding the Medium of Exchange"

The Money Paradox - Printing More Leads to Having Less

You have probably figured out that governments are fond or printing more money. This has become abundantly clear of your own government since 2007, as the Federal Reserve and the Treasury have gone on a rampant money creation spree that has increased the numbers of dollars around the world by three hundred percent.

Despite this mass creation of money, printing more of it does not give you any more money, but actually takes purchasing power away from you. This is referred to as a money paradox.

How More Money is Created

You may be surprised to learn how easy it is for the Fed to literally create money right out of the air. They can in fact do this through one of several means that you have seen them employ over the last few years.

By purchasing assets from banks, such as mortgage backed or asset backed securities, they do it. They also can purchase U.S. government debt like Treasuries, as well as stocks and corporate debt to infuse cash into the still fragile financial system. When they do this, they are not sending checks or enormous stacks of cash to the banks and other entities. Instead, they are printing money to pay for them.

Understand that the Fed does not have its own printing press hidden in a back room office. They have no power to literally create physical dollar bills. In fact, physically printed dollar bills only represent five percent of the U.S. dollars circulating around the world. Most of those actually printed ones are held by people in other countries, too. Truthfully only the Treasury can create more physical dollar bills, and they only bother to when it is time to replace old bills that are being taken out of circulation.

The way that the government through the Fed actually creates additional money is far more subtle. They do it by going to the commercial banks' reserve balances and simply crediting them electronically. Through doing this, and especially through purchasing Treasuries, the Federal Reserve has shown that it is able to create and move as great a quantity of money as it feels necessary into the economy. In theory, no limit exists as to the quantity of money that the Federal Reserve is able to electronically create and Congress is then able to spend.

Supply and Demand Consequences of the Fed Creating More Money

The Fed has engaged on a rampant money printing spree for the last several years. Once more, in the month of September, they have indicated that they are looking seriously into doing this form of quantitative easing, or massively increasing the money supply, yet again.

In their September statement, many analysts read between the lines that this will happen as early as October. This creating of still more money electronically from thin air is not without its consequences, though, as most any sound economist will tell you.

When the Fed engages in this repeated creation of new dollars electronically, they are dramatically impacting the critical and underlying supply and demand laws. Supply and demand tells you that as the supply of dollars increases, and demand for these dollars remains basically the same, then the value of the dollars is going down. Another way of putting it is that the Fed is devaluing, or even debasing, the dollar currency that you have.

On top of this, they are other effects to the money paradox. More dollars available create an increasing demand for the basically flat quantity supply of goods and services. This inevitably leads on to higher prices down the road. As the prices for such goods and services increase, the purchasing power, or real value, of your dollars in hand continues to go down. Just because you have not yet seen this happen on a significant scale, does not mean that it is not coming in the near to medium term future.

Why You Do Not Benefit from the Fed Creating More Money

In the vast majority of cases, you do not benefit when the Fed creates more money. You will see the reason why when you consider again what you read above, that the way the Fed creates and injects more money into the system is by crediting the account balances of banks and entities that have accounts with them.

Unfortunately, you and other individual Americans do not and can not have an account with the Fed. This means that when they start passing around the new electronically created dollars, you are left completely out of the process.

Banks are given the money, which they then loan out as mortgages, lines of credit and credit card balances, and car loans. They are not giving you any of this money, but only loaning it out to you in consideration of repaying a higher principal amount plus interest. The system may see the new dollars given out, but you and the vast majority of other Americans do not.

The only amount that you were given in the first massive round of money distribution once again known as quantitative easing is in the form of the one time stimulus check for $700 to $1,400, depending on whether you were single or not. This was not given out from from created dollars though, but by the government taking on additional debt, which you as the tax payer will have to repay some day.

How the Money Paradox Works

This is how the money paradox works then. The Fed is creating new money electronically out of thin air. Banks receive the lion's share of it. It does not directly benefit you at all, nor increase the number of dollars in your hand.

But it does cost you terribly when inflation rears its ugly head. At the point when that starts to filter through the system, as it assuredly will, then the money that you are holding will actually become less valuable. Even though more money will have been created, you will have less purchasing power in your static number of dollars than you did before.

In case you are still unclear on how this can actually happen to you and your money, look at this example. Pretend that you have $100 in savings. If bread were $1 per loaf, then you would literally have 100 loaves of bread in savings.

Meanwhile, the Federal Reserve comes along and increases the money supply of existing dollars by fifty percent in a dashing example of quantitative easing. You do not receive any of this money, as it is credited directly to banks' reserves and the Federal government's accounts.

Over the next year or two, inflation jumps massively as the number of dollars existing to chase the relatively stable amount of loaves of bread goes up by almost fifty percent. Within a few turbulent years, the price of bread has risen to $1.50 per loaf. Alas, your same $100 will now only purchase sixty-six loaves of bread.

This is exactly how the money paradox robs you. Your money is only valuable to you in terms of what it will actually purchase. When your purchasing power falls significantly, or even by a little, your fixed number of dollars in your hand will actually be worth less, regardless of how many more dollars have been magically created.

What You Always Wanted to Know About The Dollar Bill

If you are like many Americans, then you have occasionally held up a one dollar bill and looked at the various symbols and words found on it with interest.

Probably you have never received a good explanation for what these words and symbols mean and from where they came.

For example, you probably did not know that the current design of the one dollar bill only dates from 1957. In the following paragraphs, the important elements of the dollar bill are explained so that the next time that you look at the bill, you will know what they mean.

What is A Federal Reserve Note?

Federal reserve notes are the official name for United States bank notes, more commonly known as dollar bills. The United States BEP, or Bureau of Engraving and Printing, prints these Federal Reserve Notes on a unique paper that is produce by the Dalton, Massachusetts company Crane and Company. Federal Reserve Notes are the one kind of American bank notes that are still being produced to this day. You should not mix them up with Federal Reserve Bank Notes that were discontinued back in 1945.

Such Federal Reserve Notes are officially authorized by the United States Code in Section 411 of Title 12. Once they are printed and packaged, they are issued out to the various Federal Reserve Banks. These Federal Reserve branch reserve banks then place them in circulation.

Such Federal Reserve Notes prove to be fiat currency of the United States, which means that they are only backed up by the full faith and credit of the U.S. government rather than gold or silver assets kept in a vault, as proved to be the case until 1971.

The Phrase This Note is Legal Tender

All U.S. Federal Reserve Notes include the words on the front of each of them that state that this note is legal tender for all debts, public and private. This statement means that the printed paper dollar acknowledges a debt and guarantees its payment. It is interesting to note that the original dollar bills in the 1700's and 1800's did not carry this exact statement.

Instead they said that this certificate is receivable for all public dues and when so received may be reissued. This signified that they could be used for all debts owed to various governing agencies, and it did not specify that private transactions had to incorporate them. At the time, various private bank institution notes were also utilized between private parties, as well as gold and silver, to make payment on any transactions.

About The Great Seal

All dollar bills also feature the Great Seal on the back of the bill. This seal was designed by Benjamin Franklin with the assistance of other men including John Adams and Thomas Jefferson.

A process that occurred in three different committees, it required four years to be fully accomplished. After this, another two years passed before it would finally be approved. Secretary of Congress Charles Thompson submitted the ultimate version, having brought in elements from each committee's ideas.

Since it came about as a result of the American revolution, the Great Seal is a particular mixture of natural elements, including olive branch, eagle, stars, light rays, cloud, and eye, and universal symbols that included arrows, a pyramid, and a shield. President Franklin Roosevelt actually made the decision to place the two sides of this Great Seal on the one dollar bill's back.

Although elements of the seal have been altered over the years with each succeeding generation of Americans and their particular tastes, it is more or less the same as when the founding fathers originally created it.

The Pyramid Symbol and Its Significance

Looking on the back of the dollar bill at the left hand circle on the Great Seal, you can recognize a pyramid. This pyramid only appeared in the Great Seal with the additions of the third committee. Neither Benjamin Franklin, Thomas Jefferson, nor John Adams suggested its inclusion.

Charles Thompson claimed that the pyramid stood for duration and strength, and so it found its way on to the final design. The credit for first using the pyramid on American money is given to Francis Hopkinson.

The pyramid has tremendous symbolism and significance. On the Egyptian styled pyramid are thirteen steps that lead up to the pyramid. These represent the original thirteen states that were a part of the newly independent nation. Another thirteen steps are found approaching a summit of the pyramid that is not finished. These represent the anticipated future expansion of the country.

Above the pyramid rests an all seeing eye on a keystone. The eye is called the Eye of Providence. It is encompassed by rays of light. This all seeing eye has been referred to as a Freemasonry symbol in the past. Freemasonry proved to be a secretive fraternal organization with roots going back to the Medieval Knights Templar.

Those who believe this to be a Freemasonry symbol argue that it is evidence that the original Founding Fathers held beliefs in Masonry and Masonic principles. The conspiracy theorists claim that the Founding Fathers wished to embed this Masonic order into the entire United States.

Below the pyramid you can see a variety of Roman numerals and Latin writing. At the bottom of the pyramid are found the Roman numerals MDCCLXXVI. These translate to the year 1776, which stands for the year that the United States became independent from Great Britain.

You also see Latin writing found around the pyramid and the eye. Beneath the pyramid itself are found the Latin words "Novus Ordo Seclorum."

These stand for A new order of the ages when translated. The phrase references the founding of the United States in 1776, as well.

The all seeing eye also has Latin writing above it. It states "Annuit Coeptis." When translated, this phrase means that He has favored our undertakings. By He, the founding fathers meant God, or Providence. This phrase relates to the all seeing "Eye of Providence" once again.

The Motto In God We Trust on the Bill

No doubt you have seen the U.S. motto on all coins and bills. The phrase In God We Trust is hard to miss. What may be surprising to you is that this phrase only became the national motto and appeared on the one dollar bill in the last fifty or so years.

The eighty-fourth Congress actually passed the law that made In God We Trust the national motto. The President approved it on July 30th, 1956. The two groups made a joint resolution that declared In God We Trust to be the national motto for the United States. Only the following year in 1957 did the phrase begin to appear on paper money.

It first found use on the one dollar silver certificate. This paper money with the new national motto appeared for the first time in circulation on October 1st, 1957. At this time, The Bureau of Engraving and Printing began converting to a new printing process, the dry intaglio process. While they were affecting the conversion, the organization began working the In God We Trust Motto on to the back of all denominations and types of paper currency.

The New 100 Dollar Bill - A Return to the Gold Standard?

If you have not seen the new hundred dollar bill yet, then you should look at one at your first opportunity.

The new hundred dollar bill is totally unique in the history of the U.S. Treasury for a variety of reasons.

The most noticeable of these is that half of it features shiny gold coloring. This gold and a variety of other differences in this unique bill have suggested to some that there might be a hidden symbolism in the hundred dollar bill. If it is true, this could have tremendous impacts on your investments going forward.

New Features in the Hundred Dollar Bill

For those of you who have not seen what this exciting new bill looks like, you can get a good idea by going to the following link to look at it. Here, you will see that the new hundred dollar bill is specially designed with several new security features.

These include a blueish three dimensional security ribbon and a golden bell inside of a gold colored inkwell. Besides this, it also features a color shifting number 100, a golden 100, raised printing, micro printing, and a portrait watermark.

These are all interesting and practical design and security features, yet they do not at once explain what hidden symbolism may be a part of this last of redesigned hundred dollar bills.

Symbolism in the New Hundred Dollar Bill

The United States possesses a unique history of placing hidden meanings inside of bills. This is important to remember as you go through the various unusual differences in this new one hundred dollar bill. It helps you to see where the conspiracy theorists are coming from with the new bill, particularly in light of the economic crisis that has recently shaken the nation and world.

The symbolism in the new hundred dollar bill centers around all of the gold coloring and ink found on it. Not only is there plenty of gold coloring found in the bell and inkwell, as well as on one of the number hundreds, but the bill turns still more gold when you shift it in the light.

Besides this, there are still other dramatic differences between this bill and all of the other bills that the Bureau of Engraving and Printing has made. Some are suggesting that all of this gold recalls the days of the gold standard that the U.S. participated in for so long, until only forty years ago in fact.

Consider the most obvious difference between this new hundred dollar bill and the various other colored bills that have been printed in recent years. You can not miss the enormous blue stripe, called a security thread, that runs down the middle of the bill. Red, white, and blue contain certain special meanings within the American flag.

The white stands for innocence and purity. The red stands for valor and hardiness. The blue color signifies perseverance, vigilance, and justice. This blue stripe divides the hundred dollar bill into roughly two halves. When you look at the two halves and think about them carefully, you notice that they are entirely different from one another.

The Two Sides of the One Hundred Dollar Bill

Keep in mind that there are two groups in the U.S. where money backing is considered. One, which currently has the upper hand, believes that paper money, also known as fiat money, is the best path for the nation. The other group holds to an intrinsic money that is actually backed up by gold. Look at the two sides of the hundred dollar bill with this in mind.

The Left Side of the One Hundred Dollar Bill

To the left of the blue stripe are features that agree with the fiat money group. The left side does not have any gold on it, for example, only the standard green found in U.S. paper bills. It contains the typical elements that you would expect to see in a bill, including the Fed's official seal, Federal Reserve Note, and also the just moved signature of the Treasury Secretary, formerly on the right side of the bill.

This is consistent with a Fiat money theory, since Tim Geithner is a firm believer in paper money. The centerpiece of the left side is Ben Franklin, who is placed just to the left of this blue stripe. You probably do not know this about Benjamin Franklin, but he proved to be a huge supporter of Fiat money in his time.

Franklin did not like the Imperial bankers of the British Empire who wished to make the colonists operate on a Gold or Silver standard. He knew that the overseas trade imbalance would deplete the colonies' gold and silver so there would not be sufficient money for the colonies to engage in their own trade with each other. So it is no accident that Franklin is on the left side of the blue stripe, representing paper money.

The Right Side of the One Hundred Dollar Bill

To the right of the blue stripe representing justice, vigilance, and perseverance you find all of the gold on the front and back of the bill. Here you see a golden Liberty Bell, a golden Ink Well, gold 100, a gold Feather pen, background gold writing, a gold Watermark, and a golden colored July 4, 1776.

On the back of the right side, you see an enormous golden 100 also. There can be no mistaking all of the gold on the right side of the security thread. Clearly it has to stand for something. Here are some possible interpretations that have been suggested for all of the elements on the gold side of the new bill.

The ink well in gold represents Congress' power to make laws that could take down the paper money system that would only need a pen stroke. The liberty bell all in gold inside of the ink well stands for the power of Congress to restore the liberty to the citizens that the banking system has taken from them.

The statement "This note is legal tender for all debts, public and private" used to be on the left side of the bill, but it has now been moved to the gold standard side. Besides this, the 100 on the front bottom shifts from green color to gold color.

Finally, the words written just atop the gold 100 on the far right are significant. They say "the People to alter or abolish it, and to institute new." This statement taken from the Declaration of Independence falls in with the argument of abolishing the current money system in favor of a return to the gold standard.

There are people who believe that the United States has been preparing for quite some time to return to the Gold Standard, since its abandonment has depreciated the dollar by over seventy percent. These people point to all of the symbolism in the new one hundred dollar bill and say that the time for the return to the Gold Standard has at last come.

They point to the unexpected delay in the release of the bill from February 10, 2011 as further evidence that the financial crisis has only encouraged the government to return to it, and that they will announce this when the hundred dollar bill actually comes out.

<u>TOOLS</u>

"Instruments for Building a Wealth Foundation"

The Formula and Predictive Successes of Jim Sinclair

You will find in your quest for good ongoing education that there are not too many valuable for free sources of information available, even over the Internet.

One such invaluable source for keeping on top of events going on in the world that affect the values of your stocks, bonds, and gold and silver investments is JSmineset.com.

The purveyor of this extremely helpful informational website is the legendary gold and silver adviser and investor Jim Sinclair.

About the Author of JSmineset.com - Jim Sinclair

Jim Sinclair is an interesting expert on precious metals of whom it is said that he has already forgotten more about gold than most of you ever knew about it. He is principally a specialist in the precious metals and a trader of commodities and foreign currencies.

Back in 1977, he established his Sinclair Group of Companies that provided customers with a full range of brokerage services covering stocks, bonds, and a variety of other types of investments. His companies had branches located in New York, Chicago, Kansas City, Toronto, Geneva, and London. He sold these companies in 1983.

As he was running these companies and following their sale, Jim Sinclair served as the precious metals adviser to the Hunt family and Hunt Oil in liquidating their massive silver position that they had built up in an attempt to corner the limited silver market. The Hunt Brothers had acquired enormous amounts of futures contracts on silver that gave them the right to buy physical silver at a certain set price.

In controlling increasingly larger silver positions, they were successful in drastically driving up the prices of silver to an amazing high of $42 per share. The regulators stepped in and ordered them to unwind their positions. Jim Sinclair was instrumental in assisting them to do this, and in helping to negotiate a $1 billion loan that Paul Volcker, then Chairman of the Federal Reserve Board, arranged to help them in their efforts to close out the silver positions.

Jim has also been an executive committee member and General partner of two firms on the New York Stock Exchange. He has additionally served as President of a commodities clearing firm Sinclair Global Clearing Corporation as well as President of a dealer in currencies and metals, Global Arbitrage. Since then, Jim Sinclair has been involved as Chairman of Tanzanian Royalty Exploration, heading up its endeavors to transform itself into a gold royalty company.

The legendary gold and silver dealer and investor has written three books and a great number of magazine articles. These cover the investment subjects of strategies for trading, acquiring precious metals, and geopolitical events as they pertain to the markets and economics of the world.

As a regular and hugely popular speaker at gold conferences and events, his commentary on financial issues and especially gold receives widespread media coverage in the United States and around the world.

Jim launched his extremely useful and free website Jim Sinclair's Mineset at JSmineset.com back in January of 2003. This free service to members of the gold community hosts his daily commentary on gold and events influencing its current and future pricing. Much more than simply gold prices is dealt with on this informative website that you should read and follow.

Mission of the Website JSmineset.com

This website has a mission of being a teaching forum that is service oriented. They use the everyday markets for the backdrop of their texts and as their classroom blackboard. Jim Sinclair and three other contributors provide commentary that is intended to teach you a lesson about the mistakes being made by the world's policy makers that are affecting you and your money and investments. It is a proactive website that counsels you how to invest to protect yourself from the troubles that are ensuing from the world leaders' tragic mistakes.

Wealth of Experience in the Contributors

Besides Jim Sinclair, the purveyor of the website, there are three other regular contributors. These men have specialties in different areas of investments and advising. Dan Norcini proves to be a professional on floor trader of commodities.

He contributes charting performed through technical analysis covering gold and silver bullion, crude oil and copper prices, the American dollar, the Canadian dollar, and the Euro. Monty Guild is a contributor who runs an investment management services company that helps advise American and foreign investors and foreign and domestic investment firms.

Finally, David Duval turns out to be an internationally known author on the specialty of mining and minerals. As co-founder of JSmineset.com, he is managing editor when he is not acting as a consultant on minerals and technical adviser to the United Nations.

What the Site Offers You

This enormously popular web site informational service has much to offer you. Each and every day, they post twenty-four hour charts in the upper left hand corner covering the prices of gold bullion, the U.S. dollar index, and the Euro. They then re-print articles from a wealth of sources from literally around the world covering every bit of news related to the financial crisis, the inflationary printing of money, the state of the U.S. and other major economies, and other geo-political concerns that have tremendous impact on your investments.

They similarly offer brief commentary on and lessons to be learned from these articles. From time to time, they write their own articles about events going on in the political and financial worlds and how they affect the prices of gold and other commodities and investments. You will not find a comparable site offering such a wealth of time saving and valuable information, and all at no charge, anywhere else on the Internet.

The Website's Formula and Predictive Successes

The website was partially founded as Jim Sinclair and the other contributors became concerned about a coming financial collapse that they began predicting way back in 2003. They saw that complicated financial instruments, called derivatives, had been created based on inflated real estate prices and bundled up risky home loans.

As the dollar amounts of these shadowy and unregulated investments began to grow into the trillions and then tens of trillions this past decade, Jim and the contributors referred to these derivatives as financial weapons of mass destruction that would blow the western based world economy to pieces one day.

They predicted that when this began to happen, that the price of gold would rise to $1,225, $1,250, then $1,650 an ounce, and all by or before 2011. Jim came up with a formula that he posted in September of 2006 to explain how it would all come to pass. When he made these astonishing predictions, gold prices were in the $500-$600 per ounce range. Gold drove to literally $1,225 per ounce on its first thrust above $1,200 before pulling back, as Jim Sinclair suggested that it would. It has since surged past $1,250 and is now on its way to $1,300.

Since gold has moved so quickly, and the U.S. and other countries have begun to print money at rates that are unprecedented by the leading economies in recent decades, he has since revised his predictions for gold prices to surpass $1,650, potentially going to as high as $5,000 per ounce in the coming years.

Ultimately the goal of this website is to help you to protect your assets and investments against what the authors see as coming hyperinflation.

They do this by encouraging you to invest in physical gold bullion and to have the stay in power to hold on to this insurance through the ups and downs of the price movements in gold. As such, the website really is looking out for your best interests.

Learn The Economics of Wealth Cycles with Michael Maloney

Among the many useful sources of information available to you on the Internet is a site by Michael Maloney. This is called WealthCycles.com.

On this site, you will find much helpful and useful advice for protecting your middle class assets and growing your wealth in the wild times that are ahead for the United States and world economy.

About Michael Maloney

Michael Maloney has been an entrepreneur since he turned seventeen years old. In his years as an entrepreneur, his goal morphed into one of being a worthy steward of the financial trust his family had placed in him. Because of this, Maloney began studying the economy of the world and the United States, as well as the financial markets.

What he uncovered may surprise you to hear. Michael Maloney learned that identical economic patterns repeated themselves again and again in history, starting back in the Ancient World and continuing to our own time. Literally each time that the currency of a state grew over inflated, it became devalued. Then the citizens understood that a journey back to silver and gold as the safe haven money proved to be essential for survival.

Maloney understood that what you see going on nowadays has occurred time and time again. His greatest revelation turned out to be that this same pattern is about to transpire once more. This time it will be far more intense than in the past, to the tune of several multiples greater.

Because of this understanding, Michael Maloney became convinced that in order to grow and safe guard the wealth of his family, he would need to buy into silver and gold. In time, Maloney opened a wildly successful silver and gold dealership. He wanted to do more than just buy into the precious metals. His goal lay in working with the naturally occurring economic cycles to do this.

After years of research and study, he realized his dream to begin helping others to understand the economic and wealth building cycles of the market. This led to his writing the Guide to Investing in Gold and Silver that has already been read by tens of thousands of individuals.

It took Michael Maloney countless years as an entrepreneur, business owner, inventor, and even author to reach the point of starting up his dream company. WealthCycles.com is the product of the overwhelming demand of people like you in need of useful facts and practical financial guidance that they can use in their everyday lives to grow and protect their own wealth.

About WealthCycles.com

The WealthCycles website is actually a resources website for financial education. It provides you with an all inclusive kit of tools of information that comprises historical viewpoints and pragmatic approaches to applications, as well as explanations for present day economic situations, helping individuals to find the ability to save their families, as well as to prosper and to secure their families' futures in the wake of the coming worldwide economic instabilities.

At this site, Maloney and company offer you easy to understand guidance for getting through the challenging financial system of today. In the process, they seek to stimulate your mind, entertain you, and motivate you as well. The site promises to help you through the most exciting opportunities for building up wealth that history has to offer, which Maloney and WealthCycles insist are just around the corner.

Wealthcycle.com Site Mission

The site has a stated goal of helping you to learn all about the economics of wealth cycles so that you can take care of yourself and your family in the future.

WealthCycles.com has been created to provide comprehensible and timely information pertaining to the economic cycles of wealth. As such, the site and company realize that information is becoming more and more important to your life in this age. Because so much information has become available, it is almost overwhelming to go through it and sift it for value and truth.

Although there are countless resources available online, alongside the twenty-four hour news cycle of both television and radio, WealthCycle.com knows that this proves to be far more financial information than you can possibly absorb. Besides this, far too much of the financial information on offer proves to be no more than propaganda or statistical noise. Much of this exists to frighten you rather than to help you learn.

Because of this, too many people are confused and bewildered by all of the data firing at them. You may feel the same way. One sided conversations and points of view are quoted out of and without the proper context on a seemingly daily basis.

WealthCycles.com Goal

The goal at Wealthcycles.com is to merge content and context together seamlessly. They do this through utilizing technology to help you with the learning and comprehension of the economic wealth cycles that they constantly bring up. This way, they offer you tools that will help you to secure both your future and that of your family's well being.

Helping you to become both financially educated and a well informed person of what is really happening is part of this goal. The site and company see the need for a site to help people sift through the noise to get the most timely and correct financial information into your hands and lives in time to help you.

This means that their website concerns both educating you and teaching you to take critical and timely actions. First, you will have to understand what to do, so that you can take the necessary actions. To help you with this, they will show you the historical past and how it explains the future.

They will combine the historical view with practical and present day analysis. Finally, they will teach you how to sift through all of the constant barrage of information to put the best content into the proper perspective that will mater for you and your family.

The Different Sections of the Site

WealthCycles.com has four different principal sections on the site to help carry out these goals of assisting you to protect yourself and your family from upcoming turmoil and disaster. The Current Analysis section looks at the things that are occurring right now, as well as what the talking heads are gabbing about, and the news that is on the front page these days. This is all done within The Wealth Cycle Principle that it has happened before now and is happening yet again.

The Classic Essay by Michael Maloney proves to be the site owner's essays pertaining to many things. The Wealth Cycle Principle is covered. Other essays explain the ways that these constantly repeating trends can help you to make the best financial decisions right now.

In the Wealth Cycle basics and fundamentals. Maloney and company explain the hardware of this Wealth Cycle principle. This is done so that you will understand the economic cycles and how to react to them properly.

Finally, there are the Tools and Tips to help you secure your Financial Future section. These are how to maps and manuals for those who are inexperienced investors or new to the study of economics. These provide fast reads for the basics and dangers that can way lay even the most experienced of investors.

Take Control of Your Finances with iPhone BudgetCare App

There are so many different apps for the iPhone anymore that much of the time it is difficult to separate the good ones from the hyped ones. With literally thousands of them on the market, finding the most effective ones is not easy.

One iPhone App that you should seriously consider investing the $1.99 sum into is BudgetCare. This helpful App is reviewed in the subsequent paragraphs.

Uses for BudgetCare iPhone App

No one can argue that saving money is the popular trend these days. As the global Great Recession has seized hold of the global economy, all people everywhere are interested in saving money wherever and however they can.

The first principal of saving money is to establish a good budget for yourself and then discipline yourself to actually follow it consistently. Sticking to a budget forces you to stay accountable for all of your spending, as it assists in keeping track of each of your individual expenses. Suponix has created an electronic version of this most ideal tool that you can have with you and use on the go, where you are. This is called BudgetCare, the most convenient tool for performing all functions of a budget literally in the very palm of your hand.

Functions of BudgetCare

BudgetCare features four main functions when you first open it. These main choices permit you to accomplish all of your necessary budgeting tasks. On the opening screen, you will see the options New Transaction, Statistics, Budget and Balance, and Settings.

Establishing Your Budget with BudgetCare iPhone App
Creating your new budget is easy with this BudgetCare iPhone App. From the main options on the first screen, you start out by choosing the category of Budget and Balance. The flexibility with BudgetCare permits you the user to establish a different new budget literally every month if you wish.

Alternatively, you are able to stay with the one that you have and simply roll it forward. This lets you maintain a pre set limit of spending literally every month. After you have set up this initial budget or the new month's budget, you are able to look at your total amount of money that you have spent for the month and compare it to the budget that you are presently using by the month, by the week, or by the day.

Entering Your Transactions with BudgetCare iPhone App

Actually putting in your spending transactions proves to be very easy. All that you have to do is to go to the main screen and select on the category of New Transaction. Next, it prompts you for a dollar amount of your expenditure. Simply enter the dollar amount total spent and then pick out one of the categories for spending. You will find that the App actually offers thirteen different categories from which you can select.

These spending categories include all of the most important possibilities. Among them are areas ranging from insurance and bills, to health care, to education, to car expenses. One of the great things about the App is that should your latest expenses not fall under one of the pre existing categories, you are able to create your own unique category and easily add it to the original line up of thirteen categories.

The BudgetCare iPhone App starts out with a default currency of United States dollars. If this is not your principal currency, it is not a problem. The option to change it to either British Pounds, European Euros, Japanese Yen, or Russian Rubles is similarly built into the App.

In practice, changing the underlying currency actually only impacts the symbol that is displayed, since the program does not perform any currency conversions as part of its standard budgetary operations. Still, it will make you feel more at home with your budget to see your native currency displayed if you are transacting in Pounds or Euros rather than American dollars. Not only this, but the feature gives the App a more truly international feeling for users outside of the United States.

Using the Statistics Option to Create Charts and Graphs with BudgetCare iPhone App

After you have inputted a variety of pieces of data, you will find that the BudgetCare iPhone App offers you other functions that are interesting and practical to use. With enough information put into the budget, you become capable of generating both pie charts and bar charts. You accomplish this by going to the main screen and selecting the category of Statistics.

On the statistics screen, you will next select the type of information that you wish to display, and then the format of graph. Data that you can choose from is found arranged by category. This makes it really easy to look at and, more importantly, to understand from where most of your actual spending comes. In this way, you will be able to focus on categories that you can cut back on to realize practical and manageable savings.

Using the Settings Category of BudgetCare iPhone App

The last category on the main screen is Settings. As with most App's that you find, this will allow you to set up the particulars of the program. In this fashion, you are able to personalize the App to suit your personal preferences.

Final Verdict on BudgetCare iPhone App

It is true that more complicated and involved personal finance management applications exist among the tens of thousands of iPhone apps available. BudgetCare does not aspire to be the most all inclusive and comprehensive personal financial management program. Instead, it is aiming for simplicity and ease of use. This is its primary attraction, and it lives up to its aspirations very well.

The biggest deficiencies that it has center on its lack of choice for either importing data or exporting it once you have finished inputting it. Still, at only $1.99 to purchase, BudgetCare provides you with an affordable and easy to understand, utilize, and follow budgeting tool for tracking your actual spending.

To use BudgetCare iPhone App, you will need the 2.1 upgrade in software. The App works not only with the iPhone, but also with the new iPod Touch.

What You Can Expect From a Financial Mentor or Teacher

Two words that are often used interchangeably are teacher and mentor. Even though you might have confused these words, or used them for each other, in the past, teacher and mentor are not the same thing.

In the following paragraphs, you will come to understand what the subtle differences are and why each of them has their purposes in helping you to build up your personal finances.

The Meaning and Role of A Teacher

Teachers are educators that assist students with learning. This is commonly done in a school, college, or university setting. The goal with a teacher is typically to go through a curriculum, applicable skill, or lesson plan. Teachers focus on things like thinking and learning skills.

Besides this, teachers make a conscious decision to go into teaching and to perform their teaching trade. They do this by verbally sharing and imparting knowledge to you as a student. Teachers are usually people with whom you have less of a personal connection too. Still, they are useful in helping you to gain a financial education.

The Meaning and Role of A Mentor

Mentors stand for something beyond the role and capacity of a teacher. They are trusted guides and counselors. A mentor will possess a greater, more personal connection with you as an individual than would a teacher. Mentors also make it their business to help you to achieve your goals in life. Mentoring is the act of actually supporting you as you strive to realize your life's ambitions.

How Mentoring and Teaching Differ From One Another
Even though these two labels are utilized fairly interchangeably, they are not the same thing at all. Mentors turn out to be different than teachers because they do much more than only relate information to you. They guide you in your endeavors, aspirations, and plans.

Mentors have usually accomplished what it is that you are attempting to do. Because of this, they know about the vision that you have and the dangers that lie along your path, since they have already been there to see the landscape in person. Mentors live their whole lives as examples, not only sharing and talking about them.

As an example, a medical school professor is undoubtedly a teacher. They help you to learn the things that you need in order to become a doctor. Yet a medical professor who took a particular interest in you and inspired you to actually become a doctor, more than simply through classroom instruction, is a mentor.

Teaching no doubt has its time and place. Without good instruction, you will not accomplish much in life. But mentoring is commonly more effective for you. This is because it proves to be more personal, applicable, and deeper in nature. Mentoring is so much more than simply discussing where you hope to get in life and your finances.

Mentoring is about the personal experience and relevant knowledge that will assist you in reaching that hoped for place with the least amount of difficulties, setbacks, and overall problems.

The Qualities that You Should Seek Out in A Financial Teacher or Mentor

When you are seeking a financial teacher, then you are looking for different qualities than you will be looking for in a financial mentor. A good financial teacher should be someone who is well schooled in all the basic and advanced concepts of personal finance and investing. They should have credentials to prove this.

Probably they will have a good amount of teaching experience in the subject of finance as well. With a financial teacher, you are probably talking about a professor of economics or business. They might also be a thoroughly experienced high school or community college teacher of finance or economics, as well.

Financial mentors are likely to be those individuals with real world practical experience rather than those with an extensive teaching background. Whether they have ever taught a class on personal finance, business, or investing or not, they have certainly been involved in these things in their own lives. A good financial mentor has likely established and run a successful business, excelled at investing, and done wonders with his or her own personal finances.

They have likely made their money and become wealthy already, or they are well on their way down that path. In other words, accomplished financial mentors have great successes and experience to boast of in the practical application of personal finance, business, and investing.

Besides this, a financial mentor should be someone who makes himself or herself available to guide, lead, and inspire you. It does not matter how wildly successful financial mentors have been if they are unwilling to share this positive experience, lessons learned, and mistakes made along the way with you individually. Financial mentors have to be available and willing to share with you.

Finally, financial mentors should be clear and understandable. They should know what they want to say and then impart their wisdom, experience, and knowledge in a manner that can not be misconstrued. Otherwise, you will only be attempting to understand the lessons that you are supposed to take away from their helpful sessions and time spent. Nothing is more frustrating than having the time and attention of a greatly successful financial mentor to whom you can not properly relate.

What You Can Expect From Financial Mentoring

When you become involved with a financial mentor, you should be able to expect a number of things. The first of these is useful and direct feedback that includes concrete examples and choices. They should lay them out in ways that you understand without difficulties. Every mentor will have his or her own style though, which you should keep in mind.

Financial mentors will also be honest with you. This is not always so comfortable, particularly if you are wrestling with doing the thing that you know you should do but do not want to do. Tough and honest criticism is something that is necessary for you to get out of your financial mentoring relationship. You should expect them to not only tell you what you are doing right, but also what you are doing wrong, and the reason that it is wrong.

Financial mentoring should also offer you a relationship that is clearly defined. You should not have any doubt as to how frequently you will get together. You should also be comfortable knowing when you can contact your mentor in between your get together meetings, and how many times is acceptable. Besides this, you should know if your mentor will give you oral or written feedback on your discussions and ideas.

You should also be able to expect that a mentor will assist you in deciding what to concentrate your discussions on when you sit down together. Even though the mentor is outside of your financial affairs, they need to have a good working knowledge of what you are doing and where you stand financially. By working together in the sessions, you will mutually decide what areas are best topics to discuss to help you improve your financial condition and reach your financial goals for your business and investments.

In all of these ways, financial mentors will help you to build up your wealth. They will coach you on your career and business path and goals. They will share with you ideas that have worked well for them with finance and investing. And they will make an excellent sounding board for you with any untested ideas that you have also.

The Disease That Infected The Entire American Economy

If you have paid attention to the media since the financial melt-down of 2007 and 2008 began, then you have become aware that many different articles, books, and movies have been both written and made concerning the debacle that led to the crash that spawned the now infamous Great Recession.

While many have attempted to sum up the causes and players in the past, none have done it so convincingly and effectively as has a movie that came out in the second half of 2010 called "Inside Job."

The following paragraphs consider the movie that in under two hours manages to explain how the whole sordid affair went down, and who is ultimately responsible for the enduring mess with which we have been left.

Goals of the Movie "Inside Job"

Charles Ferguson is the creative director behind this latest financial crisis movie. He set out to create a documentary that would lay out the naked truth of the events leading to the financial collapse in his at once comprehensive, interesting, and maddening film "Inside Job." Ferguson is able to do in under two hours what no one else has so far accomplished.

He lays out the historical basis for the near collapse of the financial industry back in September of 2008.

He then goes through the actions that occurred to allow it to happen in the first place. Not satisfied with only these accomplishments, Charles Ferguson through narrator Matt Damon goes on to assign blame to the different financial and corporate moguls who permitted it to happen, as well as to show you the people who stood the most to gain from the events. "Inside Job" does not leave you with a rosy scenario of the economic outlook under President Obama, since his administration is heavily infiltrated by the identical individuals who assisted all of these events in taking place.

Substance of the Movie "Inside Job"

Inside Job proves to be the most convincing presentation of an argument possible. It first throws down the thesis gauntlet. Next, it presents a greater body of evidence than you have imagined to convince you that this argument is actually the case.

Complicated ideas that surrounded and led to the crash are carefully and clearly explained so that you do not require an economics PhD to understand them. In fact, any individual who will sit down and carefully watch the movie will walk away with a clear understanding of what happened and who made it possible. This is done with a skill and style that does not take the subject and tone it down to too an overly simple level.

The Events that Made The Crisis Possible

"Inside Job"gets to its core point early on in the film. During the tenure of the much beloved President Ronald Reagan, the financially based rules and regulations that had ensured that no major financial crisis since the time of the Glass Steagall act had been enacted were simply repealed.

The idea in removing such legislation from the time of the Great Depression lay in efforts to allow businesses, and especially financial businesses, to have a free reign in their affairs and investments. The problem with these new found freedoms is that they permitted gradually greater and more frequent gross misconduct to occur in the financial sector.

The banking and investment industries, whose entire goal is to make greater and more profits, simply could not resist the opportunities to take massive advantage of the situation when the government removed all of the restrictive rules and limits. Ferguson demonstrates in his "Inside Job" again and again the ways that the financial services group expanded constantly after that point until it became a disease that infected the entire American economy.

In the process, they developed complicated, misunderstood, and extremely hazardous financial instruments that became the financial weapons of mass destruction which wrecked the world economy. Why would they choose to do this, you might ask? The answer is upsetting and disgusting. Their goals lay in increasing the bottom line without regard for the danger to the banks, their customers, and their investors, all so that the executives and managers could reap increasingly enormous bonuses each and every year.

The People Who Allowed this Inside Job To Happen

The truth is that not only one single party is to blame for the events that took place. The greedy financial barons gained this ability as a result of not only both President Reagan's and the two President Bush administrations, but also during the Wall Street dominated Treasury Department years when Bill Clinton sat at the helm of the ship of state.

It may surprise you to learn that the guilty parties have not changed much at all in the last three decades. Among the final points of the "Inside Job" film is that they are still running the economic show nowadays, even after the crisis has happened.

The guilty individuals, who have the blood of countless individuals destroyed by the crisis on their hands, are laid bare in the movie. The ones who did not let President Obama take on Wall Street with major reforms and regulations after the collapse of both Bear Stearns and Lehman Brothers in the late summer of 2008 are all still in the most important positions of economic power and authority. The film reveals that they are none other than Fed Chairman Ben Bernake, Treasury Secretary Timothy Geithner, and White House Economic Policy head Lawrence Summers.

"Inside Job" is not satisfied with these conclusions. It goes after the unethical conflicts of interest found in the halls of academia in influential economic schools at Columbia and Harvard. The professors here were mostly busy writing, talking, and teaching about market deregulation, free market capitalism, and so on.

All the while, these types were busy creating scholarly sounding works that claimed that credit default swaps, derivatives, and other dangerous investments posed no danger to the country and economy and should not be closely regulated.

The truth is out about all of these insidious investments now, but it is too late for the countless millions who have lost all of their investments and savings, not to mention their jobs and livelihoods. Perhaps the greatest punishment that many of the guilty parties will receive will prove to be the fact that they were asked uncomfortable questions by film director Ferguson that left them with no better responses than sputtered through half admissions of guilt and deflections of blame.

Verdict of the "Inside Job" Movie

Inside job leaves the ending of the economic crisis story open. It does not tell you that all of the problems have been resolved or corrected. This is because they have not. The same credit default swaps and derivatives that enabled the entire mess to take place are still being traded in huge and dangerous numbers, and mostly without regulation, yet again.

With the revelations of insatiable American greed and complicit government officials that it puts on display, "Inside Job" ought to be watched by all Americans. Every economics class in both high schools and colleges should watch the film to better understand the unbridled greedy nature of people in positions to profit when they are left to their own devices.

The critics have loved the movie; hopefully more people will see the film than those who already know the story. These are the only ways that we might hope to learn from the past mistakes made surrounding the economy and the great economic crisis of 2007-2010.

Martin Armstrong's Global Perspective on Economics

There are a number of good and useful websites containing helpful information that are currently available to you in your financial education. Some of them are remarkable for not costing you anything to access.

Among these is Armstrong Economics, the website of respected and well known economist Martin Armstrong. In the following paragraphs, you will learn all about the wealth of perspective that both he and his website offer you.

About Martin Armstrong

Martin Armstrong claims a number of impressive accomplishments to his credit. He founded Princeton Economics, personally overseeing the Princeton Economics Institute's computer system and economic model development. In his endeavors, he also formulated and developed the Economic Confidence Model that concentrates on the little known influence of the 8.6 year cycle of business on the global economy.

Martin Armstrong is furthermore the author of 'The Greatest Bull Market in History." This work proves to be a complete examination of the financial markets and global economy from 1900 forward. He has been voted Equity Magazine's honor of "America's Top Economist" in 1990.

The website owner is also an expert who has been sourced for high level testimony on a number of economic issues. He has provided such testimony to the Joint Economic Council of Congress and the Brady Commission, where he offered his insight on the Black Monday 1987 stock market crash that he had successfully forecast long before the crash actually happened.

Martin Armstrong is often quoted by various respected news sources, including the Wall Street Journal, the New York Times, and Bloomberg. He has made appearances on CNBC the money channel, along with different financial channels, in order to offer his view points on major economic issues that affect the world.

Martin spends his time studying business cycle history, analyzing different financial markets, and looking into monetary systems of the world and market crashes. He is presently researching on the world economy. His wealth of knowledge and perspective on numerous ranges of issues are shared with you for free on Armstrong Economics, his website.

About Armstrong Economics Website

Armstrong Economics the website brands itself as Martin Armstrong's global perspective on economics. His ArmstrongEconomics.com website provides a wide ranging body of research from this famed around the world economist and developer of the Economic Confidence Model.

The resource not only provides his insights on issues in the world economy, but it also keeps you and the other viewers up to date with Martin Armstrong's individual accomplishments in business, as well as his ongoing legal battles that he has struggled through against the United States' government throughout the first ten years of the new century.

Format of Armstrong Economics

The most important section of the Armstrong Economics site for regular readers is the Writings section of the website. Here, posted chronologically, you will find from one to five lengthy articles per month stretching from the present month all the way back to the last two years. These articles are wide ranging, but most of them include diagrams and charts, many of them drawn by the hand of Martin Armstrong himself.

Themes of Armstrong Economics

Martin's themes are both topical and timely for events that are taking place in the world economy today. His most recent writing posts deal with "The Rising Frustration with the Debt Crisis" that is enveloping various developed countries around the world, "The Fractal Nature of Markets" pertaining to how mathematics relate to and provide insight on economics, and "So You Thought Stocks Only Go Up In Boom Times" that discusses the various reasons that stocks are gaining in value even though the world economy is still firmly in the grips of the next phase of the financial crisis.

Among the many things that Martin Armstrong is dealing with and concerned about these days relates to the spreading contagion of collapsing banks and the sovereign debt crisis around the world.

He warns you that the Irish banks' sickness will spread throughout Europe and the United States, that they have not and will not be contained.

Like in America, Irish banks made bad loans and over leveraged themselves in the process. This has led to similar problems with their banking sector and overall economy as you have seen at home in the U.S. As the bad debt and the banks implode, Armstrong says that you see the real estate values depressed, which cuts down on economic growth.

This resulting fall in economic growth causes consumers to cut back on their spending and try to hold on to their dwindling savings. This of course bites into the Irish government's eventual tax revenues. Now they are being forced to get bailouts and massively cut back on government spending and programs, including critical pensions and social services. The tragedy of it all, Armstrong admits, is watching the various factors feed into each other and multiply the negative effect.

The biggest mistake that Armstrong sees being made in all of these banking problems is that the governments are misunderstanding and incorrectly diagnosing the root problems. He says they see it as simply a giant liquidity crisis. In reality it is far more than this. The resulting and serious problem, according to Armstrong, is that pouring even trillions of dollars into these banks will not fix, or even address, the significant issues.

Armstrong says something very interesting in these pieces on the various sovereign debt crises and over leveraged and failing banks throughout the developed world.

Hugely different ways of doing things are necessary in order to stop these vicious cycles of pumped up bubbles that blow up in the poor defenseless citizens' faces.

He believes that both Great Britain and Ireland will be the first to make these necessary reforms. On top of this, Martin Armstrong claims that he has the answers to save these and other countries from the vicious cycles that they are trapped within now. He does not give out the details of these specific solutions, but he does say that he will happily come to these two countries' aid when they are serious about making the necessary changes to the ways of doing things economically.

Armstrong is pretty negative on how long he believes that the depression will last in real estate in not only Ireland but also in the United States and other developed countries. He believes that the real estate markets died an ignoble death in 2007 and that you have not seen the last of it by far.

In fact, Armstrong predicts that real estate will not fully come back for a long twenty-six years. He illustrates his point on housing by directing your attention to the Nasdaq stock market bubble encouraged by the many dot coms. These imploded back in the year 2000, and the Nasdaq stock market values have still not recovered fully ten years later.

Armstrong tells you that the point is that the old model for both banking and developed economies is dead and has to be buried, the sooner the better. Until a new economic model is created from the ground up, things simply will not get better, he opines on his Armstrong Economics site.

Will Peak Oil Collapse the Financial System of the World?

You may have noticed that since the Financial Crisis and Great Recession began, people are producing more and more books, articles, and movies about a dramatic decline in our standard of living and future economic prospects.

While some experts call the events surrounding the recent economic crisis a paradigm shift, you can not yet be sure that they will bring down the world economic system. One film that argues that things are certainly going to get that much worse in the near future is called "Collapse."

The Premise of "Collapse"

You prefer to hear good news. Most all Americans are optimistic people who sincerely believe that new Presidents will be able fix the problems in the country and the world. You hope that we will replace polluting oil and carbon dioxide emissions with clean energy and fix the shattered economy with new ideas and better policies.

Even the American media and talking heads shun pragmatism and choose to hope that we will see the best outcome. This begs the question, has anyone made preparations for the worst case scenario?

The movie "Collapse" looks seriously and grimly at the worst possible outcome. It puts up a staggering amount of facts and figures to show you in interview format that things are not simply going to improve. What will probably upset you the most about it is that the movie and its presentation may convince you.

The Character In "Collapse"

"Collapse" is done in an interview format. The real life character Michael Ruppert turns out to be an unusual sort of American. The man possesses a life story that sounds very much like a thriller. Ruppert's parents are intelligence agents. He makes the claim that the CIA once came to him and asked him to run drugs on their behalf. Naturally, he refused them. Ruppert says that the government has been after him for this ever since.

Admittedly, Michael Ruppert sounds like a crazy nut case with this introduction, but the truth is that he is actually very intelligent, informed, and sane. Ruppert is a one time police officer in Los Angeles who became an independent reporter and writer.

He gained some credibility by publishing his newsletter "From the Wilderness" that forecast today's financial crisis back in 2005 when the majority of Washington politicians and economists and Wall Street investors said that nothing is wrong. Besides this, he also blew the whistle on the CIA being involved in drug trafficking within the United States, a claim that turns out to have some truth to it.

The Director of "Collapse"

"Collapse" is directed by Chris Smith, an experienced film maker who lists "American Movie" and "American Job" among his credits. In this movie, Director Smith draws on the lively interview film making style of Errol Morris. Morris perfected the concept of making movies that are interviews with persons interspersed with footage, newsreels, and industrial films.

This film represents a real break from the documentaries that Chris Smith has made before. "Collapse" proves to be a deep study of main character Michael Ruppert's apocalyptic mind, the man who sincerely and deeply holds that modern capitalist society is nearing a complete collapse.

Main Argument of the Movie "Collapse"

The film "Collapse" picks up with Michael Ruppert's true life story. He has been warning the world not just for years, but for decades about the doom of the capitalist industrialized world that lies just around the corner. No one has listened to him in the past. He wrote a book that sells only a handful of copies. His critics call him a fringe lunatic. Even the movie has not been watched by many people in the country. Yet the truth is that some very convincing facts underlie Michael Ruppert's assertions.

His biggest claim rests on the idea that the world's oil reserves have more or less run out. Without oil to support the modern industrial world, the whole notion of unending growth falls apart. This idea of peak oil is not original to Ruppert, since it has been argued and embraced by respected figures in the oil and gas business for three decades now.

Hubert first made the claim that the world had exhausted the easiest to extract half of oil from the earth, and that there would always be less of it found and brought up to use in the future. The dire facts behind Hubert's peak oil are that oil production will continue to decline. This will cause the prices of gasoline, pesticides, plastics, and all oil related products to rise to impossible to afford levels.

Because of this peak oil point that you saw reached around 2005, Ruppert predicted then that the financial system of the world would collapse. He argues that the world economy will never really recover either. These are grim claims to be sure, but they are backed up throughout the film by impossible to refute facts and figures. Almost every statement that the chain smoking Michael Ruppert says has statistics to support it.

His tale is backed up by events in American history too. One of these that is very convincing are the details he provides about former American Presidents. All Presidents from Jimmy Carter to President George W. Bush with Dick Cheney have made serious efforts to secure more energy sources.

President Carter launched initiatives to encourage American to develop and deploy solar power energy. Vice President Cheney headed up a task force to locate additional oil reserves to keep America's oil supplies flowing. His efforts possibly helped to lead us to Iraq.

Other Arguments of the Movie "Collapse"

Michael Ruppert is not simply discussing the peak oil theory causing the collapse of the modern world. As the movie moves along, he gets into discussions on global food production, alternative energy possibilities, financial chaos, government scandals, and Americans' emotional response to it all.

All of these other elements will have a hand in the collapse, according to Ruppert. Foods that companies engineer genetically, currencies that do not have gold backing, and peak oil will all conspire together to bring down the modern world.

This is not all simply information of the gloom and doom variety being fired at you. It is an intelligent and intriguing movie where Michael Ruppert goes clearly through the issues at hand and tells you the hard facts and their accompanying truth like no one else will. However right he will prove to be, you can say for sure that some kind of shift in the world economy will happen. Science teaches us that nothing can grow forever.

In the human future that comes, everything will operate on a local scale, Ruppert says. He is right to call many forms of alternative energy, such as ethanol, impractical. Still, he can not say with certainty what other more efficient alternatives to energy scientists will devise.

Director Chris Smith acknowledges this after Ruppert is off camera. The possibilities created by human ingenuity are left out by Ruppert, who does not address them. Instead, Ruppert prefers to look at the whole future of the world through the lens of technologies and policies that have failed you.

Whether you deny Michael Ruppert's claims or not, you can not be unmoved by how seriously he takes them. When you see him convincingly burst into tears talking about how important community will become, or ask for a break because he is overwhelmed by it all, you can not argue that the man is sincere and fully convinced.

WEALTH

"Pursuing Prosperity with Financial Education"

Do We Really Need Money If There Is Abundant Wealth?

Can you imagine a world where wealth was so abundant and widespread that money was no longer necessary for society to function?

If you are like many people living in America today, then you are probably scratching your head at the mere suggestion of such a concept.

A movement does exist to move away from the use of money to an economy based on resources, and it is interesting to be aware of and understand. It is called a resource based economy.

Background to the Resource Based Economy Conception
Jacque Fresco is the man who founded an outfit called the Venus Project. With this organization, he promotes a vision of the future that gets away from profit based economics to one of resource based economics. He and his supporters believe that you can simply improve society by abandoning capitalism and embracing instead this resource based economy.

A resource based economy in their view is one that is built around the design and creation of sustainable cities, effective management of natural resources, the efficient utilization of energy, and highly advanced automation of technology.

They concentrate on a number of Utopian sounding benefits that Fresco and the Venus Project believe would accrue to society as a result of this radical transformation in economics as you know it.

Downsides to the Role of Money and Profit Motive

Fresco and the Venus Project point to the present day world, which is underpinned by capitalism, as the motivating factor for a major change. They make interesting points regarding the picture of the world today under its present system.

Crime, poverty, war, and corruption all come from the scarcity of resources that the world's current economic system based on profits only encourages and serves to reinforce. This is true on both an individual, national, and regional world level.

They also suggest that the drive for profits furthermore holds back the advance of technology that benefits society as a whole. Simply put, if a technology is not economically viable in a relatively short span of time, then no company in their right mind would pursue it under the current economic system in place in the world.

Technologies that benefit people as a whole or that encourage the efficient use of resources but that require substantial investment upfront and long times to recuperate costs are far too often sacrificed in favor of far shorter term gains.

Benefits of Assigning the Resources to the People

This resource based economics movement believes that technology would progress in a far more beneficial way for society and humanity as a whole, if it were carried out in an environment that did not consider how profitable it was in the short run. It argues that more resources would subsequently become available to a greater number of people as a result. This would happen as such technologies would lead to the creation of vastly more abundant materials and end use products.

The results of such a newly discovered abundance of physical resource wealth would have several positive effects. Humanity's proclivity towards greed, corruption, and a rampant form of individualism would be significantly reduced. Rather than these vices, you would see more acts of individuals helping each other out.

As a result of the fair distribution of such abundant resources for all people everywhere, people could lead healthier, longer, and more satisfying lives in peace and relative harmony. Competition between individuals add different groups of peoples would be greatly lessened as a direct result.

Fresco and his supporters offer several other thoughts on a world without money. They propose that by doing away with the current form of monetary systems in the world and all that they entail, significant improvements could be made. Competition and unfair labor practices harm society, they argue.

These limitations that are imposed keep people from achieving their ultimate potentials, as people all around the world are engaged in a desperate and often competitive struggle to survive, many times at another person's expense.

Such a resource based economy and economics would instead be geared to benefit as many people as possible to a maximum potential, instead of only benefiting the five percent of the world's population that presently has all of the money and most of the resources of the world for their personal domain.

How Such a Radical Transformation Could Come About

The Venus Project and those who suggest that this is possible do not envision a violent overthrow of the political and economic system, as with communism or Marxism. Rather they believe that the present economic situation that has resulted in the U.S. and around the world will lead people naturally to this conclusion on their own.

They feel that the Great Recession with its hallmarks of high unemployment and destruction of investment wealth will cause individuals to choose to abandon the free market system of capitalism as they gradually lose confidence in the monetary system and establishment. In time, they see a ground swell of grass roots support for the elimination of the world's present day economy based on money to one that they consistently refer to as an economy based on resources.

What A World Without Money Would Look Like

There are two examples to consider of how a world without money might look. One is historical and the other is based in popular science fiction. The historical example is demonstrated by hunter and gatherer societies. It was showcased in the 1980's film entitled, "The God's Must Be Crazy."

If you remember this film about a simple African hunter and gather society, everyone in the tribe helped and looked after one another because there was no money to divide them and place them in competition against one another. Resources were shared as they were obtained from the hunting and gathering.

The harmonious system only broke down with the untimely arrival of a shiny glass Coca Cola bottle that was thrown out of a plane flying overhead. Since there was only one of these, and everyone desired it, it created a form of money and intense competition. Soon, everyone in the tribe was fighting to have this form of money. Eliminating this struggle and competition, to return back to a time when one person shared with and helped out his neighbor, is much of what a world without money would look.

Another, more appealing example of how a world without money would look can be seen in the newer series of Star Treks that began with Star Trek: The Next Generation. Whether you are a Star Trek fan and watcher or not, you can admire the idea that society had progressed to the point that replicators had been invented to create literally anything needed practically out of thin air. This was accomplished simply by telling the computer what you needed or wanted. Naturally, energy was used in the process.

Yet technology had advanced to the state of creating a vast abundance of resources so that the struggle for them between people ceased to exist. As a result of this, people pursued their passions for work, in an effort to better the lives of the whole of mankind.

While not a perfect world, this universe without money, salaries, and exclusive possessions has fired the imagination of legions of people since you first saw it begin its multi-decade run phenomenon on television and in the movie theaters.

Four Expenses That Keep You From Becoming Wealthy

There are many different expenses in the world that conspire to keep you from becoming wealthy. Finding a way to diminish their impact on your finances and investments is necessary if you are to escape from their draining effects.

Among the various elements that you will find consistently hold you back from achieving wealth are taxes paid to the government, debt owed to banks, the rising costs of inflation, and expenses associated with retirement accounts.

The Negative Effects of Taxes to the Government

There is likely no single factor that has such a drastic impact on your wealth, income, and assets as do the taxes that you have to pay the various branches of government. Between income tax, sales tax, property taxes, and inheritance taxes, experts estimate that more than fifty percent of your money goes to taxes.

This is before you ever realize any of it. Avoiding taxes completely is impossible, as Benjamin Franklin some wisely reminded you with his famous line about two things being certain in this life, both death and taxes.

Still, there are things that you can do to minimize the impacts of taxes on your income and assets. If your business or job situation permits, you can move to one of the states that does not have state income taxes as a starter. The biggest of the more than two hundred different taxes levied on you as an American by far is Federal income tax.

This can easily consume a good thirty percent of your annual income if you do not take steps to reduce your tax liability.

Finding the greatest number of deductions for your income can be accomplished by working with a good tax accountant. There are many of these professionals available to help you to reduce your income tax burden. Their costs are well worth the amount in the tax bill that they can save you, if you let them.

The Negative Effects of Debt to Banks

Debts to banks include loans and credit card bills. These two expenses can be ruinous for any person's income and ability to save and invest. Interest rates on credit cards commonly run from fifteen to twenty-five percent in the wake of the financial crisis and credit crunch of the Great Recession.

If you are having to service personal debts at such exorbitant interest rates, you are never going to become wealthy. This is why it is so very important to understand how much of your money is going ever month to service interest on debts. It is similarly important to make a plan to escape from the prison of these debts.

Paying off debts takes discipline and will power. To do it, you have to find a way to reduce your monthly expenses to the point that you have extra money to put towards paying down the smallest balance first. All extra money should be applied to this single balance. Once the first balance is paid down, then you can use that bill's monthly payment amount with the extra money each month to pay down the next smallest balance.

This creates a snowball effect over time that allows each bill to be paid down at a significantly faster rate than the one before it. Eventually like this, you will have paid off your obligations and escaped from the debt trap.

In the meantime, anything that you can do to reduce the higher interest rates in favor of lower ones is a good idea. Balance transfers that permit you to lock in lower rates are one way of achieving this. Going through debt consolidation is another way. The crippling effects of paying usurious interest rates to banks on personal debts must be overcome before you can achieve real wealth.

The Negative Effects of Inflation

Inflation is yet another insidious factor that conspires to keep you from ever becoming wealthy. Inflation involves constantly rising prices on essential items like energy, food, and medical costs. The government figures in the CPI show this to be an average of two to three percent per year over a given amount of time.

Over ten years, this reduces your purchasing power and real wealth by as much as twenty to thirty percent. You as an individual can not avoid these higher costs, which happen as a result of government debt and money creation policies.

There is something that you can do to reduce the net impact on you and your income and investments though. This is in putting a percentage of your assets into vehicles that appreciate with inflation. Precious metals are the best example of assets that go up at the same and even a higher rate than does inflation over time.

By putting five to ten percent of your investment dollars into gold or silver, you will at least reduce the net effect of that great thief inflation. The rising value of your gold and silver assets will help to offset your currency's lost purchasing power.

The Negative Effects of Retirement Account Expenses

You may be like many Americans who use the services of an investment bank to manage your retirement accounts and their investments. While there is nothing inherently wrong with having a Morgan Stanley, John Hancock, or Wachovia Securities handle this on your behalf, there are considerable expenses and fees associated with their services.

Money managers of whatever type they may be skim a few percentage points of the account's entire value off the top to cover their expenses every year. A portfolio that is only gaining five to eight percent per year on average can hardly afford to pay even one to two percent each year in fees. In years where the value of the account even drops, this is more crippling.

There is a way around this utilization of money managers with your IRA's and 401k's that you can take advantage of with your investment accounts. This is known as a self directed IRA. Such a self-directed IRA has you making your own decisions on investments for the retirement plan.

A custodian holds the assets on your behalf and executes your orders for buying and selling of investments. They will also file all necessary updates with the IRS and issue the client statements, along with handling administrative duties for you the account owner.

These self-directed IRA accounts have advantages besides typically coming with lower fees than traditionally managed ones. They also permit investors to engage in a far wider range of investment types than traditional IRA's permit. Not only can stocks, mutual funds, and bonds be purchased, but a wide variety of other assets are allowed to be acquired in these accounts. These include precious metals, real estate, foreign stocks, franchises, mortgages, private equity, partnerships, tax liens, and even foreign real estate.

Unfortunately, no one can completely escape from the effects of government taxes and inflation. These harmful impacts can be lessened through careful and proper planning and taking proactive steps. Debts and interest to banks and overly high fees charged by investment banks can be avoided through making serious efforts.

By eliminating the negative effects of these four specters where possible, and reducing them where they can not be totally done away with, you will remove many of the impediments that keep you from becoming wealthy over time.

How to Build Your Wealth With These Four Asset Classes

If you are like many people, you have looked around for ways to build up your wealth and been frustrated by the overwhelming numbers of choices that you have found.

There are so many different places that you can invest your money. Most of them offer the competing claim of being the best or safest return available to you.

In reality, there are four asset classes that you should not miss out on when you are looking for the best ways to build your wealth. These include owning a business, real estate, certain paper assets, and commodities.

Building Your Wealth by Owning A Business

Owning a business is a terrific way to build up residual income. When you start a business, it will require a great amount of work in the initial stage. There are some businesses that you will probably want to avoid, since they will only become masters to which you are a slave.

Restaurants and hotels are examples of these. They only create residual income for you if you work at them almost all of the time until you get them to a point that you can look for a good manager to run them while you are away.

Smarter business models are online businesses, such as e-commerce sites. Once you get this kind of business up and running, it can generate income for you on an ongoing basis, without you having to micromanage it.

Once again, some significant time and money investments are involved in setting up this kind of business. You will have to first get the website professionally designed and created, and then have the site indexed and search engine optimized with the search engine majors like Google, Yahoo, and Bing.

After you build up a steady stream of visitors that start to become customers who buy your products or informational services, you will find that a substantial income stream can be built up that does not require huge amounts of work to manage and maintain. Remember that the overwhelming majority of wealthy people in the world today did not get rich working for someone else, but through starting their own successful businesses. Residual income from such businesses is one of their best known secrets.

Building Your Wealth by Owning Real Estate

A second effective way to build up your wealth is through owning real estate. Real Estate offers you three advantages that few other investments can equal. On the one hand, you can acquire it with the intention of holding on to it for capital appreciation. Assuming that you buy a property at a reasonable price, you can count on it rising in value over time. This is because historically real estate has always increased in value over the long term.

Real Estate also offers you the ability to leverage your investment in a way that few other asset classes do. How many other forms of investments can you name that you are able to become an owner of for only ten to twenty percent of the investment price put down? Real estate provides you with an effective way to achieve between ten to one and twenty to one leverage on your investment dollars. Because of this, capital gain appreciation can be a substantial percentage return on your original investment.

Think of it like this, if you purchase a property for $100,000 using only $10,000 of your own money and $90,000 of a bank's money, then you achieve a ten to one leverage. If the property appreciates $10,000 in value, then when you sell it and repay the bank, you will have made a one hundred percent return on your original $10,000 investment. This major return that helps you to build up wealth at an accelerated pace is all a result of leverage.

Real Estate can also provide you with residual income while you wait for capital appreciation. Houses, townhouses, or condominiums can all be rented out to bring in extra income. If you can find a stable tenant who will stay with the property long term, then you can more than cover your mortgage payments and maintenance costs, and perhaps even have a few hundred extra dollars a month coming in on top of this. Many wealthy people have achieved their wealth through smart, strategic investments in real estate and rental properties.

Building Your Wealth by Owning Paper Assets

Paper assets can include a wide variety of different investments, such as stocks, bonds, mutual funds, treasury bills, and certificates of deposit.

They all have the commonality of being investments represented by pieces of paper. Some of these are better means of building wealth than are others.

By buying stocks in really good companies with proven track records and strong balance sheets, you gain the possibility for both capital gains and residual income through cash flow. While you are waiting for the long and short term growth of the company to be realized in higher stock prices, you can also benefit from dividends that solid, proven companies pay out.

Dividends are profits from publicly traded companies that are returned to the stock holders who are invested in the company. In recent years, you have seen dividends become more popular and significant. Returns of even five percent from major outfits like IBM, Microsoft, Coca Cola, and Wal-Mart are no longer uncommon.

Getting these residual income checks on a quarterly basis is an effective way to increase wealth while you wait for the long term trend of rising stock prices to increase the value of your paper asset investment. Historically, the stock market as a whole has increased in value at a rate of eight percent plus over the medium to long term. When you couple these returns with a nice dividend, the prospects for building wealth with paper assets become significant.

Building Your Wealth by Owning Commodities

The wealthy mostly have one thing in common, which is that they protect their wealth from unexpected disasters like runaway government spending, terrorism, and rampant inflation. All of these objectives can be accomplished by owning commodities, in particular precious metals.

The long term trend is for precious metals like gold, platinum, and silver to increase in value over time. More than simply keeping pace with inflation, gold often outperforms returns in other investment classes, especially given time. In the last ten years as an example, gold has been involved in a major bull market. It has increased in value by more than five hundred percent while equities were basically flat or only marginally improved over the same time frame.

Precious metals are easily bought and sold. You can choose to own physical bars and coins that you buy from area coin shops or large established dealers with stores over the Internet. You can also buy them in stock form as Exchange Traded Funds like GLD. There is even a depository company with a site called GoldMoney.com that allows investors to put as much of their wealth into gold as they would like. It can then be used to make purchases for things over the Internet, much like PayPal currency.

Building your wealth through owning commodities makes good sense, in particular as a hedge to your paper investments and real estate holdings.

Why High Energy Prices Are Destroying the Nations Wealth

You have been hearing about the importance of being energy independent for many years now. It is no exaggeration to say that the United States is massively dependent on foreign oil imports to run its economy, since over nine point nine million barrels of oil are imported per day, or over three billion, six hundred and ten million barrels of oil per year.

The truth is that high energy prices paid to other countries are destroying the wealth of the nation, and have to be addressed.

The Magnitude of the Problem

It is no exaggeration to say that America is completely addicted to foreign oil. This addiction hangs over our national security and economy. It has a grip on every portion of your daily life, tying our hands nationally. The addiction to oil has only grown worse since the 1970's. In 1970, the U.S. only imported around twenty-four percent of its oil needs. Today, this amount has increased to sixty-five percent and it is only growing with time.

The Importance of Being Energy Independent

It is critical that the United States be energy independent from a security stand point. Of the massive oil and gas imports going on every day, just under half of that amount comes from OPEC countries, many of whom are either opposed to the interests of the United States or actively working against us in the world, such as Venezuela and Russia.

Others OPEC members support terrorists with money that we send them, such as Saudi Arabia. Even the ones who are friendly to us, like Canada, Mexico, Nigeria, and Colombia, take your money away in exchange for the energy that the country simply can not do without. These countries that are our allies are harming our financial security when they drain off a huge part of the national resources for oil and natural gas.

We simply can not send away the vast billions of dollars to people whose intentions towards us are questionable. When the country relies on its critical energy sources from foreign supplies to the tune of two-third of its oil consumption, it stands in an uncertain position in a dangerous world that can not be predicted.

The Money Factor of Energy Imports

The issue of energy independence is not simply one that concerns placing the country's security in the hands of possibly unstable and unfriendly foreign countries. It has everything to do with a draining transfer of wealth that is underway with every increasing barrel of oil that the country imports.

In just the year 2008, the U.S. spent $475 billion on importing for-
eign oil. This is an enormous amount of money taken out of the
country and its economy to send away to foreign countries. So long
as you see this happen, oil imports will drain away the life blood of
the economy until the bleeding is finally stopped.

From 2009 to 2018, over a ten year period, the United States oil
imports will cost a staggering $10 trillion dollars, all sent away to
foreign countries. Legendary oil man T. Boone Pickens has called
this the upcoming largest transfer of wealth in all of human history.

This size of the problem and dollar amount only gets worse as the
price of oil increases. As the oil prices rise, the nation's wealth
falls, since you are witnessing the country sending away so many
trillions of dollars at current oil prices. Every extra dollar America
sends away is one that could be invested in the country's own desperately needing improvement ares of infrastructure or education.

Creating Wealth by Investing in Alternative Energy Sources that Cost Less than Oil

Shifting away from costly foreign oil imports is not only possible,
it has already been done by several countries around the world.
Both Japan and Brazil have made this happen with concerted national efforts. In so doing, they have created wealth for themselves
as well as significant numbers of jobs in new industries of alternative energy sources.

How did Japan and Brazil do this, and can the United States accomplish it as well?

Japan made a heroic effort to design and produce millions of fuel efficient cars. Like this, they slowed down their oil consumption substantially and also created numerous high paying jobs in the process. Brazil had a serious problem of its own as it was importing eighty percent of all crude oil it required. Because they invested heavily in the technology of biofuels, they found that they could replace their cars' and trucks' power sources of gasoline with a fuel made from sugar.

The new cars are being produced at home, as is the fuel that is grown entirely in Brazil. This leads to more jobs kept at home in two new industries and far less money sent away to foreign countries for oil.

The U.S. similarly has the ability to develop alternative energy sources that cost less than oil. The nation's natural gas and wind reserves are vast. By using natural gas to power trucks and other heavy vehicles, the oil imports could be cut down substantially. Natural gas can also help to power electricity generation plants. Wind is also another possible answer for the national energy dilemma.

Windmills are starting to be built to take advantage of this, but not yet on the scale that will make a huge difference. Using wind energy, as much as twenty-two percent of the electricity for the national grid can be created.

Building wind mills in conjunction with solar panels would lead to literally millions of new jobs in these high technology industries.

Commercial buildings and home owners can be given incentives to employ other energy saving options too. Along with the wind generation, a new electrical transmission grid could be built for the twenty-first century. All of these new industries would lead to more jobs and wealth kept at home. The newly generated electricity could find its way to electric powered cars.

Electric powered cars are a technology that has existed for more than thirty years. The auto manufacturers, in concert with the major oil producers like Exxon-Mobil, BP, Shell, and Chevron-Texaco, conspired to kill the concept back in the nineteen eighties. The design for the first electric car found itself bought and buried. The lost opportunity from this American created invention so many years ago can not be over-exaggerated.

No Significant Improvement on Fuel Efficiency

Instead, the car companies continued to manufacture cars without serious efforts at significantly improving fuel efficiency. The result today is that you see far too many American cars that still do not boast greater fuel efficiency, as is evident in Japan's domestic car manufacturing industry.

The first domestically manufactured electric car is called the Volt. It is build by General Motors, and it is just rolling into production for the next year.

Already, the critics are saying that the new Volt will be a failure before it is even launched. This is because its operating efficiency is not significant enough to compete with foreign built electric cars. On top of this, the Volt will be too expensive to be competitive with its foreign manufactured rivals. It is an effort that proves to be too little and too late.

The United States can do better than this. For the sake of your country's future, it has too.

Don't Mistake Your Life Insurance With Building Wealth

Life insurance turns out to actually be a contract that you make with an insurance company. In this contract, the insuring company consents to paying your beneficiaries a pre set amount of money if you die or potentially if you either become terminally or critically ill.

In exchange for this, you the policy holder pay pre arranged amounts of money, usually in routine monthly payments, although this can also be done in one or more lump sum amounts.

Although you will hear many times that life insurance can be used to build up wealth, this is generally not the case.

The Two Types of Life Insurance

There are two types of life insurance that are available to you when you are looking after your financial needs. One is term life insurance that you simply pay premiums on in exchange for life insurance coverage.

The other is cash value life insurance that accrues some value in the policy over time. Although a cash value life insurance policy does offer some recompense for premiums invested, its cost is significantly higher than simply term insurance.

In the subsequent paragraphs, the reasons for why you should not confuse cash value life insurance with truly building up wealth are explained.

Myth Versus Reality of Cash Value Life Insurance Products

Cash value life insurance is commonly touted as a wonderful product that not only provides protection against the financial problems associated with your untimely demise, but also offers you some tangible value that grows over time.

Because of this second benefit, more than seventy percent of all of the life insurance policies that are sold to people today prove to be cash value life insurance policies. Although you are always told by life insurance agents that insurance policies that offer the combination of such insurance and savings together in one vehicle are the most ideal ways to go, the truth is starkly different.

The myth that such cash value life insurance will actually aid you in retiring wealthy is false.

In fact, these cash value life insurance policies turn out to be among the worst available financial products on the market. The reason for this is that life insurance policy returns are predictably terrible. Sure, your insurance sales representative will bedazzle you with amazing sounding projections of value. In reality, the policies never actually perform anywhere near the levels at which they are projected.

Cash Value Insurance Policies Example

Look at the example of a thirty year old male to better understand why these cash value insurance policies are pretty horrible investments. If this man actually has the ability to spend one hundred dollars every month on life insurance premiums, then he will discover that he is capable of buying around $125,000 in life insurance from the biggest five cash value insurance companies, with which to protect his family.

The companies are all suggesting that he buy a life insurance policy that will similarly accrue value towards retirement. This is accomplished by cash value policies. Yet, if your man in this example instead buys a twenty year length of term life insurance with the same $125,000 of coverage, then he will pay only seven dollars premium every month instead of the hundred dollars monthly premium of the cash value policy.

You are probably thinking that by going with this $100 premium per month, the remaining $93 going out of his pocket each month will be applying towards savings for retirement. This is not actually the case, since expenses are involved on the part of the insurance company.

The Expenses Associated with Cash Value Life Insurance Policies
It will shock you to learn that for the first three years of insurance premiums, the entire extra $93 each month vanishes into the black holes of expenses and commissions. This is a full 36 different payments, representing $3,350 of the savings for retirement.

After this period of time has elapsed, the savings and returns finally get started. The return on the savings will then vary depending on which type of cash value life insurance is elected. Whole life averages about 2.6% a year.

Universal life pays around 4.2% a year, and the latest variation on cash value life insurance, called variable life, averages at a better 7.4% per year. Variable life achieves these superior returns by investing in mutual funds.

The identical mutual funds when invested in aside from this policy pay an annual average of twelve percent, per Fortune magazine and Kiplinger's Personal Finance. Even the returns that these policies provide prove to be significantly less than they would be adopted independently of these insurance policies.

The Real Disadvantage to Cash Value Life Insurance Policies

These meager returns and high costs associated with opening cash value life insurance policies are not the only downsides to them, although they are bad enough for anyone attempting to build up wealth.

They have another provision that you have probably missed when you were listening to a presentation of such products. This is the death benefit. In both universal life and whole life versions of the cash life insurance policies, the only thing that your heirs receive upon your demise is the policy's actual face value, that in this particular case amounted to $125,000.

The extra $93 per month in savings that your man cheerfully accrued with all of those premium monthly payments simply vanishes into the pocket of the insurance company. So, if you paid into this kind of policy for thirty years with $93 per month supposedly going to the retirement pool, then you would have built up at least $33,500 in retirement savings.

Your heirs would not see a single penny of this money at your death.

It will make you laugh to think that you would be better off financially to simply purchase the $7 term life insurance policy and sock the difference of $93 per month into a mayo jar. When three years had passed, you would have the $3,000 plus that would have disappeared into commissions and fees of the cash value life insurance policy.

And if you paid into it the full thirty years discussed above, this would be $33,500 without any investment gains returns. When you passed away, you would have something besides only the life insurance policy face value to leave to your family.

Building up Wealth with the $93 per Month

Instead of enriching the insurance company, you should take this extra $93 per month and invest it wisely and well. Over a life time span of thirty years of achieving good returns on it even commiserate with the eight percent per year stock market average return, you would have at least $67,000 built up. This could either go towards your retirement costs or if you died, instead to your heirs, along with the $125,000 face value of the term life insurance policy that you paid only $7 per month for all those years.

The thing to take away with you from this lesson is that you should not purchase cash value life insurance under any circumstances. This does not build up wealth for you at any meaningful level. You are always better off to instead buy term life insurance at the far lower rates and simply invest the remaining savings every month.

The Tax Scheme Is A Secret Weapon of Wealth Creation

You may wonder how the rich seemingly get richer and richer all the time while the working people are still struggling to get and stay ahead.

This is because the tax scheme in the United States favors business owners and investors. It allows them to keep a far greater percentage of the money that they earn than the working class are allowed to retain.

The Change in the Tax Code that Advantaged the Rich

There is a reason for this present tax advantage that the rich benefit from that dates back to World War II. In 1943, Congress changed the tax code so that those who worked to earn their money lost the majority of their tax breaks that they possessed. Up to this point, workers paid their taxes at the end of the year. Once this tax code change went through, you saw the main advantages in the tax system default to those who invested and employed others.

In particular, the best tax breaks go to those who put their money into real estate, oil, and gas, as well as to the owners of businesses. The reasoning behind this varies for each type of investment. With the self employed, these business owners create jobs. These jobs provide employees with salaries on which the highest taxes are then assessed.

The logic with oil and gas investments boils down to the fact that since the economy requires huge amounts of oil and gas, any person who is involved in gas and oil exploration receives huge tax breaks. Investors who put their money into real estate are providing housing for the workers that the government tax system desperately needs. For this they are rewarded with significant tax breaks, since they save the government from having to offer housing to the workers.

The Myth About 401K Tax Advantages

You may be confused concerning these tax advantages that are supposed to only benefit the rich. Likely you are wondering why 401K's have not been mentioned as a significant tax benefit for the working class. This is because 401K's are not truly tax advantaged. Employees these days may work hard and save to their 401K's, but they are still earning less with this savings vehicle than the rich do with their investments.

This is because the IRS taxes the pay of workers at the highest rates available. This may sound far fetched, but when you compare workers' tax rates to those of business owners and investors, it really is true. While savings invested into 401K's and the income that they generate are tax deferred, they are still taxed when they are withdrawn as ordinarily earned income. This means that they suffer from the highest tax rates available, though the day of reckoning is delayed until retirement time.

Examples of the Real Estate Tax Breaks That the Rich Receive Money made from real estate investments, especially those that are passive income producing, commonly turns out to be the lowest taxed income that you can obtain.

You might have an apartment complex that you own that creates $6,000 per month in income. This will accrue to you practically tax free.

Should you decide to sell the property later, then you are able to receive these capital gains without being required to pay a capital gains tax. This represents a savings of greater than twenty percent in some states. Even bonds, stocks, mutual funds, and real estate investment trusts do not offer this kind of nearly tax free income, though they are taxed at lower capital gains rates than the earned income rates.

Examples of the Oil and Gas Exploration Tax Breaks That the Rich Receive

Similarly, people who invest in projects that explore for or produce gas and oil receive enormous tax breaks. These run to the tune of seventy percent tax deductions on money invested in the project that are taken off of income made from the oil and gas money income.

They also provide allowances for depletion, which are other tax breaks. This means that should you invest $20,000 in oil and gas projects, then you receive $14,000 in deductions off of your income for this. On top of that, you would receive another tax break on income made from selling the gas and oil.

Examples of the Business Owner Tax Breaks That the Rich Receive

Business owners also receive substantial tax breaks, particularly when they are able to create more jobs. For hiring certain types of employees that are job challenged, they receive significant tax breaks. They are allowed to depreciate costs of property and offices, as well as equipment purchased for the use of the business.

As much as fifty percent of these costs can now be depreciated against income in the first year that they are purchased. Businesses have many other tax deductions and advantages that allow them to massively reduce their amount of taxable income.

These examples serve to illustrate a very important point regarding the wealthy and their ability to only get richer. Among the greatest factors for how the rich manage to do this seemingly all of the time is that they possess significant control over the greatest single expense in every American's life, that of their taxes paid.

Reasons that The Wealthy Are Given These Tax Breaks

The government has its reasons for rewarding such investors and business owners with better tax breaks than they give the hard working individual. The rich are performing useful services that benefit all of society with their activities.

These include providing jobs for the population, as well as creating housing and renting opportunities for these same people. For accomplishing these important tasks for the country and its working population, they are rewarded with the biggest and best tax breaks.

You may be thinking to yourself that the government is playing favorites with the wealthy in the ways that they treat them for taxing purposes. This is a correct assessment of the situation. As far as the government is concerned, the wealthy prove to be more useful to government in their goals of taking care of society and all of the nation's employees as a whole.

Without the rich to create jobs for them, there is not a large group of people who are capable of paying the taxes. Since the rich make this possible for the government, they could said to be in alliance with them. The business owner allies in this arrangement are rewarded significantly when it is tax time.

Similarly, since the government has determined that certain investors were more useful to them than others, they decided to reward these investors with the best tax breaks. Not only the providers of housing are covered by these provisions, but also those who make oil and gas exploration possible. All of these groups are concentrated on providing value for the members of society in their normal endeavors. They are rewarded for this as well.

If you only work for your money and save it, then you will have a hard time getting ahead. Though 401K's are supposed to be tax advantaged accounts, they really are not. Accountants can not do much to protect people from taxes who only have these deductions to fall back on. This is why being engaged in passive income real estate investments, oil and gas exploration investments, and small businesses pays off.

Wealth Building Strategies in Energy And Metals Markets

You have heard about the huge profits being made in gold and oil over the last five to ten years practically every time you turn on the financial channels or even the general news. You may feel like you have missed out on all of the fantastic opportunities, but this is actually not the case.

In Chris Waltzek's new book "Wealth Building Strategies in Energy, Metals and Other Markets", you are given another chance to catch the bull market run that still has another five or ten years to go. This important and useful book is reviewed in the following paragraphs.

About The Author - Chris Waltzek

Chris Waltzek proves to be an executive producer, show host, and writer for Goldseek.com Radio. This popular program is a two hour broadcast that happens every week and deals with the financial industry. The show has interviewed guests including Jim Rogers, Steve Forbes, and Ron Paul. Besides this, Waltzek additionally puts out the Spotlight Picks Newsletter that Goldseek.com owns.

In his past career, he filled a role as an industry analyst working for Jones, Day, Reavis, and Pogue, among the biggest lawyer firms in America.

With an MBA in both information systems and business economics, he is presently involved in the undertaking of getting his PhD for business administration.

Disenchanted by Banks And The Stock Market?

Chris Waltzek set out to write a book that would offer help and guidance to people who have been disenchanted by both banks and the stock market. He points out that neither places are sure bets for you money anymore.

Banks continue to fail in dangerous numbers, on track to surpass their levels of the past few years in 2010. Wall Street has proven that it can be up for a day, week, or month, then down thousands of points in the following ones. Because both places represent gambles for your money, Chris offers this book to show you how to make your investments as good as gold.

He provides an insightful work that that will teach you how to invest practically and profitably in this difficult economic scenario where anything can happen and no one can tell you with any real certainty what next month will hold.

Optimal Types of Investments for Many Years in the Future

Chris Waltzek the author provides you with a tremendous amount of historical, technical, and fundamental forms of evidence in support of precious metals in his book "Wealth Building Strategies in Energy, Metals, and Other Markets." He claims that they are and will remain the optimal types of investments for many years in the future.

Making more than just this claim, Waltzek spends a good portion of the work convincing you that if you are looking for the very best investment possibility out there, precious metals, and in particular gold, will be the very best choice in protecting your wealth.

How to Find Diverse Wealth Building Opportunities

"Wealth Building Strategies in Energy, Metals, and Other Markets" does not simply tout precious metals as the only investment of choice though. His book comes along at the right moment to help you discover safe havens that you can use to change economic downturns into opportunities for building wealth. The author Waltzek makes the case that so long as stocks go from new highs to shocking lows, you will have to engage in versatile and changing strategies if you are going to make money.

The investment book identifies several tools that are necessary for achieving success in investing. Chris Waltzek relates that you must have effective money management as well as the ability to pick out long term trends in order to do well in the markets.

Included in Wealth Building Strategies in Energy, Metals, and Other Markets is a proprietary investing system that pursues the greatest number of potential global indexes with limited correlations which you can follow and trade. It focuses heavily on precious metals and energies among its core components.

Other Financial Information Contained in Wealth Building Strategies

Besides dealing with precious metals and investing systems, Chris Waltzek covers a number of other important topics in the book. He looks at where both the energy and housing markets are headed next. The author also deals with a number of complicated but important financial concepts like credit, banking, deflation and inflation, and the mortgage bubble.

As he goes through these, he demonstrates to investors what trends they can anticipate in these areas. Finally, "Wealth Building Strategies in Energy, Metals, and Other Markets" provides a proven method for getting control of runaway finances in order to turn them around so that they can be utilized to support successful investment ideas.

Many different concepts are covered in the various topics of "Wealth Building Strategies in Energy, Metals, and Other Markets." Author Waltzek goes through insurance plans for every portfolio that are comprised of gold. He talks about peak oil and the dramatically increasing global energy demands that make investments in energy necessary.

He makes the argument for maintaining cash reserves in a safe in your home as a sensible idea. Waltzek suggests getting rid of your credit cards and instead having an emergency cash fund in their place. He also goes through the ideas underlying trend investing and price behaviors of investments.

Besides all of this, he addresses investor psychology and how you can discover and overcome your own individual weaknesses in order to greatly improve both your discipline in trading and the results that you obtain from your investment portfolio.

Professional Investment Advice

The book is organized into useful chapters on the various investment classes and topics that it covers. At the end of every chapter is a critical takeaway section for investors to ponder. Besides, this, there are applicable frequently asked questions from the listeners of Chris Waltzek's Goldseek.com Radio, along with expert answers to them provided. Professional investment advice is found here that will benefit all investors.

Much More than a Financial Advice

There is no doubt that many of the concepts that the author Chris Waltzek is promoting are not completely new. In the past, effectively managing your money to limit your losses and learning to identify trends for investments have proven to be winning formulas for great investing success. Such time tested ideas that the book is promoting have not declined in importance, but have only become more critical than they have ever before been.

Wealth Building Strategies in Energy, Metals and Other Markets ultimately proves to be much more than a financial advice or self help book, though it does offer a good amount of this type of wisdom. In the end, it represents a useful and sophisticated guide for surviving and profiting in the new economy.

To this effect, it provides thought provoking looks at both secure and profitable opportunities for investments that any investors can take advantage of, no matter what their income amounts or experience levels prove to be. The best point of "Wealth Building Strategies in Energy, Metals and Other Markets" is that it offers you all of the ideas and strategies that you need in order to make money in today's increasingly globally based economy.

Can We Accelerate Technology to Create Abundant Wealth?

Those of you who keep up with scientific advances will have likely heard of a theory called the Singularity. The singularity is a concept relating to the possibility of accelerating technology being able to create wealth for everyone.

The possibility of this and real potential that it has to impact your life and investments make it important for you to have a good understanding about this singularity and what it will entail in the coming years.

About the Singularity

The singularity is a construct that became popular when author Ray Kurzweil published his book "The Singularity Is Near" In it, he detailed an idea of a potential moment in time when readily available technology will become so common place, and the capability of utilizing this technology itself so potent, that intelligence will saturate the entire world around you.

A few other experts have also declared that such a technological singularity will occur at some point. When this happens, a greater amount of wealth will be created as a result than has ever before been conceived of, so that there will finally be enough to go around to everyone.

An example of this rapidly increasing technology and knowledge is evident in Moore's Law pertaining to computers. Moore's Law reveals how the power of computers doubles in literally every two year period. If you have any doubt of the veracity of this law, you only have to look at both current cell phones and lap tops and then compare them against the earlier models.

Not only are such devices far smaller nowadays, they also contain a much greater number and more powerful group of programs on them than ever before. Technology has improved to the point that even laptops can be purchased for under $500 these days. Remember when they were $2,000-$3,000 and only available to those who had significant money? This is all evidence of the dramatically improving rate of speed for technological advances and the approaching singularity of knowledge.

Factors That Speed Up the Advance of Technology

Information is literally exploding as you read this article. It may shock you to learn that in excess of three thousand different books are currently published every day. More stunning is the fact that 1.5 exabytes, or 1.5 quintillion bytes, of new information will be created this very year. Technical information is similarly doubling at the rate of every other year.

What does this mean in practical terms for you and your family?

The resulting explosion of technology and information will cause you to live not only longer, but also better. This will happen as energy sources that you never dreamed of become commonplace. Artificial intelligence will make dramatic improvements in your life too. In time, you will be able to use more of your brain power than in the past, in particular with regards to virtual reality.

Results of this Increasing Technology and Spread of Knowledge
In the past, you have always seen technology improve the quality of life and wealth that spread as a result of it. Consider the telephone. One simple invention brought the nation and the entire world together, increasing productivity massively as it did. And yet only a few years before the telephone appeared on the market, no one could conceive of it at all. Look at the fax machine as a more recent example. You probably remember when it was a novel invention that only major corporations could work with to send documents around the nation and world.

Now, even many people have them in their own homes. Businesses could barely operate without them today. The resulting increase in wealth and productivity from the Internet revolution has proved to be even more dramatic than these. Every single information and technological revolution has significantly increased personal wealth and given a boost to economies around the world. This is possible because technology really is intelligence being replicated repeatedly.

As a result of even more dramatic advances in technology that are coming in the next few years, you are going to see quantities and sources of wealth come into existence of which you can barely dream. Futurists and technology experts are quick to point out that this trend is only just getting started. The author Ray Kurzweil referenced earlier in the article is also a futurist, or future trends predictor. He states that we are soon to reach an age where wealth is exponentially created.

Historical Comparison of the Explosion of Wealth

As the rate of progress continues to grow faster and faster, so too will the wealth that it creates. It may surprise you to learn that some of these dramatic advances in technology have already happened. Author Stephen Waite has discussed some of these in his recent book entitled "Quantum Investing"

He stated that the first stages of the new singularity in wealth began in the last century of the 1900's. In fact, a greater quantity of wealth came into existence in the last hundred years than in all of previously recorded history combined. In this time period, the GDP, or production of all goods and services, in the United States increased from only $500 billion back in 1900 to over $9 trillion in 1990.

That represents an astonishing eighteen fold growth in under a hundred years. And this occurred despite the terrible setbacks of the Great Depression and two destructive World Wars. Even severe economic setbacks, as painful as they turn out to be, do not derail the dramatic growing of wealth created by the accelerating advance of technology and the spread of knowledge.

Future Technologies That Will Accelerate of the Explosion of Wealth

With the advances of the last century and the rise of the Internet and World Wide Web over the past ten to twenty years, you continue to see the acceleration of knowledge and wealth created by the advance of technology.

These are only the beginnings.

Majorly transforming technologies are set to propel the world forward to the technology, knowledge, and wealth created by reaching the singularity. Technological advances that are set to dramatically impact he world that you live in, as well as the opportunities for the explosion of wealth all around you, include several fields that are only beginning to make their impacts felt.

This includes molecular advances and quantum computing, robotics, nano technology devices, and bioengineering. All of these fields are anticipated to make massive break through discoveries and astonishing applications in the next ten to twenty yeas. Imagine what the unanticipated discoveries, which are commonly the really world changing ones, will be like.

The impacts of these technological revolutions are already starting to impact the investment world and stock markets. Consider an example of one that is presently considered to be a negative innovation. This is the concept and advance of High Frequency Trading, also known by its acronym of HFT.

High Frequency Trading makes use of incredibly powerful computers and artificial intelligence in order to take advantage of market imbalances, in advance of people who are employing technology that is less potent. The High Frequency Traders are simply benefiting from arbitrage, or inconsistencies that their computers spot in prices.

Individual traders have been able to do this for decades, but not at the speed and accuracy that computers can. Huge sums of money can be made in less than seconds using this technology. It is only one example of the dramatic changes that are coming to your world as technological advances allow wealth to be created for everyone.

RESOURCES

"Free Bonus Content"

For additional 'Wealth Advisor' editions please check our website or go to amazon.com.

Get All 'Wealth Advisor' Editions
www.wealthbuildingcourse.com/wealth-advisor

At present we are offering a free membership to the Wealth Building Course. This membership is free as long the full course is in development. The current release date will we in 2012 and the course will be priced at $799.

Sign Up For Your Free Wealth Education Membership:
www.wealthbuildingcourse.com

If you have additional interest in preserving your wealth and invest in silver please check out the author's book: 'Building Wealth with Silver', which is available at amazon.

Building Wealth with Silver Book:
www.wealthbuildingcourse.com/silver-book

The author also developed a very sophisticated course around silver investment, which is available for purchase online. The 'Silver Fortune Formula' course reveals every detail for successful silver investing.

Silver Investment 101:
www.wealthbuildingcourse.com/silver

Resources

Thomas Herold, CEO – Co-founder Wealth Building Course

Thomas Herold is a successful entrepreneur and personal development coach. After a career with one of the largest electronic companies in the world, he realized that a regular job would never fully satisfy his need for connection on a deep level.

The only way to live his full potential was to start building his own business and find new ways to be in service to others.

For over 25 years he has helped many people – including himself – build their dream businesses. Toward that goal, he focuses on education – simplified and enhanced by modern technology. He is the author of three books with over 200,000 copies distributed worldwide.

Other than his passion for creating businesses, Thomas has spent over 20 years in the self-development field. Placing emphasis on the exploration of consciousness and building practical applications that allow people to express their purpose and passion in life, Thomas's work in this area has provided ample and happy proof that this approach works.

He believes that every person has at least one gift and that, when this gift is developed and nourished, it will serve as a fountainhead of personal happiness and help contribute to a better, more sustainable world.

For the past three years Thomas Herold has studied the monetary system and has experienced some profound insights on how money and wealth are related. He has recently committed to sharing this knowledge in a new venture – the Wealth Building Course, a website along with educational materials that designed to help people get started on their own money makeover and get a financial education in the process.

Thomas's ultimate vision for the Wealth Building Course is to empower people to adopt a wealthy mindset and to create abundance for themselves and others. His ability to explain complex information in simple terms makes him an outstanding teacher and coach.

www.ingramcontent.com/pod-product-compliance
Lightning Source LLC
Chambersburg PA
CBHW051438170526
45166CB00001B/31